GOSPEL PARALLELS

A Synopsis of the First Three Gospels

With alternative readings from the Manuscripts and
Noncanonical Parallels

Text used is the Revised Standard Version, 1 9 5 2

The arrangement follows the Huck-Lietzmann
Synopsis, Ninth edition, 1 9 3 6

Edited by Burton H. Throckmorton, Jr.

THOMAS NELSON INC., PUBLISHERS
Nashville / New York

Fourteenth printing

Fourth Edition, revised
Copyright 1949, 1957, 1967, 1979

by

Division of Christian Education of the National Council of
the Churches of Christ in the United States of America.

Permission to use the text of the Revised Standard Version
granted by the Division of Christian Education of the National Council of the Churches of Christ in the United States
of America

The International Council of Religious Education expresses
its deep appreciation to J. C. B. Mohr (Paul Siebeck) Pub-
lisher of the Huck-Lietzmann *Synopsis,* Ninth Edition, 1936,
which inspired the plan followed by the Editors in the preparation of *Gospel Parallels.*

International Standard Book Number 0-8407-5150-8 (Trade Ed.)

MANUFACTURED IN THE UNITED STATES OF AMERICA

PREFACE TO THE SECOND EDITION

A thorough study of the gospels is possible only when they are printed in parallel columns for comparison. Therefore, the American Standard Bible Committee requested a sub-committee to prepare a synopsis based on the Revised Standard Version so that the new version might better meet the needs of students. Before the work was undertaken, advice was sought from representative college and seminary professors in order to obtain their ideas on the features which should be included. The principles of arrangement in this volume were adopted on the basis of the suggestions which were made.

It seemed advisable, first of all, to compile a synopsis of the English text which could be used conveniently with a Greek synopsis. The obvious choice was the latest edition of Albert Huck's *Synopsis of the First Three Gospels* (9th ed. by Hans Lietzmann; English by Frank Leslie Cross, 1936). This edition is available to American students through the American Bible Society. During the two generations since "Huck" first appeared (1892), it has steadily come into ever wider use, until now it is known by New Testament students the world over. It prints each gospel in order (with quite minor exceptions); it repeats each gospel when out of order, and contains adequate subdivisions without being too complex. Hence, we have used the same section numbers and a similar marginal apparatus in order that the books may be used in the same class, where some can profitably follow the Greek and others only the English text.

Gospel Parallels offers two advantages never before available in a synopsis in English. First, the noncanonical parallels are given in full in addition to the parallels in the other canonical gospels. Most students do not have immediate access to the Gospel according to the Hebrews or to the quotations and gospel allusions in the Church Fathers. Yet these are a valuable part of our tradition about Jesus. Secondly, in connection with variant readings, the chief manuscript support has been cited. We believe that students who know no Greek can learn the significance of the most important manuscript witnesses. We have included all of the variants noted in the Revised Standard Version and have added others which seemed important enough to bring to the attention of serious Bible students.

The titles of some section headings have been changed from those used in the latest edition of "Huck." In some cases this was required by the new translation. Another difference will be found in the printing of the parallels from the Gospel of John, except where a very long passage is involved.

The Hazen Foundation made a generous subsidy toward the cost of the plates in order that the book might be available to students at as reasonable a price as possible. The committee supervising the preparation of the Synopsis was composed of Henry J. Cadbury, Harvard University Divinity School, Frederick C. Grant, Union Theological Seminary, and the late Clarence T. Craig, formerly of Yale University Divinity School and later Dean of Drew Theological Seminary. The detailed work of preparing the present volume was done by Burton H. Throckmorton, Jr., then instructor in New Testament at Union Theological Seminary and lecturer at Columbia University, now Professor of New Testament at Bangor Theological Seminary, Bangor, Maine. In the typing of the manuscript, the verification of references, and the completion of the manuscript citations, he has made an indispensable contribution. Professor Kendrick Grobel of the Vanderbilt University School of Religion kindly assisted in reading the proof.

It has been eight years since *Gospel Parallels* was first published. Its use of the Revised Standard Version, its arrangement following that of Huck's *Synopsis,* and its fairly extensive footnotes—the three major features of this particular "harmony" or "synopsis"—have apparently proved useful to a large number of students. It is therefore reappearing in a second edition.

In spite of much proofreading, the first edition contained a number of errors. Most of these have been eliminated in subsequent printings; and it is our hope that in this edition all initial mistakes have been corrected.

The major change in this edition, however, is in the form of an addition. It has been increasingly evident that the references used in the footnotes required a more adequate explanation than what has been provided. The significance of the Greek manuscripts, the versions, the church fathers, and the noncanonical gospels referred to has in no way been indicated. Manuscript support for various readings is cited in the footnotes; but the book has not revealed what combinations of manuscripts constituted strong support for any given reading. In other words, without consulting a number of different sources, the student has not been able to use the apparatus satisfactorily. It has therefore seemed advisable to prepare an introduction to the references made in the footnotes.

The following introductory material deals only with writers or documents which are referred to in the footnotes of this book. It is intended to help the non-specialist appreciate the meaning and significance of these notes; and it is hoped that some, at least, will be led to inquire further.

PREFACE TO THE THIRD EDITION

Because of the continuing and widespread use of *Gospel Parallels* it has seemed important that it be published in a third edition, primarily to correct and supplement the footnote references which have proved to be one of the more helpful aspects of the book. In this edition I have for the first time included references to the Gospel of Thomas, in some cases quoting the whole saying or logion, in others indicating only the logion number. (Numbers of the logia are taken from *The Gospel according to Thomas,* translated by A. Guillaument, *et al.,* Harper & Brothers, 1959.)

A detailed checking of the textual apparatus disclosed a number of errors which have been corrected in this edition. I have also included support from four papyri not formerly referred to: P^1, P^{25}, P^{67}, and P^{75} A few additional corrections and improvements have been made throughout the book, and the Introduction to Footnote References has been brought up to date.

I am extremely grateful to Mrs. Bernice C. Rich of Thomas Nelson & Sons whose discernment has brought to light a number of errors and inconsistencies. I should like also to thank Edwin B. Chatfield for his interest and helpfulness in the preparation of this edition.

Bangor, February, 1967   Burton H. Throckmorton, Jr.

EXPLANATION OF SIGNS

Greek Manuscripts cited

S	Codex Sinaiticus (4th, or perhaps 5th cent.)
A	Codex Alexandrinus (5th cent.)
B	Codex Vaticanus (4th cent.)
C	Codex Ephraemi (5th cent.)
D	Codex Bezae Cantabrigiensis (6th cent., perhaps 5th)
W	Washington (Freer) Manuscript (5th cent.)
Θ	Koridethi Gospels (7th to 9th cent.)
λ	The "Lake Group" (minuscules 1, 118, 131, 209, etc.)
φ	The "Ferrar Group" (minuscules 13, 69, 124, 346, etc.)
ℜ	The "Koine" or "Byzantine" text (EFGH etc. and most minuscules)

P^1	Philadelphia Papyrus (3rd cent.)
P^3	Vienna Papyrus (6th–7th cent.)
P^4	Paris Papyrus (3rd cent.)
P^{25}	Berlin Papyrus (4th cent.)
P^{37}	Ann Arbor Papyrus (3rd–4th cent.)
P^{45}	Dublin Papyrus (3rd cent., Chester Beatty Collection)
P^{67}	Barcelona Papyrus (ca. 200 A.D.)
P^{75}	Geneva Papyrus (ca. 200 A.D., Bodmer Collection)

Versions cited

it	Itala (the Old Latin version, as reconstructed by Adolf Jülicher)
vg	Vulgate (ed. Wordsworth and White, 1889-98)
sy^c	The Old Syriac (edited by Cureton, 1858)
sy^s	The Sinaitic Syriac (discovered in 1892)
sy^p	The Peshitta Syriac version (ed. by G. H. Gwilliam, 1901)
sa	The Sahidic version (ed. by G. Horner, 1911ff.)
bo	The Bohairic version (ed. by G. Horner, 1898ff.)

Introduction to Footnote References

DEFINITION OF TERMS

Uncial—refers to capital letters; manuscripts written in capital letters are "uncials" and predominated until the ninth century A.D.

Minuscule—refers to manuscripts written in small, cursive letters, often joined to each other. Minuscules and uncials overlapped during the ninth and tenth centuries, and only minuscules occur from the eleventh century onward.

Cursive—refers to small, joined, "longhand" letters used in minuscules.

Palimpsest—a manuscript which has been written on twice, the first writing having been erased.

Roll—refers to the way in which a book was put together. If a book were a "roll," the writing material was rolled—sometimes, in the few cases of expensive books, on rollers. To be read, the manuscript had to be unrolled with the right hand and re-rolled with the left. There were no "pages" and, even in the case of the Bible, no chapter and verse divisions; so references could not be made except to rolls themselves, or to works appearing in a roll. Titles and authors were noted at the end of the roll, which was somewhat inconvenient. Greek rolls seldom exceeded 35 feet and were usually closer to 25 feet; a gospel such as Matthew or Luke would have used about 32-35 feet. The material was written in a series of columns about two to three inches wide; there were usually 25 to 45 lines to a column depending on the width of the roll and the size of the letters. Sometimes the rolls were wrapped in parchment for protection. When rolled up, they were about 9 or 10 inches tall and an inch to an inch and a half in diameter. Words were not separated and there was little punctuation.

Codex—a bound book. With the introduction of codices, page references could be given, and much more material could be included in one book. The papyrus codex goes back probably to the first century A.D., and the Gospels surely appeared together in a codex in the second century. The earliest extant example of the Gospels in codex form comes from the third century, but codices were not universally used even then. Of 304 pagan manuscripts of the third century, 275 are papyrus rolls, 26 are papyrus codices, and 3 are vellum codices.

Papyrus—refers to the writing material and to the writing itself. The material was used surely from the sixth century B.C. Single sheets usually did not exceed 13 by 19 inches. To make a roll, pieces were glued together end to end. Writing was usually done on only one side of the papyrus (the recto) where the fibers ran horizontally; sometimes, however, the other side (the verso) was also used. In the fourth century A.D. the use of papyrus declined probably because larger books than papyrus could provide were needed, and because the manufacture of vellum was improved, but papyrus was still being used in Egypt in the sixth century A.D.

Vellum—skins of cattle, sheep, and goats, seldom of pigs and asses. These skins were washed, scraped, rubbed with pumice, and chalked. They made an excellent writing material. The two earliest vellum documents known were found at Dura in Mesopotamia, and date from 190–189 and 196–195 B.C. But vellum was rare this early. All references in Roman literature as far as the end of the first century A.D. are to papyrus. But toward the end of the first century A.D. vellum was fairly common outside of Rome, although it had by no means displaced papyrus. In the fourth century vellum displaced papyrus both in the roll and in the codex. Vellum books, some of which were the most beautiful books ever made, were used for about a thousand years.

TYPES OF TEXT

Before we take up the manuscripts themselves we must remember that more important than the manuscripts are the types of text or "families" they represent. None of the original manuscripts of the New Testament have survived nor, presumably, any direct copies of the original manuscripts.

What we have are copies of copies. Into these copies crept errors; moreover additions and "corrections" were sometimes made by the copyists, for the only Bible of the early church was the Old Testament, and it was not imperative to copy the gospels and epistles—still uncanonized—exactly word for word. The manuscripts of the New Testament can be classified by groups or families, descended from common ancestors and supporting distinctive types of text. Indeed, the chief value of the majority of manuscripts is not their approximation to the original text of the New Testament, but their support of one or another of these groups or families. No manuscript can be better than that from which it was copied. Textual criticism since the publication of Bengel's study of the New Testament in 1734 has shown that manuscripts, like animals, can be classified into families, which families are related to each other in varying degrees of intimacy. It is the family, then, that is far more significant than the manuscript, and one manuscript copied from a good family gives far more support to a reading than a hundred manuscripts, no matter how accurately copied, from a poor family which *as a family* is late or inaccurate. First must be asked, how good is the family? and second, how accurate is the copy or text at hand?

How did these families, or types of text, arise? It is quite obvious that errors, corrections and additions made in Rome would be perpetuated in manuscripts copied at Rome, and not at Alexandria or Antioch or Caesarea. Each religious center in the church would preserve and add to its own peculiar readings and gradually the texts in and around the various leading communities took on their own characteristics. Moreover, when bishops and scholars edited New Testament texts for local use by copying from the various manuscripts in their own communities, the character of the text in these communities became the more fixed; so that today, with the help of the early versions (translations into other languages) and quotations from the Church Fathers, we can assign manuscripts to their proper families. There are, of course, cases in which manuscripts seem to fit more than one family, and there is always the possibility of a new family being isolated by the discovery of new manuscripts or by the re-arrangement of old ones. Textual criticism is by no means a closed study! It should be added in conclusion that because we are dealing now primarily with differences among the manuscripts, they loom far larger than their actual significance should allow. The fact is that in about 90 per cent of the New Testament the manuscripts all agree; the differences occur in a small percentage of passages, and do not affect fundamental Christian doctrine.

The main types of text now recognized are:

(1) *The Alexandrian text* (called "Neutral" by Westcott and Hort because of their belief that it was uncontaminated) represented chiefly by B, S, and the Coptic versions. It is identified by the absence of aberrations found in other groups. Its center was Alexandria, hence its name; but it was found throughout the Eastern church. As it is represented by the oldest extant uncials, B and S, this type of text is very significant.

(2) *The Byzantine text,* also called Syrian, Antiochene, Koinê, and Received (*Textus Receptus*), originated in the late third century around Antioch—hence its designation as Antiochene and Syrian. It was adopted in Constantinople and so predominated in the Byzantine world. It is also referred to as the "Received text," or *Textus Receptus,* because it was this text which was found in almost all late manuscripts and so became the basis of the first printed editions of the Greek New Testament in the sixteenth century, beginning with Erasmus' edition of 1516. Through these editions, it was the text which was first translated into the modern European tongues. Our King James (Authorized) Version is a translation of this type of text. The oldest and best manuscripts of this text are A and parts of C in the Gospels; W in Matthew and most of Luke, and often the Peshitta: then follow most of the late uncials and minuscules. By the eighth century it was practically the only Greek text being used. It is characterized by conflations (combinations of readings from other manuscripts) and revisions in the interest of smoothness and intelligibility. The late uncial and minuscule manuscripts of this text are referred to by the German capital ℜ, the first letter of the Greek word *koine,* "common," which term is often used to refer to this family.

(3) The term "Western text" was once used to refer to all pre-Byzantine, non-Alexandrian readings, but it more properly refers to the Graeco-Latin manuscripts of western Europe such as D; to the Old Latin version; and to quotations from western Church Fathers such as Cyprian. Other non-Alexandrian, pre-Byzantine readings must be classified in another way. This type of text is marked by omissions and insertions sometimes the length of several verses, and by eccentric read-

ings. The text originated in the middle of the second century, and so its readings cannot easily be dismissed. The so-called "Western non-interpolations," chiefly found in the last three chapters of Luke, are readings found in all but the Western manuscripts and believed by Hort to be late; hence they were not interpolated in (or added to) Western manuscripts. This designation begs the question of the authenticity of the readings: it implies that they were not in the original autographs but were interpolated in the non-Western manuscripts, or not interpolated in the Western manuscripts. It would seem wise not to consider the readings as a unit, but to decide on the authenticity of each one separately, on other grounds. The Western text probably originated in North Africa or Egypt, in Greek, and was early translated into Latin.

(4) *The Syriac text,* to be distinguished from the Syrian (Byzantine), was once thought to belong to the Western text but is now considered by many scholars to be an independent text. It was originally associated with the Western type of text, but it was also closely akin to the Alexandrian type. Its Western readings probably came by way of Tatian's *Diatessaron,* which was written in Rome but was widely circulated in Syria in the Syriac language. The Syriac family is represented primarily by the manuscripts sy^c and sy^s. It was later revised by Rabbula under Byzantine influence and became the Peshitta (sy^p) which is the authorized Bible of the Syrian Church.

(5) *The Caesarean text* is found in Θ, λ, ϕ, W (in Mark), P^{45}, and quotations in the later works of Origen and in the works of Eusebius. It was used in Caesarea (hence its name) but the discovery of the third century P^{45} in Egypt, together with the knowledge that Origen used this type of text in Alexandria as well as in Caesarea, makes it probable that it originated in Egypt, perhaps as early as the second century. This text lies between the Alexandrian and the Western. It is as significant a group as we possess because it is as early as the Alexandrian type, but lacks the extravagant readings of the Western.

Greek Manuscripts of the New Testament Referred to in the Footnotes

S—*Codex Sinaiticus,* middle fourth century; included both the Old and New Testaments plus the Epistle of Barnabas and the Shepherd of Hermas. The text is Alexandrian. It often agrees with B, but not always, for it has been influenced by another tradition similar to the Western. Among the versions, the Bohairic comes nearest to it, with much support coming also from the Sahidic. The manuscript may have originated in Palestine or in Alexandria.

The story of its discovery is one of the most fascinating true stories of modern times. In 1844 Constantin von Tischendorf made his first visit to St. Catherine's Convent on Mount Sinai, looking for manuscripts. While browsing around the library, he saw a large basket full of parts of old manuscripts containing fragments of the Old Testament in Greek. As they were in a basket whose contents, according to the librarian, had already twice been burned as fuel, Tischendorf asked and received permission to take the leaves to his room. He might as well have them, as far as the librarian was concerned, because they were about to be burned anyway. But when the librarian became aware of the fact that the leaves were valuable, he refused Tischendorf permission to see the source from which these comparatively few sheets had been taken. So Tischendorf took back the sheets, forty-three in all, to the University of Leipzig, and gave them the name of the reigning king of Saxony, Frederick Augustus. These leaves remain to this day in the University library, catalogued as Codex Friderico-Augustanus, and containing several chapters of 1 Chronicles, some of 2 Esdras, all of Esther, part of Tobit, most of Jeremiah, and about half of Lamentations.

In spite of all the publicity which these sheets received, Tischendorf managed not to disclose the place where they had been found. He was determined to return to that convent and secure the other fragments, whatever they might be. In 1853 he did return, but in vain; for no information was given him. In 1859 he returned for the third time under the auspices of the Czar of Russia. Again he looked through the library but found nothing like the forty-three leaves he had taken back to Leipzig. On February 4th while he and the steward were taking a walk around the convent garden, they discussed the Septuagint and various texts of it which they had seen. When they returned to the convent, the steward invited Tischendorf to join him in his cell for some refreshments. From a corner he took an object wrapped in a cloth, which he placed before Tischendorf on a table. Tischendorf unwrapped the cloth, and before him lay Codex Sinaiticus—"the Bible of Sinai." He soon noticed that the whole New Testament was there. Having received permission to take this treasure to his room, Tischendorf was so filled with emotion that he could neither sleep nor even lie down on a bed; and so in a cold room, by the light of a small lamp, he spent the night copying the Epistle of Barnabas. "All my boldest dreams," he writes, "were surpassed. I was certain of having found the most important manuscript in the whole world—a veritable pillar to sustain Divine Truth." [1] Not successful in obtaining permission to take the manuscript to Cairo, he nevertheless went to Egypt without it; and by playing a little game of politics, he succeeded in getting it sent to him there. In 1869 these leaves, 347 in all, were "given" to Czar Alexander II of Russia in exchange for money amounting to about $7000—a gift which was somewhat slow in arriving but was finally presented to the monastery at Mount Sinai and the affiliated convent of Mount Tabor. In addition to this money, some Russian decorations were awarded to certain Sinai fathers. In the 1930's when the Soviet government was in need of funds—and not particularly interested in Biblical manuscripts—a group of Americans was asked to consider the purchase of the new manuscript from the Soviet government. The figure proposed was a million dollars; but due to the depression it could not be raised. In 1933 the British people and government bought the famous manuscript from the Soviet government for £100,000, and it was moved to the British Museum in London, where it may now be seen. In addition to the leaves at the University of Leipzig, there is a small fragment of the manuscript in the Library of the Society of Ancient Literature in Leningrad.

As Tischendorf considered this the oldest extant manuscript of the Bible, he referred to it by the sign ℵ (*Aleph*), which is the first letter in the Hebrew alphabet. The letter A had already been used to designate Codex Alexandrinus. In this book the letter S is used as more significant than *Aleph* to students who do not know the Hebrew language.

A—*Codex Alexandrinus*, first half of fifth century; contained originally both the Old and New Testaments, plus I and II Clement (see p. xiv) and the Psalms of Solomon, which follow the Book of Revelation. Matthew 1:1–25:6 (most of this Gospel) is lost; also missing from the New Testament are John 6:50–8:52 and 2 Corinthians 4:13–12:6. The text is Byzantine in the Gospels and Alexandrian in the Pauline epistles.

The manuscript is said to have been given to the patriarchate of Alexandria in 1098. In 1621 it was perhaps taken from Alexandria to Constantinople by Cyril Lucar who left Alexandria as patriarch to take up the same position in Constantinople. Cyril Lucar offered the codex as a gift to James I of England, through Sir Thomas Roe, the English ambassador to Turkey; but James having died in 1627 when the codex arrived in England, it was received by Charles I who deposited it in the Royal Library. When George II presented that Library to the nation in 1757, the codex passed into the possession of the British Museum. The Byzantine text of Alexandrinus in the Gospels is the earliest representative of this text (sometimes called "Syrian") which, as early as the fourth century, had come to predominate over all other texts. The Authorized (King James) Version is the English equivalent of this type of text. In the Acts and Epistles, however, the text of this codex is of the Alexandrian type, the chief exponents of which are Sinaiticus and Vaticanus. In the Book of Revelation the text is also Alexandrian and is, with the possible exception of P[47], the best extant text of that book.

B—*Codex Vaticanus*, fourth century; contained originally both the Old and New Testaments, but Hebrews 9:14–13:25, the Pastoral Epistles, Philemon, and the Apocalypse—and perhaps, as in S and A, parts of the Apostolic Fathers—have now been lost. The text is Alexandrian. It was considered by Westcott and Hort, and after them by many other scholars, to be the best single extant text of the New Testament. The text of the Gospels and Acts is the best Alexandrian text we have, but there is a considerable Western element in the text of the Pauline epistles. Vaticanus and Sinaiticus are textually closely related, but their common birthplace cannot now be determined.

This codex appears in the earliest catalogue of the Vatican library, published in 1475, but no one knows when it was taken there or any of its earlier history. There is, then, no interesting story in connection with a "discovery" of this manuscript, as it has been preserved in the Vatican for almost five hundred years. But the way in which it was guarded by Vatican authorities is interesting. For hundreds of years nobody in the outside world knew what Vaticanus' text was like, as no one was allowed to copy it or to study a section long enough to remember it. It was first made known in 1553 when a correspondent of Erasmus, one Sepulveda, sent him some selected readings from it. In 1669 a collation (or list of its various readings) was made by Bartolocci, a Vatican librarian, but it was never published and no one knew anything more of it for a hundred and fifty years. Napoleon carried the manuscript off to Paris as a victory prize, and while there it was studied

---

[1] This quotation, as well as the story narrated, may be found in Tischendorf's own record of his discovery of Sinaiticus read by him at a meeting of the Royal Society of Literature, February 15, 1865, and entitled: *Mémoire sur la Découverte et l'Antiquité du Codex Sinaïticus.*

by Hug. He was the first to make known its great age and supreme importance (1810). In 1815 it was returned to its home as were the many other treasures which Napoleon had robbed from the various libraries of Europe. Again it became practically inaccessible to scholars. In 1843, after waiting for several months, Tischendorf was finally permitted to look at it for six hours. In 1844 de Muralt was allowed to examine it for nine hours. In the next year the great English scholar, Tregelles, was permitted to see it on condition that he would not copy a word. And so before he entered the precinct where the manuscript was kept, his pockets were searched for all potential writing materials; and when he seemed to be looking too intently at any particular passages, the two guards who stood next to him snatched the manuscript away. Meanwhile in 1857 Cardinal Mai published an edition of the work, and in 1866 Tischendorf again applied for the opportunity to study it. His request was granted on condition that he examine it for no longer than three hours a day, and not copy any of it. By the end of eight days, however, he had managed to copy out eight whole pages. His permission was then revoked, but on special entreaty it was renewed for a period of six days. This gave Tischendorf enough time to enable him to publish, in 1867, the best edition of the manuscript then available. Finally, in 1889–90 a photographic copy was made of the whole manuscript and it became the common property of all scholars.

C—*Codex Ephraemi,* first half of fifth century; a palimpsest containing parts of both the Old and New Testaments. The text is Alexandrian in general but has many other mixed readings, so it is not so important as the texts of Sinaiticus, Alexandrinus, and Vaticanus, because it does not represent as consistently any one type of text.

In the twelfth century a scribe expunged the Biblical text and re-used the vellum to record the thirty-eight discourses of Ephraem (a Syrian Father [d.373] often referred to as Ephraem Syrus) translated into Greek. It was therefore very difficult to recover the original Biblical text but most of it has now been deciphered by the use of chemicals. The first complete edition of the manuscript was published by Tischendorf in 1843–45. He was able to read almost every word of it, and had even discovered several notes by some of the correctors of the text. The manuscript seems to have been brought from the East to Florence in the time of Lorenzo de' Medici by a Greek named Andrew John Lascar. When Lascar died in 1535 the manuscript, together with all his library, was bought by Pietro Strozzi. It then belonged to Cardinal Niccolò Ridolfi, of Florence, of the de' Medici family, and later Queen Catherine de' Medici owned it. As she was the wife of King Henry II of France, the codex was brought to Paris and became part of the Bibliothèque Royale (now the Bibliothèque Nationale).

D—*Codex Bezae,* later fifth century or early sixth; a bilingual manuscript of the Gospels and Acts, written in Greek on the left page and in Latin on the right, and the oldest known manuscript written in two languages. The text is Western.

The Bishop of Clermont borrowed the manuscript from the Monastery of St. Irenaeus in Lyons to take to the Council of Trent in 1546. It was then returned to the monastery whence it was rescued when Lyons was sacked by the Huguenots in 1562. In some way it got into the hands of Théodore de Bèze, the Geneva scholar and reformer; and he presented it to the University of Cambridge in 1581. Since then it has been called by his name, the letter D being used to refer to it. See under *Types of Text* for a discussion of its textual characteristics.

W—*Washington Codex,* fifth century or perhaps late fourth; includes Deuteronomy, Joshua, the Gospels, and the Pauline epistles, with two small lacunae in the Gospels, Mark 15:13–38 and John 14:25–16:7.

The manuscript is unusually interesting because it contains four types of text, not corresponding to the four Gospels: the Alexandrian type of text is found in Luke 1:1–8:12 and in the Gospel of John; the Byzantine type is found in the rest of Luke and in Matthew; the Western type is found in Mark 1:1–5:30; and the Caesarean in the rest of Mark. The manuscript is quite independent with regard to its reading; for this reason its origins are difficult to determine. An addition following Mark 16:14 is of special interest because it is rather lengthy and is not to be found in any other known manuscript. A translation of this addition follows:

And they replied saying, "This age of lawlessness and unbelief is under Satan who by means of unclean spirits does not allow men to comprehend the true power of God; therefore reveal now Thy righteousness." Thus they spoke to Christ; and Christ answered them, "The limit of the years of the authority of Satan is fulfilled; but other horrors draw near and for the sake of them that sinned was I delivered unto death that they might return to the truth and sin no more; that they might inherit the spiritual and incorruptible glory of righteousness which is in heaven."

ix

If these words are inserted between verses 14 and 15 of Mark 16, it will be seen that they fit well into the context. Apparently they were inserted by a scribe to soften the reference to Jesus' strong rebuke of the disciples in verse 14. The "quotation" from Jesus was probably composed *ad hoc* somewhere around the end of the second century or the beginning of the third. The first part of this reading is quoted by Jerome in his treatise against the Pelagians (ii.15).

The manuscript was bought by Charles L. Freer from an Arab dealer named Ali in Gizeh, near Cairo, on December 19, 1906. It was taken to Detroit and later deposited in the Freer Gallery of Art in Washington, D.C.; hence the letter W refers to it. It had once been located, perhaps, in the Monastery of the Vinedresser, which was situated near the third pyramid in Egypt, until the monastery was destroyed between 1208 and 1441. What happened to the manuscript between this date and 1906 we do not know, but when Professor H. A. Sanders of the University of Michigan began to study it, he found sand in the wrinkles and incrusted on the outside. It had apparently not been opened for centuries.

Θ—*Koridethi Codex,* probably ninth, perhaps seventh century. It is difficult to date because no other specimen of the same kind of writing has yet been found. It contains only the Gospels and is referred to as *Theta,* Θ, the eighth letter of the Greek alphabet. The text is Caesarean in Mark and Byzantine in the other Gospels.

Colonel Bartholomée discovered it in Swanetia on the slopes of the Caucasus in 1853. In 1869 it was taken to St. Petersburg by the military governor of Kutais; but it was later taken back to the Caucasus and sent to the Gelaty convent near Kutais. It was then forgotten for about thirty years; and in 1901 was rediscovered by Bishop Kirion in the treasure room of St. Andrew's Cathedral, in which were preserved the codices belonging to the Gelaty monastery. Bishop Kirion then took the manuscript to Tiflis in Russia where it is now to be found. Scholars were first informed of its existence by von Soden in 1906, in the prolegomena to his edition of the New Testament. It takes its name from the monastery of Koridethi, near the Caspian, to which it formerly belonged. It was edited in 1913 by Gustav Beermann and Caspar René Gregory.

λ—*The Lake Group* (Family 1)

We are now dealing not with one manuscript, but with families or groups of manuscripts which have so much in common that they are presumably derived from a common ancestor. Moreover, these manuscripts are not uncials but minuscules, and are known by their numbers as they stand in the commonly accepted catalogue of minuscule manuscripts of the Greek New Testament. We shall consider only two—Families 1 and 13. Family 1 was isolated for separate examination and edited by Kirsopp Lake in 1902 (hence its name). This group, also referred to by the Greek letter *Lambda,* λ, consists of several manuscripts, numbers 1, 118, 131, 209, etc. of which Codex 1 is the most important. The family is known by the number (1) of this codex as well as by the name of the scholar who edited it. Codex 1 is a Basel manuscript dated in the tenth to twelfth centuries. It is impossible to establish a place of origin for any of these manuscripts.

φ—*The Ferrar Group* (Family 13)

The other group of manuscripts is the Ferrar Group named after W. H. Ferrar who helped edit them, and known by the Greek letter *Phi,* φ. In 1877 T. K. Abbot published *A Collation of Four Important Manuscripts of the Gospels,* which manuscripts had been examined by Abbot and Ferrar and were published after the latter's death. Many peculiar readings had been found which pointed to a common parent. The four manuscripts studied were related to each other but not to any other known family; so it was thought that they belonged to a separate family of manuscripts which in turn were derived perhaps from an uncial. These four manuscripts are minuscules, written in the twelfth, thirteenth, and fifteenth centuries. They are: codex 13 (12th or 13th century, in the Bibliothèque Nationale, Paris); codex 69 (the Leicester Codex, 15th century, in possession of the borough of Leicester, England); codex 124 (12th century, Imperial Library, Vienna); and codex 346 (12th century, Ambrosian Library, Milan). The parent of these manuscripts has never been found, but other manuscripts, similar to them, have since been seen to be additional members of the same family. They are codices 543 (12th century); 788 (11th century); 826 (12th century); 828 (12th century), etc. Most of these manuscripts seem to have an Italian-Sicilian origin and their texts are Caesarean in character. Codex 69, however, was written in England.

ℜ—*Koine*—see under the Byzantine text, page vi.

THE PAPYRI

The papyri referred to in this book are as follows:

P[1]—at the University of Pennsylvania, Philadelphia, Pennsylvania; third century; containing Matthew 1:1-9, 12-20, 23.

P[3]—in the Österreichische Nationalbibliothek, Vienna; sixth–seventh century; from a lectionary; containing Luke 7:36-45; 10:38-42; the text is Alexandrian.

P[4]—in the Bibliothèque Nationale, Paris; third century; from a lectionary; containing Luke 1:58-59; 1:62-2:1, 6, 7; 3:8-4:2, 29-32, 34-35; 5:3-8; 5:30-6:16; the text is Alexandrian.

P[25]—at the State Museum, Berlin; late fourth century; containing Matthew 18:32-34; 19:1-3, 5-7, 9-10.

P[37]—in the University of Michigan Library, Ann Arbor, Michigan; third–fourth century; containing Matthew 26:19-52.

P[45]—in the Chester Beatty Library, Dublin, and the Österreichische Nationalbibliothek, Vienna: known as Chester Beatty Papyrus 1; third century; contains parts of all the Gospels and Acts; the text is chiefly Caesarean in Mark, Alexandrian and Western elsewhere—very mixed. This collection of Gospel papyri represents a large collection of Biblical manuscripts acquired around 1930 from a dealer in Egypt by A. Chester Beatty, an American collector of manuscripts, now living in Dublin. These leaves of both the Old and New Testaments vary in age from the second to the fourth centuries and are believed to have been found on the banks of the Nile near Memphis.

P[64]—in Oxford; from about 200 A.D. See P[67].

P[67]—at the Fundación San Lucas Evangelista, Barcelona; ca. 200 A.D.; belongs with P[64]; contains Matthew 3:9, 15; 5:20-22, 25-28.

P[75]—Bodmer Papyrus XIV and XV, in the Bodmer Library, Geneva; ca. 200 A.D.; containing Luke 3:18-18:18; 22:4-24:53 with lacunae; also John 1:1-15:8 with lacunae.

The Oxyrhynchus Papyri, were first known in 1897 when B. P. Grenfell and A. S. Hunt published a fragment of papyrus from Oxyrhynchus, Egypt, dating from the middle of the second century and containing some sayings of Jesus. Six more sayings were found in 1903 and published the year following. Their great significance lies in the fact that they offer parallels to all four Gospels and must have been copied from a manuscript written as early as 110-130 A.D. (2207 papyri from Oxyrhynchus, mostly un-Biblical, have so far been published in twenty-three volumes.) The numbers used in this text (1, 654, 655, 1224) refer to the numbers of the documents as numbered by Grenfell and Hunt. Number 1 is found in vol. I of this edition of the papyri; numbers 654 and 655 are found in vol. IV; number 1224 is found in vol. X.

The Egerton Papyrus 2, dated in the middle of the second century and belonging perhaps even earlier in the century, is the second oldest specifically Christian manuscript yet discovered. (The oldest is the John Ryland's Papyrus, P[52], giving parts of John 18:31-33, 37-38, and dating from the first half of the second century.) Its provenance is unknown because it was bought with many other manuscripts from a dealer who had collected them; Oxyrhynchus, however, is not an unlikely place, and like the Oxyrhynchus papyri this papyrus contains sayings of Jesus which are not recorded in our canonical Gospels. It has been edited by H. I. Bell and T. C. Skeat in *Fragments of an Unknown Gospel,* British Museum, 1935, with three other Egerton papyri.

The Fayum Fragment (Frag. Fajjumense), parallel to Mark 14:27-30, but omitting vs. 28, third century. It was discovered in Vienna, in 1885, in the great papyrus collection of the Archduke Rainer There is a question as to whether it comes from a gospel text or is only a homiletical paraphrase of the passage.

VERSIONS OF THE NEW TESTAMENT

In the beginning the Church read what was to become its New Testament altogether in the Greek language in which it had been written; but when the Gospel was taken to people who did not speak Greek, it had to be translated immediately into the language of its new hearers. These early translations from the Greek are known as "versions," and this book refers to three of them: the Latin, the Syriac, and the Coptic (Sahidic and Bohairic). We shall deal with them in this order. Other versions of less value from a textual point of view are the Ethiopic, the Gothic, the Armenian, the Georgian, the Arabic, the Slavonic, and the Persian.

The Latin Versions (it vg)

The Latin version is divided into two groups—the Itala (it) and the Vulgate (vg). The Itala (also known as the Old Latin) refers to all the Old Latin manuscripts which are not derived from Jerome's Latin translation known as the Vulgate. Jerome tells us that Pope Victor (*ca.* 190) was the first man to write theological treatises in Latin; and Tertullian, who died around 223, also wrote in Latin. Latin then became more and more the language of the Roman Empire, and the New Testament had to be translated into that language. In 383, in his preface to his revised Latin text of the Gospels, Jerome wrote that he had compiled one Latin text because there were so many floating around which differed both among themselves and from the Greek manuscripts; and Jerome's contemporary, Augustine, in his *De Doctrina Christiana*, attests the same wide variety of Latin interpretations. It was in order to give the church what he considered the best available Latin text and to rid the Latin New Testament of its variety of readings, that Jerome, at the behest of Pope Damasus, published his edition of the Gospels in 383; this was followed by the rest of the Bible, completed in 405. It was Jerome's edition of the Bible which in the eighth century became standard in the Roman Catholic Church. There is a question as to whether the extant Vulgate of the Acts, the Epistles, and the Apocalypse goes back to Jerome; but at present there seems to be no better explanation of them.

It is the earlier Latin manuscripts with their great variety of readings to which we refer as the Itala, or the Old Latin. We have no whole Bibles in the Old Latin, but only groups of books or fragments, dating from the fourth to the thirteenth centuries. There are also quotations from the Itala in the Latin Church Fathers which sometimes amount to whole chapters. These date from the second century on.

The Old Latin manuscripts may be roughly divided into three groups:

(1) The African manuscripts, such as *k, e.*
(2) The European manuscripts, such as *a, b, i.*
(3) The Italic manuscripts, such as *f, q.*

It is probably group number 3 which Jerome took as the basis for his own revision, and which may itself be a modification of number 2. Number 1, the African group, represented by manuscripts *k* and *e,* is extremely important because it is the same type of text as that used in Africa by Tertullian and Cyprian in the second and third centuries. Hence the tradition is at least that old, although the manuscripts *k* and *e* are later, *e* coming from the fourth or fifth century and *k* from the fifth or sixth. In parts of the Gospels, then, we can recover a Latin text which existed in the second century.

In order to arrive at the Greek text which this Latin represents, the Latin manuscripts must be retranslated back into Greek; and before this can be done, the translator must decide whether the Latin has itself been translated from the Greek literally or in paraphrase. For a literal Latin to Greek translation of a Latin manuscript which often paraphrased the Greek it translated, will not get us back very close to the original Greek! In addition to this difficulty we must try to decide whether the Latin manuscript with which we are dealing is itself a translation of a Greek manuscript or an edition of another Latin manuscript. These are some of the difficulties which accompany all the versions—Latin, Syriac, Coptic, etc.

We do not know what Greek manuscripts Jerome used, but they were apparently of an Alexandrian rather than a Western type. As the years went on, however, Jerome's Vulgate text itself became corrupt, being made to conform to Old Latin texts which died hard; and as a result there is scarcely an Old Latin reading which cannot be found in some manuscript of the Vulgate. There were numerous commentators who preferred the Itala, and its many surviving manuscripts testify to its having been in use centuries after Jerome had made his great revision. Indeed it was still being used in Bohemia at the close of the Middle Ages. As, then, the Vulgate was corrupted by the Old Latin and by many and sundry "improvements," it likewise had to be revised. This was done as early as the sixth century by Cassiodorus. Later Charlemagne, aware of the confusion of texts in his day, asked an Englishman, Alcuin, Abbot of St. Martin at Tours, to revise the Latin Bible; and on Christmas day in the year 801, Alcuin presented the Emperor with his revision. Other revisions followed and finally Pope Sixtus V (1585–90) published a text in 1590, accompanied by a bull declaring it alone to be trustworthy. Three months later he died. The College of Cardinals then called in all copies of the Sixtine edition, which had many errors, and in 1592 Pope Clement VIII (1592–1605) issued his own edition of the Vulgate (the Clementine Vulgate), but under the names of both Sixtus and Clement. The bull which accompanied Clement's Vulgate established it as the standard Roman text, and the third edition of the *Clementina* of 1598 is still the official Latin text of the Bible of the Roman Catholic Church. No verses were to be altered and no variant readings were to be put in the margin; so that officially, at any rate, textual criticism within the Roman Church was apparently proscribed from that date.

No text of the New Testament has been so influential and significant in the western church as the Vulgate. It was from the Vulgate that the Bible was read throughout western Europe for a thousands years; and it was the Vulgate that missionaries carried with them throughout the world and later translated into the vernacular of those to whom they had borne the Gospel. The first complete book to be printed from a press in Europe was a text of the Vulgate, published in 1455 at Mainz, by Gutenburg and Fust; the first complete English Bible was a translation from the Vulgate, made by Wycliffe; it was in the Vulgate text that the present chapter divisions of the Bible were worked out, probably by Stephen Langton, later Archbishop of Canterbury, *ca.* 1228.

The Syriac Versions (sy^c sy^s sy^p)

As in the Latin there is an old text (the Old Latin, represented by many manuscripts) and an authorized text (the Vulgate), so in the Syriac there is an old text (the Old Syriac, represented by two manuscripts) and an authorized text (the Peshitta—sy^p). In the eighteenth century, the Peshitta was the only Syriac text known; but scholars like Griesbach felt certain that an Old Syriac text lay behind it. This Old Syriac text is represented by two manuscripts discovered since Griesbach's time —the Curetonian and the Sinaitic Syriac (sy^c and sy^s). In 1842 a Syriac manuscript of the Gospels arrived at the British Museum from the library of a monastery in the Nitrian Desert in Egypt. William Cureton, the English Syriac scholar and an officer of the Museum, edited the leaves which were published in 1858 and are known by his name. They come from the middle of the fifth century and were erroneously believed by Dr. Cureton to contain the words of Jesus just as he spoke them— language and all! He stated that the original of his version was made before the original of the Peshitta. This was hotly disputed by advocates of the Peshitta but it has since been generally recognized to be true.

A second aid in getting at the Old Syriac text was made available in 1836 when the Armenians of the Mechitarist Monastery of San Lazzaro, Venice, published a commentary on Tatian's *Diatessaron* by Ephraem, the Syrian Father of the fourth century, which they possessed in an Armenian translation. This was not widely known until 1876, but since then Zahn and others have reconstructed the text on which this commentary, originally in Syriac, was based. In addition to the commentary, an Arabic translation of the *Diatessaron* was subsequently found in the Vatican Library; and after that still another Arabic translation was found in Egypt. From these two manuscripts the *Diatessaron* was edited in 1888. One should not leave the *Diatessaron* without also mentioning the Dura Fragment which was found on the site of Dura-Europos, a Roman fortified city captured by the Persians in 256 A.D. One of the vellum fragments from this site proved to be fourteen imperfect lines of the *Diatessaron* in Greek. Scholars are still uncertain whether Tatian wrote his *Diatessaron* in Greek or in Syriac—we have an Arabic translation and a Syriac commentary on it in an Armenian translation—but we now know that it existed in Greek, in Mesopotamia, in the early third century.

Finally, in 1892, two Cambridge ladies, Mrs. A. S. Lewis and her sister, Mrs. M. D. Gibson, discovered some palimpsest leaves of a Syriac manuscript of the Gospels in the same monastery of St. Catherine on Mount Sinai where Tischendorf had found his great Greek uncial, Sinaiticus. The gospel text underlay a Syriac treatise dated in the year 778 and was itself of the early fifth century. It was later photographed at Sinai and the photographs were published in 1894 containing about three-fourths of the Gospels. Known as Sinaitic Syriac (sy^s), the manuscript is still at Sinai, and along with other manuscripts there, has been rephotographed by an expedition from the American Schools of Oriental Research at Jerusalem.

The Old Syriac version, to which sy^c and sy^s belong, probably originated in the late second century or early third, and was akin to the text of Sinaiticus and Vaticanus, with Western readings inserted under the influence of the *Diatessaron*. It has been observed that the two manuscripts do not represent exactly the same text. There is a great deal more difference between them than there is, for instance, between two copies of the Peshitta; and of the two manuscripts the Sinaitic Syriac represents the earlier text. It is the oldest text of the Syriac that is known. But only the Gospels survive in the Old Syriac version; the rest of the New Testament first appears in the Syriac language in the Peshitta.

The Peshitta (common language) version of the Syriac New Testament was increasingly used in the Syrian church from the end of the fifth century. Its origin is not certain. Until recently it was generally believed that this text was edited under the direction of Rabbula, Bishop of Edessa in 411-435, but perhaps it existed before Rabbula, originating in Antioch as an attempt to make the Syriac text conform more closely to the Greek. The Peshitta still remains the basis of the authorized Syriac text. It has two early, significant revisions, one by Philoxenus, Bishop of Mabug (Hierapolis), in 508, known as the Philoxenian Syriac; and the other by Thomas of Harkel (Heraclea) at Alexandria, in 616, known as the Harclean Syriac.

The Coptic Versions (sa bo)

The New Testament spread to Greek-speaking people in Egypt, thence to natives who spoke Coptic in various dialects, chief of which were the Sahidic and the Bohairic.

The Sahidic. The Sahidic or Thebaic version was current in Upper (southern) Egypt whose chief city was Thebes, and its existence was not known until the end of the eighteenth century. It is found only in numerous fragments from which, however, most of the New Testament can be put together. Many fragments date from the fifth century, some from the fourth. The text is preponderantly Alexandrian but contains some Western readings, especially in Mark and Luke. The version is dated early in the third century.

The Bohairic. The Bohairic or Memphitic version, which alone of the Coptic has the complete New Testament, was current in Lower (northern) Egypt. Bohairic, the most developed of Egyptian dialects, ultimately superseded all other dialects, until "Coptic" came to mean "Bohairic." Over a hundred manuscripts, all late, have been found. Three date from the twelfth century; the oldest, containing the Gospels, is at Oxford and is dated 1173–74 A.D. The remaining manuscripts are later; but a single leaf of Ephesians may be dated in the fifth century. The text is mainly Alexandrian, and the version is dated in the first half of the third century, a little after the Sahidic.

CHURCH FATHERS

I Clement—a letter written from the church at Rome to the church at Corinth by Clement, a leading presbyter of Rome, *ca.* 95 A.D. It admonishes the Corinthians to lead a godly life and then exhorts them to obey their presbyters who have received their leadership from the apostles. It is an early indication of Rome's initiative among the churches.

II Clement—a sermon, probably originating in Alexandria or Corinth *ca.* 150 A.D., not by Clement, but receiving its name from him because of an early association with his letter. It follows I Clement in the manuscripts.

Ignatius—bishop of Antioch in Syria who, at the beginning of the second century, *ca.* 110–117, while being led through western Asia Minor to his execution as a martyr in Rome, wrote a letter to each of six churches exhorting unity among the believers. The basis of this unity was the threefold ministry of bishop, presbyter, and deacon. The churches written to were at Ephesus, Magnesia, Tralles, Rome, Philadelphia, Smyrna; and one personal note to Polycarp, bishop of Smyrna.

Didache—otherwise known as the "Teaching of the Twelve Apostles" first appeared *ca.* 100–110 A.D. as a brief formulation of the rules of conduct Christians should observe.

Barnabas—the Epistle of Barnabas written *ca.* 130 A.D. probably in Alexandria, offered Christians a compromise solution to the problem of the proper significance for them of the Hebrew law. This compromise held that the Jewish scriptures were true, not literally as the Jews believed, but allegorically. The Epistle was accepted as Scripture by Clement and Origen, and is found in the manuscript Sinaiticus.

Marcion—a Christian heretic, excommunicated *ca.* 144 A.D. (He is cited in this book only as giving manuscript support.) He was antilegalistic, rejecting the Old Testament and its God, substituting a Docetic Christ and a New Testament canon composed of St. Paul's epistles (not the Pastorals) and the Gospel of Luke considerably excised. This was the first New Testament canon to be drawn up as far as is known.

Justin—called the Martyr from his testimony unto death in Rome *ca.* 165, was born in Samaria of heathen parents. A student of philosophy, he was gradually converted to Christianity as the oldest, truest, and most divine of all philosophies. In its defense he wrote his *Apology* (for Christianity) *ca.* 155, addressed to the Emperor Antoninus Pius and his colleagues; and his *Dialogue with Trypho,* shortly after, which defends Christianity against the attacks of Judaism by means of a discussion between Justin and a Jew named Trypho.

Tatian—from Syria or Assyria, writing in the middle of the second century. Known chiefly for his *Diatessaron* which interweaves the four Gospels into one continuous narrative.

Irenaeus—born in Asia Minor, probably in the second quarter of the second century; made bishop of Lyons, which post he held till his death, *ca.* 200. Known chiefly for his book refuting various Gnostic schools, *Refutation of Gnosticism,* or *Against Heresies*—the oldest surviving work in which the Church repudiated heresy—he also wrote several other books and many letters which must have been almost treatises. His *Refutation* is known mostly from an early Latin translation.

Theodotus—late second century; a follower of the Gnostic heretic, Valentinus of Alexandria; excerpts from his writings have been recorded by Clement.

Tertullian—born in Carthage *ca.* 150–55, studied law; converted to Christianity *ca.* 190–95, but broke with the "Catholic" Church *ca.* 207 in favor of the asceticism of the Montanists. Father of Latin theology, he wrote in Latin; when he died *ca.* 223, he had left the Montanists and founded a sect of his own. His chief polemical work was *Against Marcion* in five books written over a period of about twelve years, 200–12.

Clement of Alexandria—successor of Pantaenus as head of the Alexandrian catechetical school from *ca.* 200 till his death about 215; he was also a presbyter in the Alexandrian church. Perhaps not a great theologian, Clement was a kind of Greek puritan who understood philosophy as the handmaid of Christianity having led the Greeks to Christ. Four of his more important surviving works are: the *Exhortation to the Heathen;* the *Protrepticus,* or *Address,* designed to convert pagans; the *Instructor,* the first treatise on Christian conduct; and the *Stromateis,* or *Miscellanies* which is a scrapbook of many thoughts Clement wished to preserve.

Origen—born in 184–85 A.D., lived mostly in Alexandria where he headed the catechetical school and in Caesarea where he probably died in 254 during the Decian persecution. "He was the greatest Christian scholar and the most prolific Christian writer of antiquity," having written thousands of scrolls about the length of the Gospel of Matthew. He was a Biblical critic and exegete, interpreting Scripture allegorically. He wrote numerous commentaries and doctrinal works including *On Prayer;* a great apology, *Contra Celsum (Against Celsus),* which is a defense of Christianity against the attacks of the pagan Celsus; and what may perhaps be considered Christianity's first systematic theology, *De Principiis (On First Principles),* in four books. He was also the compiler of the famous Hexapla which contained the Old Testament in six columns—the Hebrew, a Greek transliteration of the Hebrew, the Septuagint, and the Greek translations of Aquila, Theodotion, and Symmachus. This must have been about nine thousand pages long.

Hippolytus—born *ca.* 170, spent most of his life in Rome where he was a presbyter, and bishop for about seven years (222–23 to 230) when he split with Calixtus who had been elected bishop. He was sent into exile to the mines of Sardinia in 235 and died there or in Rome probably the following year; he was buried on the road to Tivoli. He wrote many books but is known chiefly for his *Refutation of All Heresies* which seeks to show that the heresies had their source in Greek philosophy and in paganism.

Cyprian—cited in this book only as giving manuscript support. Born probably in Carthage *ca.* 200–210; spent all his life there; was bishop of Carthage from 248–49 till his death as a martyr in 258, when he was beheaded.

Eusebius of Caesarea—born *ca.* 260, probably in Palestine; bishop of Caesarea from *ca.* 315 till his death in 340. Played a prominent part at the Council of Nicea; known chiefly for his *Church History* in ten books, written between 323 and 325; also wrote *Theophany,* a brief exposition of the meaning of Christ, toward the end of his life.

Didymus—a disciple of Origen; blinded in early youth; one of the last presidents of the catechetical school at Alexandria; died *ca.* 398. Noted chiefly for his exegesis of Biblical books and his three books, *On the Trinity.* Also surviving is a treatise on the Holy Spirit in a Latin translation.

Epiphanius of Salamis—born in Palestine between 310 and 320; an ascetic; became bishop of Salamis, capital of Cyprus, in 367; spent life hunting heretics and died at sea on his way from Constantinople to Cyprus in 403. He wrote the *Ancoratus,* which is a defense of Christian doctrine, in 373; and, most important, the *Panarion*—his work against heresies—between 374 and 377. In this he tracks down eighty heresies, twenty of which precede the time of Christ, and the first of which is barbarism, from Adam to the flood.

Jerome—born in Stridon, Dalmatia, between 331 and 342; educated in Rome where he was baptized *ca.* 370, becoming an ascetic. In 385 he left Rome for Jerusalem where he presided over a monastery till his death in 420. His supreme gift to Christendom was the Vulgate—his translation of the whole Bible into Latin (cf. pp. xi–xiii). Also of great importance are his many commentaries on Biblical books; his dialogue against the Pelagians in three books (415 A.D.); and *On Illustrious Men,* written in 392 and 393, which is a list of ecclesiastical writers from the apostles to his own times, with their main works. Many of his letters are also preserved.

Augustine—cited in this book only as giving manuscript support; born in North Africa in 354, died in August, 430. Chiefly known for his *Confessions, City of God,* commentaries, etc. Tremendous influence on subsequent theology.

Peter of Laodicea—a bishop (although not always so acknowledged) of Laodicea, in the seventh century, who wrote commentaries on the four Gospels.

Peter of Riga—author of the poem, *Aurora,* written in the late twelfth century. In the thirteenth century McClean manuscript of this poem, bequeathed to the Fitzwilliam Museum, are many marginal notations in Latin. One such notation which is an answer to the question asked in the text, "Why did not the buyers and sellers resist our Lord?" is found in this book.

NONCANONICAL GOSPELS

Gospel of the Ebionites—written in the first half of the second century. It was apparently an abridged and altered form of the Gospel of Matthew, which Epiphanius incorrectly refers to as the "Gospel of the Hebrews" or the "Hebrew Gospel." Written in Greek and assuming all three of the synoptic gospels, this gospel was used by the Jewish Christian sect known as Ebionites. The Ebionites denied Jesus' birth of a virgin. They believed Jesus' sonship to God rested not on his birth in a special way, but on the union of the Spirit with him at the time of his baptism. The seven extant fragments of this work are found in Epiphanius' *Against Heresies* XXX, 13–22.

Gospel of the Hebrews—written in the first half of the second century, for Greek-speaking Jewish Christian circles. It probably originated in Egypt—one reason for this supposition being that its main witnesses are the Alexandrians Clement and Origen. The gospel is apparently not a development from any of the four canonical gospels.

Gospel of the Egyptians—probably from the first half of the second century, it was used by Christians in Egypt perhaps as their only "life of Jesus." Though it was influenced by Gnosticism, it was quoted by the author of II Clement. Clement of Alexandria also quoted it (*Miscellanies,* Book III), and not as heresy. Origen, however, regarded this gospel as heretical.

Gospel of the Naassenes—quoted by Hippolytus in Book V of his *Refutation of All Heresies.* The origin of the Naassenes, or Ophites, i.e. Serpent-Worshippers, is unknown, but they practiced heathen rites and were considered heretics by Hippolytus.

Gospel of the Nazaraeans—appeared in the first half of the second century, in Syrian Jewish Christian circles. It is apparently an Aramaic translation of a Greek form of the Gospel of Matthew.

Gospel of Peter—coming from the middle of the second century, it is a development in a Gnostic direction of the four canonical gospels. It is not, however, a full-blown Gnostic work. It was known by reference to its title only (i.e., there were no extant quotations from it) until the winter of 1886–87 when a fragment of it, coming from the eighth or ninth century, was found at Akhmim in Upper Egypt. The gospel began with Pilate's washing of his hands, and ended with a unique description of Jesus' resurrection.

Acts of Philip—a fourth century Gnostic work which we know from fragments of later revisions.

Gospel of Thomas—a late fourth century "gospel" found about 1945 near the village of Nag Hammadi, up the Nile River in Egypt. Written in Sahidic Coptic, it is a collection of sayings of Jesus, many of them strongly influenced by Gnostic thought. The sayings probably originated in Greek, about 140 A.D.

INDEX OF NONCANONICAL PARALLELS

INDEX OF NONCANONICAL PARALLELS.

INDEX OF THE GOSPEL PARALLELS.

Introductory Note.

The Index of Parallels which follows is a double one. The first set of references (in bold face) contains the main passages; the second set contains those sections which may be regarded as parallels apart from context considerations. The *italics* in the second set of references denote those passages in the Synopsis indicated only by cross-references (i.e., without the printing of the text).

The Infancy Narratives.

A. The Matthean Infancy Narrative. Matthew 1, 2.

I. The Galilean Section. Matthew 3—18 = Mark 1—9 = Luke 3:1—9:50.

		Matt.	Mark	Luke	Parallels and Doublets Matt.	Mark	Luke	Page
1	John the Baptist	3: 1-6	1: 1-6	3: 1-6	*11:10*	*1:15*	*7:27*	8
2	John's Preaching of Repentance	7-10	—	7-9	*7:19*			9
3	John's Preaching to Special Groups	—	—	10-14				”
4	John's Messianic Preaching	11-12	7-8	15-18				”
5	John's Imprisonment	—	—	19-20	*14:3-4*	*6:17-18*		10
6	The Baptism of Jesus	13-17	9-11	21-22				”
7	The Genealogy of Jesus	—	—	23-38	1:1-16			11
8	The Temptation	4: 1-11	12-13	4: 1-13				12
9	The First Preaching in Galilee	12-17	14-15	14-15				14
10	The Rejection at Nazareth	—	—	16-30	13:54-58	6:1-6a		”
11	The Call of the First Disciples	18-22	16-20	—			*5:1-11*	16
12	Jesus in the Synagogue at Capernaum	—	21-28	31-37	7:28-29			”
13	The Healing of Peter's Mother-in-law	—	29-31	38-39	8:14-15			17
14	The Sick Healed at Evening	—	32-34	40-41	*4:24* 8:16-17 12:16	3:10-11		18
15	Jesus Departs from Capernaum	—	35-38	42-43				”
16	A Preaching Journey in Galilee	23-25	39	44	*8:16* 9:35 12:15 14:35	3:7, 8, 10 6:54-55	6:17-19	”
17	The Miraculous Catch of Fish	—	—	5: 1-11	*4:18-22*	*1:16-20*		19

INDEX OF THE GOSPEL PARALLELS.

The Sermon on the Mount. Matthew 5—7.

THE INFANCY NARRATIVES

A. The Matthean Infancy Narrative.

Matthew 1–2

THE GENEALOGY OF JESUS.

Matt. 1:1–17	Luke 3:23–34 (§ 7, *p. 11*) (*In reverse order*)
1 The book of the genealogy of Jesus Christ, the son of David, the son of Abraham.	
2 Abraham was the father of Isaac,	34 Abraham
and Isaac the father of Jacob,	Isaac
and Jacob the father of Judah and his brothers,	Jacob
3 and Judah the father of Perez and Zerah by Tamar,	33 Judah
and Perez the father of Hezron,	Perez
and Hezron the father of Ram, [a]	Hezron, Arni, Admin
4 and Ram [a] the father of Amminadab,	Amminadab
and Amminadab the father of Nahshon,	32 Nahshon
and Nahshon the father of Salmon,	Sala
5 And Salmon the father of Boaz by Rahab,	Boaz
and Boaz the father of Obed by Ruth,	Obed
and Obed the father of Jesse,	Jesse
6 and Jesse the father of David the king.	31 David
And David was the father of Solomon by the wife of Uriah,	
7 and Solomon the father of Rehoboam,	Nathan
and Rehoboam the father of Abijah,	Mattatha
and Abijah the father of Asa, [b]	Menna
8 and Asa [b] the father of Jehoshaphat,	Melea
and Jehoshaphat the father of Joram,	30 Eliakim
and Joram the father of Uzziah,	Jonam
9 and Uzziah the father of Jotham,	Joseph
and Jotham the father of Ahaz,	Judah
and Ahaz the father of Hezekiah,	Simeon
10 and Hezekiah the father of Manasseh,	29 Levi
and Manasseh the father of Amos, [c]	Matthat
and Amos [c] the father of Josiah,	Jorim
11 and Josiah the father of Jechoniah and his brothers, at the time of the deportation to Babylon.	Eliezer, Joshua, 28 Er, Elmadam, Cosam, Addi, Melchi, 27 Neri
12 And after the deportation to Babylon: Jechoniah was the father of Shealtiel, [d]	Shealtiel [d]
and Shealtiel [d] the father of Zerubbabel,	Zerubbabel
13 and Zerubbabel the father of Abiud,	
and Abiud the father of Eliakim,	Rhesa
and Eliakim the father of Azor,	Joanan
14 and Azor the father of Zadok,	26 Joda
and Zadok the father of Achim,	Josech
and Achim the father of Eliud,	Semein
15 and Eliud the father of Eleazar,	Mattathias
and Eleazar the father of Matthan,	Maath, 25 Naggai, Esli, Nahum, Amos, Mattathias,
	24 Joseph, Jannai, Melchi, Levi

Matt. 1:2-6—I Chronicles 2:1-15;   3-6—Ruth 4:18-22;   7-12—I Chronicles 3:10-19.

[a] Greek: *Aram*.   [b] Greek: *Asaph*.   [c] text: S B C Θ λ it sa bo; *Amon*: W φ 𝕽 vg sy^c sy^s sy^p.   [d] Greek: *Salathiel*.

1

and Matthan the father of Jacob,
16 and Jacob the father of Joseph the husband of
Mary, of whom Jesus was born, who is called Christ. e

| Matthat, 23 Heli |
| Joseph |

17 So all the generations from Abraham to David were fourteen generations, and from David to the deportation to Babylon fourteen generations, and from the deportation to Babylon to the Christ fourteen generations.

THE BIRTH OF JESUS.
Matt. 1:18–25

18 Now the birth of Jesus f Christ took place in this way. When his mother Mary had been betrothed to Joseph, before they came together she was found to be with child of the Holy Spirit; 19 and her husband Joseph, being a just man and unwilling to put her to shame, resolved to divorce her quietly. 20 But as he considered this, behold, an angel of the Lord appeared to him in a dream, saying, "Joseph, son of David, do not fear to take Mary your wife, for that which is conceived in her is of the Holy Spirit; 21 she will bear a son, and you shall call his name Jesus, for he will save his people from their sins." 22 All this took place to fulfil what the Lord had spoken by the prophet:

23 "Behold, a virgin shall conceive and bear a son,
    and his name shall be called Emmanuel"

(which means, God with us). 24 When Joseph woke from sleep, he did as the angel of the Lord commanded him; he took his wife, 25 but knew her not until she had borne a son; g and he called his name Jesus.

THE VISIT OF THE MAGI.
Matt. 2:1–12

1 Now when Jesus was born in Bethlehem of Judea in the days of Herod the king, behold, wise men from the East came to Jerusalem, saying, 2 "Where is he who has been born king of the Jews? For we have seen his star in the East, and have come to worship him." 3 When Herod the king heard this, he was troubled, and all Jerusalem with him; 4 and assembling all the chief priests and scribes of the people, he inquired of them where the Christ was to be born. 5 They told him, "In Bethlehem of Judea; for so it is written by the prophet:

6 'And you, O Bethlehem, in the land of Judah,
    are by no means least among the rulers of Judah;
    for from you shall come a ruler
    who will govern my people Israel.' "

7 Then Herod summoned the wise men secretly and ascertained from them what time the star appeared; 8 and he sent them to Bethlehem, saying, "Go and search diligently for the child, and when you have found him bring me word, that I too may come and worship him." 9 When they had heard the king they went their way; and lo, the star which they had seen in the East went before them, till it came to rest over the place where the child was. 10 When they saw the star, they rejoiced exceedingly with great joy; 11 and going into the house they saw the child with Mary his mother, and they fell down and worshiped him. Then, opening their treasures, they offered him gifts, gold and frankincense and myrrh. 12 And being warned in a dream not to return to Herod, they departed to their own country by another way.

Matt. 1:23—Isaiah 7:14, 8:8.   2:2 cf. Numbers 24:17.   2:6—Micah 5:2.   2:11—Isaiah 60:6.

---

e text: P¹ S B C W λ ℜ it (some MSS.) vg syᵖ sa Tert.; *Jacob the father of Joseph, to whom the virgin Mary having been betrothed bore Jesus who is called Christ:* Θ φ it (some MSS.); *Jacob the father of Joseph. Joseph, to whom was betrothed the virgin Mary, was the father of Jesus who is called the Christ:* syˢ; *Jacob the father of Joseph, to whom was betrothed the virgin Mary who* (fem.) *bore Jesus the Christ:* syᶜ; *Jacob the father of Joseph the husband of Mary who bore Jesus who is called Christ:* bo. f text: P¹ S C Θ λ φ ℜ syᵖ sa bo; *Christ Jesus:* B; *Christ:* it vg syᶜ syˢ; *Jesus:* W. g text: S B λ φ it syᶜ sa bo; *her firstborn son:* C D W ℜ vg syᵖ; *and she bore him a son:* syˢ.

THE FLIGHT INTO EGYPT, HEROD'S MASSACRE OF THE BABIES, THE RETURN FROM EGYPT.
Matt. 2:13–23

13 Now when they had departed, behold, an angel of the Lord appeared to Joseph in a dream and said, "Rise, take the child and his mother, and flee to Egypt, and remain there till I tell you; for Herod is about to search for the child, to destroy him." 14 And he rose and took the child and his mother by night, and departed to Egypt, 15 and remained there until the death of Herod. This was to fulfil what the Lord had spoken by the prophet, "Out of Egypt have I called my son."

16 Then Herod, when he saw that he had been tricked by the wise men, was in a furious rage, and he sent and killed all the male children in Bethlehem and in all that region who were two years old or under, according to the time which he had ascertained from the wise men. 17 Then was fulfilled what was spoken by the prophet Jeremiah:

18 "A voice was heard in Ramah,
    wailing and loud lamentation,
    Rachel weeping for her children;
    she refused to be consoled,
    because they were no more."

19 But when Herod died, behold, an angel of the Lord appeared in a dream to Joseph in Egypt, saying, 20 "Rise, take the child and his mother, and go to the land of Israel, for those who sought the child's life are dead." 21 And he rose and took the child and his mother, and went to the land of Israel. 22 But when he heard that Archelaus reigned over Judea in place of his father Herod, he was afraid to go there, and being warned in a dream he withdrew to the district of Galilee. 23 And he went and dwelt in a city called Nazareth, that what was spoken by the prophets might be fulfilled, "He shall be called a Nazarene."

B. The Lucan Infancy Narrative.
Luke 1, 2

THE PROLOGUE TO THE GOSPEL.
Luke 1:1–4

1 Inasmuch as many have undertaken to compile a narrative of the things which have been accomplished among us, 2 just as they were delivered to us by those who from the beginning were eyewitnesses and ministers of the word, 3 it seemed good to me also, having followed all things closely[h] for some time past, to write an orderly account for you, most excellent Theophilus, 4 that you may know the truth concerning the things of which you have been informed.

THE PROMISE OF THE BAPTIST'S BIRTH.
Luke 1:5–25

5 In the days of Herod, king of Judea, there was a priest named Zechariah,[i] of the division of Abijah; and he had a wife of the daughters of Aaron, and her name was Elizabeth. 6 And they were both righteous before God, walking in all the commandments and ordinances of the Lord blameless. 7 But they had no child, because Elizabeth was barren, and both were advanced in years.

8 Now while he was serving as priest before God when his division was on duty, 9 according to the custom of the priesthood, it fell to him by lot to enter the temple of the Lord and burn incense. 10 And the whole multitude of the people were praying outside at the hour of incense. 11 And there appeared to him an angel of the Lord standing on the right side of the altar of incense. 12 And Zechariah was troubled when he saw him, and fear fell upon him. 13 But the angel said to him, "Do not be afraid, Zechariah, for your prayer is heard, and your wife Elizabeth will bear you a son, and you shall call his name John.

Matt. 2:15—Hosea 11:1. 2:18—Jeremiah 31:15. 2:23—cf. Isaiah 11:1, (in Hebrew). Luke 1:5—I Chronicles 24:10.

[h] Or, *accurately.*   [i] Greek: *Zacharias.*

To Matt. 2:15 cf. **Gospel of the Nazaraeans,** (in Jerome, *On Illustrious Men 3*)—"Out of Egypt have I called my son" and "For he shall be called a Nazaraean." Cf. also margin of codex 1424—This was to fulfill what the Lord had spoken by the prophet, "Out of Egypt have I called my son . . ."

14 And you will have joy and gladness,
and many will rejoice at his birth;
15 for he will be great before the Lord,
and he shall drink no wine nor strong drink,
and he will be filled with the Holy Spirit,
even from his mother's womb.
16 And he will turn many of the sons of Israel to the
Lord their God,
17 and he will go before him in the spirit and power
of Elijah,
to turn the hearts of the fathers to the children,
and the disobedient to the wisdom of the just,
to make ready for the Lord a people prepared."

18 And Zechariah said to the angel, "How shall I know this? For I am an old man, and my wife is advanced in years." 19 And the angel answered him, "I am Gabriel, who stand in the presence of God; and I was sent to speak to you, and to bring you this good news. 20 And behold, you will be silent and unable to speak until the day that these things come to pass, because you did not believe my words, which will be fulfilled in their time." 21 And the people were waiting for Zechariah, and they wondered at his delay in the temple. 22 And when he came out, he could not speak to them, and they perceived that he had seen a vision in the temple; and he made signs to them and remained dumb. 23 And when his time of service was ended, he went to his home.

24 After these days his wife Elizabeth conceived, and for five months she hid herself, saying, 25 "Thus the Lord has done to me in the days when he looked on me, to take away my reproach among men."

THE ANNUNCIATION.
Luke 1:26–38

26 In the sixth month the angel Gabriel was sent from God to a city of Galilee named Nazareth, 27 to a virgin betrothed to a man whose name was Joseph, of the house of David; and the virgin's name was Mary. 28 And he came to her and said, "Hail, O favored one, the Lord is with you!"[j] 29 But she was greatly troubled at the saying, and considered in her mind what sort of greeting this might be. 30 And the angel said to her, "Do not be afraid, Mary, for you have found favor with God. 31 And behold, you will conceive in your womb and bear a son, and you shall call his name Jesus.

32 He will be great, and will be called the Son of the Most High;
and the Lord God will give to him the throne of his father David,
33 and he will reign over the house of Jacob forever;
and of his kingdom there will be no end."

34 And Mary said to the angel, "How shall this be, since I have no husband?" 35 And the angel said to her,

"The Holy Spirit will come upon you,
and the power of the Most High will overshadow you;
therefore the child to be born[k] will be called holy, the Son of God.

36 And behold, your kinswoman Elizabeth in her old age has also conceived a son; and this is the sixth month with her who was called barren. 37 For with God nothing will be impossible." 38 And Mary said, "Behold I am the handmaid of the Lord; let it be to me according to your word." And the angel departed from her.

Luke 1:15—Numbers 6:3, I Samuel 1:11.   1:17—Malachi 4:5-6, Ecclesiasticus 48:10.   1:18—Genesis 15:8.   1:31—Isaiah 7:14.   1:32f.—cf. Isaiah 9:6-7 and II Samuel 7:12-16.   1:37—Genesis 18:14.

---

[j] text: S B W λ sa bo; add, *Blessed are you among women!* A C D Θ φ 𝕽 it vg sy^p.   [k] text: S A B D W φ 𝕽 it (some MSS.) vg sa bo; add, *of you:* C Θ λ it (some MSS.) sy^p.

MARY'S VISIT TO ELIZABETH.
Luke 1:39–56

39 In those days Mary arose and went with haste into the hill country, to a city of Judah, 40 and she entered the house of Zechariah and greeted Elizabeth. 41 And when Elizabeth heard the greeting of Mary, the babe leaped in her womb; and Elizabeth was filled with the Holy Spirit 42 and she exclaimed with a loud cry, "Blessed are you among women, and blessed is the fruit of your womb! 43 And why is this granted me, that the mother of my Lord should come to me? 44 For behold, when the voice of your greeting came to my ears, the babe in my womb leaped for joy. 45 And blessed is she who believed that there would be a fulfilment [1] of what was spoken to her from the Lord." 46 And Mary [m] said,

> "My soul magnifies the Lord,
> 47 and my spirit rejoices in God my Savior,
> 48 for he has regarded the low estate of his handmaiden.
> For behold, henceforth all generations will call me blessed;
> 49 for he who is mighty has done great things for me,
> and holy is his name.
> 50 And his mercy is on those who fear him
> from generation to generation.
> 51 He has shown strength with his arm,
> he has scattered the proud in the imagination of their hearts,
> 52 he has put down the mighty from their thrones,
> and exalted those of low degree;
> 53 he has filled the hungry with good things,
> and the rich he has sent empty away.
> 54 He has helped his servant Israel,
> in remembrance of his mercy,
> 55 as he spoke to our fathers,
> to Abraham and to his posterity forever."

56 And Mary remained with her about three months, and returned to her home.

THE BIRTH OF THE BAPTIST.
Luke 1:57–80

57 Now the time came for Elizabeth to be delivered, and she gave birth to a son. 58 And her neighbors and kinsfolk heard that the Lord had shown great mercy to her, and they rejoiced with her. 59 And on the eighth day they came to circumcise the child; and they would have named him Zechariah after his father, 60 but his mother said, "Not so; he shall be called John." 61 And they said to her, "None of your kindred is called by this name." 62 And they made signs to his father, inquiring what he would have him called. 63 And he asked for a writing tablet, and wrote, "His name is John." And they all marveled. 64 And immediately his mouth was opened and his tongue loosed, and he spoke, blessing God. 65 And fear came on all their neighbors. And all these things were talked about through all the hill country of Judea; 66 and all who heard them laid them up in their hearts, saying, "What then will this child be?" For the hand of the Lord was with him.

67 And his father Zechariah was filled with the Holy Spirit, and prophesied, saying,

> 68 "Blessed be the Lord God of Israel,
> for he has visited and redeemed his people,
> 69 and has raised up a horn of salvation for us
> in the house of his servant David,

Luke 1:46-55—cf. I Samuel 2:1-10.   1:47—Habakkuk 3:18.   1:48—I Samuel 1:11.   1:48b— cf. Genesis 30:13.   1:49b—Psalm 111:9.   1:50—Psalm 103:17.   1:51—Psalm 89:10.   1:52— Ecclesiasticus 10:14, Ezekiel 21:31.   1:53—Psalm 107:9.   1:54—Isaiah 41:8f., Psalm 98:3.   1:55— Micah 7:20, II Samuel 22:51.   1:59—cf. Leviticus 12:3.   1:68—Psalm 41:13, 111:9.   1:69— Psalm 18:2, 132:17.

[1] Or, *believed, for there will be a fulfillment.*   [m] *Elizabeth* instead of *Mary* in Origen and some of MSS. of the Itala.

[70] as he spoke by the mouth of his holy prophets from of old,
[71] that we should be saved from our enemies,
and from the hand of all who hate us;
[72] to perform the mercy promised to our fathers,
and to remember his holy covenant,
[73] the oath which he swore to our father Abraham, [74] to grant us
that we, being delivered from the hand of our enemies,
might serve him without fear,
[75] in holiness and righteousness before him all the days of our life.
[76] And you, child, will be called the prophet of the Most High;
for you will go before the Lord to prepare his ways,
[77] to give knowledge of salvation to his people
in the forgiveness of their sins,
[78] through the tender mercy of our God,
when the day shall dawn upon [n] us from on high
[79] to give light to those who sit in darkness and in the shadow of death,
to guide our feet into the way of peace."

[80] And the child grew and became strong in spirit, and he was in the wilderness till the day of his manifestation to Israel.

THE BIRTH OF JESUS.
Luke 2:1–20

[1] In those days a decree went out from Caesar Augustus that all the world should be enrolled. [2] This was the first enrollment, when Quirinius was governor of Syria. [3] And all went to be enrolled, each to his own city. [4] And Joseph also went up from Galilee, from the city of Nazareth, to Judea, to the city of David, which is called Bethlehem, because he was of the house and lineage of David, [5] to be enrolled with Mary, his betrothed, who was with child. [6] And while they were there, the time came for her to be delivered. [7] And she gave birth to her first-born son and wrapped him in swaddling cloths, and laid him in a manger, because there was no place for them in the inn.

[8] And in that region there were shepherds out in the field, keeping watch over their flock by night. [9] And an angel of the Lord appeared to them, and the glory of the Lord shone around them, and they were filled with fear. [10] And the angel said to them, "Be not afraid; for behold, I bring you good news of a great joy which will come to all the people; [11] for to you is born this day in the city of David a Savior, who is Christ the Lord. [o] [12] And this will be a sign for you: you will find a babe wrapped in swaddling cloths and lying in a manger." [13] And suddenly there was with the angel a multitude of the heavenly host praising God and saying,

[14] "Glory to God in the highest,
and on earth peace among men with whom he is pleased!" [p]

[15] When the angels went away from them into heaven, the shepherds said to one another, "Let us go over to Bethlehem and see this thing that has happened, which the Lord has made known to us." [16] And they went with haste, and found Mary and Joseph, and the babe lying in a manger. [17] And when they saw it they made known the saying which had been told them concerning this child; [18] and all who heard it wondered at what the shepherds told them. [19] But Mary kept all these things, pondering them in her heart. [20] And the shepherds returned, glorifying and praising God for all they had heard and seen, as it had been told them.

Luke 1:71—Psalm 106:10, 18:17. 1:72a—Micah 7:20. 1:72b—Psalm 105:8, 106:45. 1:73—Jeremiah 11:5. 1:76—Malachi 3:1, Isaiah 40:3. 1:79a—Psalm 107:10. 1:79b—Isaiah 59:8.

---

[n] Or, *whereby the dayspring will visit;* text: S B W Θ sy[s] sy[p] sa bo; *since the dayspring has visited:* P[47] A C D λ φ 𝔎 it vg. [o] text: S A B D Θ λ φ 𝔎 it vg sa bo; *the Lord Christ:* W sy[s] sy[p]; *Christ of the Lord:* two MSS. of the Itala and two Syriac versions. [p] text: S A B D W it vg sa Irenaeus, Origen; *peace, good will among men:* Θ λ φ 𝔎 bo; *peace and good will among men:* sy[s]; *peace and good hope to men:* sy[p].

THE CIRCUMCISION OF JESUS AND THE PRESENTATION
IN THE TEMPLE.
Luke 2:21–40

21 And at the end of eight days, when he was circumcised, he was called Jesus, the name given by the angel before he was conceived in the womb.

22 And when the time came for their purification according to the law of Moses, they brought him up to Jerusalem to present him to the Lord 23 (as it is written in the law of the Lord, "Every male that opens the womb shall be called holy to the Lord") 24 and to offer a sacrifice according to what is said in the law of the Lord, "a pair of turtle-doves, or two young pigeons." 25 Now there was a man in Jerusalem, whose name was Simeon, and this man was righteous and devout, looking for the consolation of Israel, and the Holy Spirit was upon him. 26 And it had been revealed to him by the Holy Spirit that he should not see death before he had seen the Lord's Christ. 27 And inspired by the Spirit q he came into the temple; and when the parents brought in the child Jesus, to do for him according to the custom of the law, 28 he took him up in his arms and blessed God and said,

29 "Lord, now lettest thou thy servant depart in peace
  according to thy word;
30 for mine eyes have seen thy salvation
31 which thou hast prepared in the presence of all peoples,
32 a light for revelation to the Gentiles,
  and for glory to thy people Israel."

33 And his father and his mother marveled at what was said about him; 34 and Simeon blessed them and said to Mary his mother,

"Behold, this child is set for the fall and rising of many in Israel,
  and for a sign that is spoken against
35 (and a sword will pierce through your own soul also),
  that thoughts out of many hearts may be revealed."

36 And there was a prophetess, Anna, the daughter of Phanuel, of the tribe of Asher; she was of a great age, having lived with her husband seven years from her virginity, 37 and as a widow till r she was eighty-four. She did not depart from the temple, worshiping with fasting and prayer night and day. 38 And coming up at that very hour she gave thanks to God, and spoke of him to all who were looking for the redemption of Jerusalem.

39 And when they had performed everything according to the law of the Lord, they returned into Galilee, to their own city, Nazareth. 40 And the child grew and became strong, s filled with wisdom; and the favor of God was upon him.

JESUS AT TWELVE YEARS.
Luke 2:41–52

41 Now his parents went to Jerusalem every year at the feast of the Passover. 42 And when he was twelve years old, they went up according to custom; 43 and when the feast was ended, as they were returning, the boy Jesus stayed behind in Jerusalem. His parents did not know it, 44 but supposing him to be in the company they went a day's journey, and they sought him among their kinsfolk and acquaintances; 45 and when they did not find him, they returned to Jerusalem, seeking him. 46 After three days they found him in the temple, sitting among the teachers, listening to them and asking them questions; 47 and all who heard him were amazed at his understanding and his answers. 48 And when they saw him they were astonished; and his mother said to him, "Son, why have you treated us so? Behold, your father and I have been looking for you anxiously." 49 And he said to them, "How is it that you sought me? Did you not know that I must be in my Father's house?" 50 And they did not understand the saying which he spoke to them. 51 And he went down with them and came to Nazareth, and was obedient to them; and his mother kept all these things in her heart.

52 And Jesus increased in wisdom and in stature, t and in favor with God and man.

Luke 2:22—Lev. 12:6.   2:23—Ex. 13:2, 12, 15.   2:24—Lev. 12:8.   2:30—Isaiah 40:5.
2:31—Isaiah 52:10.   2:32—Isaiah 49:6.

q Or, *And in the Spirit.* r text: S A B vg sa bo; omit, *till:* D it sy⁸; *widow of about eighty-four:* W λ. ˢ text: S B D W it vg sy⁸ sa bo; add, *in spirit:* A Θ λ φ ℜ syᴾ. t Or, *years.*

1. THE GALILEAN SECTION

Matthew 3–18 = Mark 1–9 = Luke 3:1–9:50

1. JOHN THE BAPTIST.

Matt. 3:1–6	Mark 1:1–6	Luke 3:1–6
	1 The beginning of the gospel of Jesus Christ, the Son of God.[u]	
1 In those days		1 In the fifteenth year of the reign of Tiberius Caesar, Pontius Pilate being governor of Judea, and Herod being tetrarch of Galilee, and his brother Philip tetrarch of the region of Ituraea and Trachonitis, and Lysanias tetrarch of Abilene, 2 in the high-priesthood of Annas and Caiaphas, the word of God came to John the son of Zechariah in the wilderness; 3 and he went
came John the Baptist, preaching in the wilderness of Judea,		into all the region about the Jordan, preaching a baptism of repentance for the forgiveness of sins. 4 As it is written in the book of the words
	1:15 (p. 14)	
2 "Repent, for the kingdom of heaven is at hand." 3 For this is he who was spoken of by the prophet Isaiah when he said,	*(1:4)*	of Isaiah the prophet,
11:10, p. 48	2 As it is written in Isaiah the prophet,[v] "Behold, I send my messenger before thy face, who shall prepare thy way;	*7:27, p. 59*
"The voice of one crying in the wilderness: Prepare the way of the Lord, make his paths straight."	3 the voice of one crying in the wilderness: Prepare the way of the Lord, make his paths straight—"	"The voice of one crying in the wilderness: Prepare the way of the Lord, make his paths straight. 5 Every valley shall be filled, and every mountain and hill shall be brought low, and the crooked shall be made straight, and the rough ways shall be made smooth; 6 and all flesh shall see the salvation of God."
4 Now John wore a garment of camel's hair, and a leather girdle around his waist; and his food was locusts and wild honey. 5 Then went out to him Jerusalem and all Judea and all the region about the Jordan,	4 John the baptizer appeared in[w] the wilderness, preaching a baptism of repentance for the forgiveness of sins. *cf. 1:6* 5 And there went out to him all the country of Judea, and all the people of Jerusalem;	*cf. 3:3b* *cf. 3:3a*

Matt. 3:3, Mark 1:3, Luke 3:4 (cf. Matt. 11:10, p. 48)—Isaiah 40:3.   Mark 1:2—Malachi 3:1. Luke 3:5-6—Isaiah 40:4-5.

[u] text: A B D W λ φ 𝔐 it vg syᵖ sa bo; omit, *the Son of God:* S Θ.   [v] text: S B D Θ λ it vg syᵖ bo; *the prophets* (minus, *Isaiah*): A W φ 𝔐.   [w] text: S B bo; *John was baptizing in:* A D W Θ λ φ 𝔐 it vg syᵖ sa.

⁶ and they were baptized by him in the river Jordan, confessing their sins.

cf. 3:4

and they were baptized by him in the river Jordan, confessing their sins. ⁶ Now John was clothed with camel's hair, and had a leather girdle around his waist,ˣ and ate locusts and wild honey.

2. JOHN'S PREACHING OF REPENTANCE

Matt. 3:7–10

7 But when he saw many of the Pharisees and Sadducees coming for baptism, he said to them, "You brood of vipers! Who warned you to flee from the wrath to come? ⁸ Bear fruit that befits repentance, ⁹ and do not presume to say to yourselves, 'We have Abraham as our father'; for I tell you, God is able from these stones to raise up children to Abraham. ¹⁰ Even now the axe is laid to the root of the trees; every tree therefore that does not bear good fruit is cut down and thrown into the fire." ʸ

Luke 3:7–9

7 He said therefore to the multitudes that came out to be baptized by him,

"You brood of vipers! Who warned you to flee from the wrath to come? ⁸ Bear fruits that befit repentance, and do not begin to say to yourselves, 'We have Abraham as our father'; for I tell you, God is able from these stones to raise up children to Abraham. ⁹ Even now the axe is laid to the root of the trees; every tree therefore that does not bear good fruit is cut down and thrown into the fire." ʸ

3. JOHN'S PREACHING TO SPECIAL GROUPS.
Luke 3:10–14

10 And the multitudes asked him, "What then shall we do?" ¹¹ And he answered them, "He who has two coats, let him share with him who has none; and he who has food, let him do likewise." ¹² Tax collectors also came to be baptized, and said to him, "Teacher, what shall we do?" ¹³ And he said to them, "Collect no more than is appointed you." ¹⁴ Soldiers also asked him, "And we, what shall we do?" And he said to them, "Rob no one by violence or by false accusation, and be content with your wages."

4. JOHN'S MESSIANIC PREACHING.

Matt. 3:11–12

Mark 1:7–8

Luke 3:15–18

15 As the people were in expectation, and all men questioned in their hearts concerning John, whether perhaps he were the Christ, ¹⁶ John answered them all,

---

ˣ Omit: *and had a leather girdle around his waist:* D it.   ʸ cf. Matt. 7:19 (§ 41, p. 30).

To Luke 3:15 cf. John 1:19–25.

To Matt. 3:1 cf. **Gospel of the Ebionites,** (in Epiphanius, *Against Heresies, XXX.13.6*)—In the days of Herod, king of Judea, when Caiaphas was high priest, a certain man named John came baptizing with a baptism of repentance in the river Jordan. He was said to be of the family of Aaron the priest, son of Zechariah and Elizabeth, and all went out to him.

To Matt. 3:4, 5 cf. XXX.13.4 of above reference—John was baptizing; and Pharisees went out to him and were baptized, and all Jerusalem. Now John wore a garment of camel's hair, and a leather girdle around his waist; his food was wild honey, tasting like manna, like a cake in olive oil.

11 "I baptize you with water for repentance, but he who is coming after me is mightier than I, whose sandals I am not worthy to carry;

he will baptize you with the Holy Spirit and with fire. 12 His winnowing fork is in his hand, and he will clear his threshing floor and gather his wheat into the granary, but the chaff he will burn with unquenchable fire."

7 And he preached, saying, "After me comes he who is mightier than I, the thong of whose sandals I am not worthy to stoop down and untie. 8 I have baptized you with water; but he will baptize you with the Holy Spirit."

"I baptize you with water; but he who is mightier than I is coming, the thong of whose sandals I am not worthy to untie;

he will baptize you with the Holy Spirit and with fire. 17 His winnowing fork is in his hand, to clear his threshing floor, and to gather the wheat into his granary; but the chaff he will burn with unquenchable fire." 18 So, with many other exhortations, he preached good news to the people.

5. JOHN'S IMPRISONMENT.
Luke 3:19–20

|14:3-4 | 6:17-18|
(§ 111, p. 78)

19 But Herod the tetrarch, who had been reproved by him for Herodias, his brother's wife, and for all the evil things that Herod had done, 20 added this to them all, that he shut up John in prison.

6. THE BAPTISM OF JESUS.

Matt. 3:13–17

13 Then Jesus came from Galilee to the Jordan to John, to be baptized by him. 14 John would have prevented him, saying, "I need to be baptized by you, and do you come to me?" 15 But Jesus answered him, "Let it be so now; for thus it is fitting for us to fulfil all righteousness." Then he consented.

Mark 1:9–11

9 In those days Jesus came from Nazareth of Galilee

Luke 3:21–22

21 Now when all the people were baptized

Matt. 3:15—*Then he consented; and when he was baptized a huge light shone from the water so that all who were near were frightened.* Two manuscripts of the Itala.

To Matt. 3:11-12 cf. John 1:24-28.　To § 6 cf. John 1:29-34.

To Matt. 3:11, Mark 1:7, Luke 3:16 cf. Acts 13:25—And as John was finishing his course, he said, "What do you suppose that I am? I am not he. No, but after me one is coming, the sandals of whose feet I am not worthy to untie." Cf. also Acts 1:5; 11:16; 19:4.

To Matt. 3:13 cf. **Gospel according to the Hebrews,** (in Jerome, *Against Pelagius III.2*)—The mother of the Lord and his brothers said to him, "John the Baptist baptizes for the forgiveness of sins; let us go and be baptized by him." But he said to them, "In what way have I sinned that I should go and be baptized by him? Unless, perhaps, what I have just said is a sin of ignorance."

16 And when Jesus was baptized, he went up immediately from the water, and behold, the heavens were opened² and he saw the Spirit of God descending like a dove and alighting on him; 17 and lo, a voice from heaven, saying, "This is my beloved Son,ᵃ with whom I am well pleased."

and was baptized by John in the Jordan. 10 And when he came up out of the water, immediately he saw the heavens opened and the Spirit descending upon him like a dove; 11 and a voice came from heaven, "Thou art my beloved Son;ᵃ with thee I am well pleased."

and when Jesus also had been baptized and was praying, the heaven was opened,

22 and the Holy Spirit descended upon him in bodily form, as a dove, and a voice came from heaven, "Thou art my beloved Son;ᵃ with thee I am well pleased." ᵇ

7. THE GENEALOGY OF JESUS.

Matt. 1:1–16 (p. 1)

1 The book of the genealogy of Jesus Christ, the son of David, the son of Abraham. 2 Abraham was the father of Isaac, and Isaac the father of Jacob, and Jacob the father of Judah and his brothers, 3 and Judah the father of Perez and Zerah by Tamar, and Perez the father of Hezron, and Hezron the father of Ram, 4 and Ram the father of Amminadab, and Amminadab the father of Nah-

Luke 3:23–38

23 Jesus, when he began his ministry, was about thirty years of age, being the son (as was supposed) of Joseph, the son of Heli, 24 the son of Matthat, the son of Levi, the son of Melchi, the son of Jannai, the son of Joseph, 25 the son of Mattathias, the son of Amos, the son of Nahum, the son of Esli, the son of Naggai, 26 the son of Maath, the son of Mattathias, the son of Semein, the son of Josech, the son of

---

To Matt. 3:17, Mark 1:11 cf. Isaiah 42:1, 44:2.

² text: S B syᶜ syˢ sa; add, *to him:* C D W λ φ 𝔐 it vg syᵖ bo.   ᵃ Or, *my Son, my (or the) Beloved.*   ᵇ text: P⁴ S A B W Θ λ φ 𝔐 vg syˢ syᵖ sa bo; *Thou art my Son; today I have begotten thee* (Psalm 2:7): D it Justin, Clement, Origen, Augustine, Gospel of the Ebionites.

To Matt. 3:13–17 cf. **Gospel of the Ebionites,** (in Epiphanius, *Against Heresies, XXX.13.7-8*)—After the people were baptized, Jesus also came and was baptized by John. And as he came up from the water, the heavens were opened, and he saw the Holy Spirit descend in the form of a dove and enter into him. And a voice from heaven said, "Thou art my beloved Son; with thee I am well pleased." And again, "Today I have begotten thee." And immediately a great light shone around the place; and John, seeing it, said to him, "Who are you, Lord?" And again a voice from heaven said to him, "This is my beloved Son, with whom I am well pleased." Then John, falling down before him, said, "I beseech you, Lord, baptize me!" But he forbade him, saying, "Let it be so; for thus it is fitting that all things be fulfilled."

To Matt. 3:16–17 cf. **Gospel according to the Hebrews,** (in Jerome, *Commentary on Isaiah 11:2*)—When the Lord ascended from the water, the whole fount of the Holy Spirit descended and rested upon him, and said to him, "My son, in all the prophets I was waiting for you, that you might come, and that I might rest in you. For you are my rest; and you are my firstborn son, who reigns forever."

To Luke 3:23 cf. **Gospel of the Ebionites,** (in Epiphanius, *Against Heresies XXX.13.2*)—"There was a certain man named Jesus, about thirty years old, who chose us." Also cf. Justin, *Dialogue 88:3*—When Jesus went down in the water, fire was kindled in the Jordan; and when he came up from the water, the Holy Spirit came upon him. The apostles of our Christ wrote this.

shon, and Nahshon the father of Salmon, 5 and Salmon the father of Boaz by Rahab, and Boaz the father of Obed by Ruth, and Obed the father of Jesse, c and Jesse the father of David the king. And David was the father of Solomon by the wife of Uriah, 7 and Solomon the father of Rehoboam, and Rehoboam the father of Abijah, and Abijah the father of Asa, 8 and Asa the father of Jehoshaphat, and Jehosaphat the father of Joram, and Joram the father of Uzziah, 9 and Uzziah the father of Jotham, and Jotham the father of Ahaz, and Ahaz the father of Hezekiah, 10 and Hezekiah the father of Manasseh, and Manasseh the father of Amos, and Amos the father of Josiah, 11 and Josiah the father of Jechoniah and his brothers, at the time of the deportation to Babylon. 12 And after the deportation to Babylon: Jechoniah was the father of Shealtiel,c and Shealtiel c the father of Zerubbabel, 13 and Zerubbabel the father of Abiud, and Abiud the father of Eliakim, and Eliakim the father of Azor, 14 and Azor the father of Zadok, and Zadok the father of Achim, and Achim the father of Eliud, 15 and Eliud the father of Eleazar, and Eleazar the father of Matthan, and Matthan the father of Jacob, 16 and Jacob the father of Joseph the husband of Mary, of whom Jesus was born, who is called Christ.

Joda, 27 the son of Joanan, the son of Rhesa, the son of Zerubbabel, the son of Shealtiel,c the son of Neri, 28 the son of Melchi, the son of Addi, the son of Cosam, the son of Elmadam, the son of Er, 29 the son of Joshua, the son of Eliezer, the son of Jorim, the son of Matthat, the son of Levi, 30 the son of Simeon, the son of Judah, the son of Joseph, the son of Jonam, the son of Eliakim, 31 the son of Melea, the son of Menna, the son of Mattatha, the son of Nathan, the son of David, 32 the son of Jesse, the son of Obed, the son of Boaz, the son of Sala, the son of Nahshon, 33 the son of Amminadab, the son of Admin, the son of Arni, the son of Hezron, the son of Perez, the son of Judah, 34 the son of Jacob, the son of Isaac, the son of Abraham, the son of Terah, the son of Nahor, 35 son of Serug, the son of Reu, the son of Peleg, the son of Eber, the son of Shelah, 36 the son of Cainan, the son of Arphaxad, the son of Shem, the son of Noah, the son of Lamech, 37 the son of Methuselah, the son of Enoch, the son of Jared, the son of Mahalaleel, the son of Cainan, 38 the son of Enos, the son of Seth, the son of Adam, the son of God.

8. THE TEMPTATION.

Matt. 4:1-11	**Mark 1:12-13**	**Luke 4:1-13**
1 Then Jesus		1 And Jesus, full of the Holy Spirit, returned from
was led up by the Spirit into the wilderness	12 The Spirit immediately drove him out into the wilderness. 13 And he was in the wilderness forty days, tempted by Satan;	the Jordan, and was led by the Spirit 2 for forty days in the wilderness, tempted by the devil. And he ate nothing in those days; and
to be tempted by the devil. 2 And he fasted forty days and forty nights		
and afterward he was hungry.	and he was with the wild beasts;	when they were ended, he was hungry.

Luke 3:27—I Chronicles 3:17.   3:31-34—I Chronicles 2:1-15.   3:32-33—Ruth 4·18-22.   3:34-35—I Chronicles 1:24-27.   3:36-38—I Chronicles 1:1-4.

---

c Greek: *Salathiel.*

3 And the tempter came and said to him, "If you are the Son of God, command these stones to become loaves of bread." 4 But he answered, "It is written, 'Man shall not live by bread alone, but by every word that proceeds from the mouth of God.' "

5 Then the devil took him to the holy city, and set him on the pinnacle of the temple, 6 and said to him, "If you are the Son of God, throw yourself down; for it is written, 'He will give his angels charge of you,' and 'On their hands they will bear you up, lest you strike your foot against a stone.' " 7 Jesus said to him, "Again it is written, 'You shall not tempt the Lord your God.' "

8 Again, the devil took him to a very high mountain, and showed him all the kingdoms of the world and the glory of them; 9 and he said to him, "All these I will give you

if you will fall down and worship me."
10 Then Jesus said to him, "Begone, Satan! for it is written, 'You shall worship the Lord your God, and him only shall you serve.' "

cf. vv. 5–7

3 The devil said to him, "If you are the Son of God, command this stone to become bread." 4 And Jesus answered him, "It is written, 'Man shall not live by bread alone.' "

cf. vv. 9–12

5 And the devil took him up, and showed him all the kingdoms of the world in a moment of time, 6 and said to him, "To you I will give all this authority and their glory; for it has been delivered to me, and I give it to whom I will. 7 If you, then, will worship me, it shall all be yours." 8 And Jesus answered him, "It is written, 'You shall worship the Lord your God, and him only shall you serve.' "

9 And he took him to Jerusalem, and set him on the pinnacle of the temple, and said to him, "If you are the Son of God, throw yourself down from here; 10 for it is written, 'He will give his angels charge of you, to guard you,' 11 and 'On their hands they will bear you up, lest you strike your foot against a stone.' " 12 And Jesus answered him, "It is said, 'You shall not tempt the Lord your God.' "

11 Then the devil left him, and behold, angels came and ministered to him.

and the angels ministered to him.

13 And when the devil had ended every temptation, he departed from him until an opportune time.

Matt. 4:4, Luke 4:4—Deut. 8:3b.   Matt. 4:6, Luke 4:10-11—Psalm 91:11-12.   Matt. 4:7, Luke 4:12—Deut. 6:16.   Matt. 4:10, Luke 4:8—Deut. 6:13.

To Matt. 4:11, Mark 1:13, cf. John 1:51, And he said to him, "Truly, truly, I say to you, you will see heaven opened, and the angels of God ascending and descending upon the Son of man."

To Matt. 4:5 cf. **Gospel of the Nazaraeans:** The Jewish Gospel has not *to the holy city*, but *to Jerusalem.*

To Matt. 4:8 cf. **Gospel according to the Hebrews** (in Origen, *Commentary on John 2:12* and *Homily on Jeremiah 15:4*)—And if any accept the Gospel of the Hebrews, here the Savior says: "Even so did my mother, the Holy Spirit, take me by one of my hairs, and carry me to the great Mount Tabor." Jerome also records these words in Latin in his commentaries on Micah 7:6, Isaiah 40:9ff., and Ezekiel 16:13.

9. THE FIRST PREACHING IN GALILEE.

Matt. 4:12–17	Mark 1:14–15	Luke 4:14–15
12 Now when he heard that John had been arrested, he withdrew into Galilee; 13 and leaving Nazareth he went and dwelt in Capernaum by the sea, in the territory of Zebulun and Naphtali, 14 that what was spoken by the prophet Isaiah might be fulfilled: 15 "The land of Zebulun and the land of Naphtali, toward the sea, across the Jordan, Galilee of the Gentiles — 16 the people who sat in darkness have seen a great light, and for those who sat in the region and shadow of death light has dawned."	14 Now after John was arrested, Jesus came into Galilee,	14 And Jesus returned in the power of the Spirit into Galilee,
17 From that time Jesus began to preach, saying, "Repent, for the kingdom of heaven is at hand."	preaching the gospel d of God, 15 and saying, "The time is fulfilled, and the kingdom of God is at hand; repent, and believe in the gospel."	and a report concerning him went out through all the surrounding country. 15 And he taught in their synagogues, being glorified by all.

10. THE REJECTION AT NAZARETH.

Matt. 13:54–58 (§ *108, p. 76*)	Mark 6:1–6a (§ *108, p. 76*)	Luke 4:16–30
54 And coming to his own country he taught them in their synagogue,	1 He went away from there and came to his own country; and his disciples followed him. 2 And on the sabbath he began to teach in the synagogue;	16 And he came to Nazareth, where he had been brought up; and he went to the synagogue, as his custom was, on the sabbath day. And he stood up to read; 17 and there was given to him the book of the prophet Isaiah. He opened the book, and found the place where it was written, 18 "The Spirit of the Lord is upon me, because he has anointed me to preach good news to the poor. He has sent me to proclaim release to the captives and recovering of sight to the blind, to set at liberty those who are oppressed, 19 to proclaim the acceptable year of the Lord."

Matt. 4:15-16—Isaiah 9:1-2.   Luke 4:18-19—Isaiah 61:1-2, 58:6.

d text: S B Θ λ φ it (some MSS.) sy⁵ sa bo; *gospel of the kingdom of God:* A D W 𝕽 it (some MSS.) vg sy^p.

To Matt. 4:12, Mark 1:14, Luke 4:14 cf. John 4:1-3—¹ Now when the Lord knew that the Pharisees had heard that Jesus was making and baptizing more disciples than John ²(although Jesus himself did not baptize, but only his disciples), ³ he left Judea and departed again to Galilee. Cf. also John 4:43; 2:12.

20 And he closed the book, and gave it back to the attendant, and sat down; and the eyes of all in the synagogue were fixed on him. 21 And he began to say to them, "Today this scripture has been fulfilled in your hearing." 22 And all spoke well of him, and wondered at the gracious words which proceeded out of his mouth; and they said,

so that they were astonished,

and many who heard him were astonished,

and said, "Where did this man get this wisdom and these mighty works?

saying, "Where did this man get all this? What is the wisdom given to him? What mighty works are wrought by his hands!

55 Is not this the carpenter's son? Is not his mother called Mary? And are not his brothers James and Joseph and Simon and Judas? 56 And are not all his sisters with us? Where then did this man get all this?"

3 Is not this the carpenter,

the son of Mary and brother of James and Joses and Judas and Simon, and are not his sisters here with us?

"Is not this Joseph's son?"

57 And they took offense e at him.

And they took offense e at him.

23 And he said to them, "Doubtless you will quote to me this proverb, 'Physician, heal yourself; what we have heard you did at Capernaum, do here also in your own country.' "

But Jesus said to them, "A prophet is not without honor except in his own country and in his own house." 58 And he did not do many mighty works there,

4 And Jesus said to them, "A prophet is not without honor, except in his own country, and among his own kin, and in his own house." 5 And he could do no mighty work there, except that he laid his hands upon a few sick people and healed them. 6 And he marveled because of their unbelief.

24 And he said, "Truly, I say to you, no prophet is acceptable in his own country.

because of their unbelief.

25 But in truth, I tell you, there were many widows in Israel in the days of Elijah, when the heaven was shut up three years and six months, when there came a great famine over all

Luke 4:25—I Kings 17:1, 18:1-2.

e Or, *stumbled*.

To Matt. 13:54 and Mark 6:2 cf. John 7:15—The Jews marveled at it, saying, "How is it that this man has learning, when he has never studied?"

To Matt. 13:57, Mark 6:4 and Luke 4:24 cf. John 4:44—For Jesus himself testified that a prophet has no honor in his own country.

To Luke 4:24 cf. *Oxyrhynchus Papyrus 1, Logion 6*—Jesus says, "A prophet is not acceptable in his own country, neither does a physician heal those who know him." Cf. **Gospel of Thomas, Logion 31.**

the land; 26 and Elijah was sent to none of them but only to Zarephath, in the land of Sidon, to a woman who was a widow. 27 And there were many lepers in Israel in the time of the prophet Elisha; and none of them was cleansed, but only Naaman the Syrian." 28 When they heard this, all in the synagogue were filled with wrath. 29 And they rose up and put him out of the city, and led him to the brow of the hill on which their city was built, that they might throw him down headlong. 30 But passing through the midst of them he went away.

11. THE CALL OF THE FIRST DISCIPLES.

Matt. 4:18–22	Mark 1:16–20	
18 As he walked by the Sea of Galilee, he saw two brothers, Simon who is called Peter and Andrew his brother, casting a net into the sea; for they were fishermen. 19 And he said to them, "Follow me, and I will make you fishers of men." 20 Immediately they left their nets and followed him.	16 And passing along by the Sea of Galilee he saw Simon and Andrew the brother of Simon casting a net into the sea; for they were fishermen. 17 And Jesus said to them, "Follow me, and I will make you become fishers of men." 18 And immediately they left their nets and followed him.	*cf. 5:1–11* (§ *17*, *p. 19*)
21 And going on from there he saw two other brothers, James the son of Zebedee and John his brother, in the boat with Zebedee their father, mending their nets, and he called them. 22 Immediately they left the boat and their father, and followed him. *(4:23f. p. 18)*	19 And going on a little farther, he saw James the son of Zebedee and John his brother, who were in their boat mending the nets. 20 And immediately he called them, and they left their father Zebedee in the boat with the hired servants, and followed him.	

Luke 4:26—I Kings 17:8-9. 4:27—II Kings 5:14.

To § 11 cf. John 1:35-42.

To Matt. 4:18-22 and parallels (and 9:9 and parallels, 10:2-5) cf. **Gospel of the Ebionites,** (in Epiphanius, *Against Heresies, XXX.13.2-3*)—There was a certain man named Jesus, about thirty years old, who chose us. (See Luke 3:23, p. 11.) Coming to Capernaum, he entered the house of Simon, who is called Peter, and said, "As I passed by the lake of Tiberias, I chose John and James, sons of Zebedee, and Simon, Andrew, Thaddaeus, Simon the Zealot, Judas Iscariot; and you, Matthew, sitting at the tax office, I called and you followed me. You, therefore, I desire to be twelve apostles, as a witness to Israel."

12. JESUS IN THE SYNAGOGUE AT CAPERNAUM.

Matt. 7:28–29 (§ 44, p. 31)	Mark 1:21–28	Luke 4:31–37
28 And when Jesus finished these sayings, the crowds were astonished at his teaching, 29 for he taught them as one who had authority, and not as their scribes.	21 And they went into Capernaum; and immediately on the sabbath he entered the synagogue and taught. 22 And they were astonished at his teaching, for he taught them as one who had authority, and not as the scribes.	31 And he went down to Capernaum, a city of Galilee. And he was teaching them on the sabbath; 32 and they were astonished at his teaching, for his word was with authority.
	23 And immediately there was in their synagogue a man with an unclean spirit; 24 and he cried out, "What have you to do with us, Jesus of Nazareth? Have you come to destroy us? I know who you are, the Holy One of God." 25 But Jesus rebuked him, saying, "Be silent, and come out of him!" 26 And the unclean spirit, convulsing him and crying with a loud voice, came out of him. 27 And they were all amazed, so that they questioned among themselves, saying, "What is this? A new teaching! With authority he commands even the unclean spirits, and they obey him." 28 And at once his fame spread everywhere throughout all the surrounding region of Galilee.	33 And in the synagogue there was a man who had the spirit of an unclean demon; and he cried out with a loud voice, 34 "Ah! f What have you to do with us, Jesus of Nazareth? Have you come to destroy us? I know who you are, the Holy One of God." 35 But Jesus rebuked him, saying, "Be silent, and come out of him!" And when the demon had thrown him down in the midst, he came out of him, having done him no harm. 36 And they were all amazed and said to one another, "What is this word? For with authority and power he commands the unclean spirits, and they come out." 37 And reports of him went out into every place in the surrounding region.

13. THE HEALING OF PETER'S MOTHER-IN-LAW.

Matt. 8:14–15 (§ 47, p. 33)	Mark 1:29–31	Luke 4:38–39
14 And when Jesus entered Peter's house, he saw his mother-in-law lying sick with a fever; 15 and he touched her hand, and the fever left her, and she rose and served him.	29 And immediately he g left the synagogue, and entered the house of Simon and Andrew, with James and John. 30 Now Simon's mother-in-law lay sick with a fever, and immediately they told him of her. 31 And he came and took her by the hand and lifted her up, and the fever left her; and she served them.	38 And he arose and left the synagogue, and entered Simon's house. Now Simon's mother-in-law was ill with a high fever, and they besought him for her. 39 And he stood over her and rebuked the fever, and it left her; and immediately she rose and served them.

To Matt. 7:28, Mark 1:22, Luke 4:32 cf. John 7:46—The officers answered "No man ever spoke like this man!"

To Mark 1:24 and Luke 4:34 cf. Judges 11:12 and I Kings 17:18.

f Or, *let us alone.*   g text: B D W Θ λ φ it; *they:* S A C ℜ vg sy⁸ syᴾ bo.

14. THE SICK HEALED AT EVENING.

Matt. 8:16–17 (§ 48, p. 34)	Mark 1:32–34	Luke 4:40–41
16 That evening they brought to him many who were possessed with demons;	32 That evening, at sundown, they brought to him all who were sick or possessed with demons. 33 And the whole city was gathered together about the door. 34 And he healed many who were sick with various diseases, and cast out many demons; *	40 Now when the sun was setting, all those who had any that were sick with various diseases brought them to him; and he laid his hands on every one of them and healed them.
and he cast out the spirits with a word, and healed all who were sick.	and he would not permit the demons to speak, because they knew him.**	41 And demons also came out of many, crying, "You are the Son of God!" But he rebuked them, and would not allow them to speak, because they knew that he was the Christ.**
17 This was to fulfil what was spoken by the prophet Isaiah, "He took our infirmities and bore our diseases."		

15. JESUS DEPARTS FROM CAPERNAUM.

Mark 1:35–38	Luke 4:42–43
35 And in the morning, a great while before day, he rose and went out to a lonely place, and there he prayed. 36 And Simon and those who were with him pursued him, 37 and they found him and said to him, "Every one is searching for you." 38 And he said to them, "Let us go on to the next towns, that I may preach there also; for that is why I came out."	42 And when it was day he departed and went into a lonely place. And the people sought him and came to him, and would have kept him from leaving them; 43 but he said to them, "I must preach the good news of the kingdom of God to the other cities also; for I was sent for this purpose."

16. A PREACHING JOURNEY IN GALILEE.

Matt. 4:23–25 (§ 11, p. 16,)	Mark 1:39	Luke 4:44
23 And he went about all Galilee, teaching in their synagogues and preaching the gospel of the kingdom and healing every disease and every infirmity among the people.***	39 And he went throughout all Galilee, preaching in their synagogues and casting out demons.	44 And he was preaching in the synagogues of Judea.h
	1:40–45 (§ 45, pp. 31–32)	

* Mark 3:10-11 (§ 71, p.53): 10 for he had healed many, so that all who had diseases pressed upon him to touch him. 11 And whenever the unclean spirits beheld him, they fell down before him and cried out, "You are the Son of God." (Cf. Matt. 4:24, § 16, p.19.)

** Matt. 12:16 (§ 71, p.53): and ordered them not to make him known.   Mark 3:12 (§ 71, p.53): and he strictly ordered them not to make him known.

*** Matt. 9:35 (§ 58, p.39): And Jesus went about all the cities and villages, teaching in their synagogues and preaching the gospel of the kingdom, and healing every disease and every infirmity.

Matt. 8:17—Isaiah 53:4.

h text: P75 S B C λ sys sa bo; *Galilee:* A D Θ φ 𝕽 it vg syp; *synagogues of the Jews:* W.

3:10, 7, 8 (§ 71, p. 53)   6:18, 19, 17 (§ 71, p. 53)

24 So his fame spread throughout all Syria, and they brought him all the sick,* those afflicted with various diseases and pains, demoniacs, epileptics, and paralytics, and he healed them. 25 And great crowds followed him ** from Galilee and the Decapolis and Jerusalem and Judea and from beyond the Jordan.

10 for he had healed many, so that all who had diseases pressed upon him to touch him;

7 . . . and a great multitude from Galilee followed; also from Judea 8 and Jerusalem and Idumea and from beyond the Jordan and from about Tyre and Sidon a great multitude, hearing all that he did, came to him.

18 and those who were troubled with unclean spirits were cured. 19 And all the crowd sought to touch him, for power came forth from him and healed them all. 17 And he came down with them and stood on a level place, with a great crowd of his disciples and a great multitude of people from all Judea and Jerusalem and the seacoast of Tyre and Sidon, who came to hear him and to be healed of their diseases.

17. THE MIRACULOUS CATCH OF FISH.

Luke 5:1–11

(cf. Mark 1:16–20 and Matt. 4:18–22, § 11, p. 16)

1 While the people pressed upon him to hear the word of God, he was standing by the lake of Gennesaret. 2 And he saw two boats by the lake; but the fishermen had gone out of them and were washing their nets. 3 Getting into one of the boats, which was Simon's, he asked him to put out a little from the land. And he sat down and taught the people from the boat.*** 4 And when he had ceased speaking, he said to Simon, "Put out into the deep and let down your nets for a catch." 5 And Simon answered, "Master, we toiled all night and took nothing! But at your word I will let down the nets." 6 And when they had done this, they enclosed a great shoal of fish; and as their nets were breaking, 7 they beckoned to their partners in the other boat to come and help them. And they came and filled both the boats, so that they began to sink. 8 But when Simon Peter saw it, he fell down at Jesus' knees, saying, "Depart from me, for I am a sinful man, O Lord." 9 For he was astonished, and all that were with him, at the catch of fish which they had taken; 10 and so also were James and John, sons of Zebedee, who were partners with Simon. And Jesus said to Simon, "Do not be afraid; henceforth you will be catching men." 11 And when they had brought their boats to land, they left everything and followed him. *(5:12–16, § 45, pp. 31–32.)*

---

* Matt. 14:35 (§ 114, p.81): And when the men of that place recognized him, they sent round to all that region and brought to him all that were sick.

Mark 6:54-55 (§ 114, p.81): 54 And when they got out of the boat, immediately the people recognized him, 55 and ran about the whole neighborhood and began to bring sick people on their pallets to any place where they heard he was.

** Matt. 12:15 (§ 71, p.53): Jesus, aware of this, withdrew from there. And many followed him, and he healed them all.

*** Cf. Matt. 13:1-2 and Mark 4:1.

The Sermon on the Mount.

Matthew 5–7

18. INTRODUCTION.

Matt. 5:1-2		Luke 6:12, 20 (§ 72, *p. 54*; § 73, *p.55*)

Matt. 5:1-2

1 Seeing the crowds, he went up on the mountain, and when he sat down his disciples came to him. ² And he opened his mouth and taught them, saying:

3:13

Luke 6:12, 20 (§ 72, *p. 54*; § 73, *p.55*)

6:12 In these days he went out to the mountain to pray; and all night he continued in prayer to God. ²⁰ And he lifted up his eyes on his disciples, and said:

19. THE BEATITUDES

Matt. 5:3-12

³ "Blessed are the poor in spirit,
　for theirs is the kingdom of heaven.
⁴ "Blessed are those who mourn,
　for they shall be comforted.
⁵ "Blessed are the meek,
　for they shall inherit the earth.
⁶ "Blessed are those who hunger and thirst
　for righteousness,
　for they shall be satisfied.
⁷ "Blessed are the merciful,
　for they shall obtain mercy.
⁸ "Blessed are the pure in heart,
　for they shall see God.
⁹ "Blessed are the peacemakers,
　for they shall be called sons of God.
¹⁰ "Blessed are those who are persecuted
　for righteousness' sake,
　for theirs is the kingdom of heaven.
¹¹ "Blessed are you when men
　　　　　　　　　revile you
and persecute you and utter all kinds of
evil against you falsely on my account.
¹² Rejoice and be glad, for your reward
is great in heaven, for so men persecuted
the prophets who were before you.

Luke 6:20-23 (§ 73, *p. 55*)

²⁰ "Blessed are you poor,
　for yours is the kingdom of God.

²¹ "Blessed are you that hunger now,

　for you shall be satisfied.
"Blessed are you that weep now,
　for you shall laugh.

²² "Blessed are you when men hate you, and when they exclude you and revile you and cast out your name as evil, on account of the Son of man!

²³ Rejoice in that day, and leap for joy, for behold, your reward is great in heaven; for so their fathers did to the prophets."

Matt. 5:5—Psalm 37:11.　　5:8—Psalm 24:4.

To Matt. 5:3 and Luke 6:20 cf. **Gospel of Thomas, Logion 54:** Jesus said, "Blessed are the poor, for yours is the kingdom of heaven."

To Matt. 5:5 cf. Clement of Alexandria, *Protrepticus X.94.4:* So the scripture naturally preached to those who have believed, "And the saints of the Lord shall inherit the glory of God and his power."

20. THE PARABLES OF SALT AND LIGHT.

Matt. 5:13–16

13 "You are the salt of the earth; but if salt has lost its taste, how shall its saltness be restored? * It is no longer good for anything except to be thrown out and trodden under foot by men.

14 "You are the light of the world. A city set on a hill cannot be hid. 15 Nor do men light a lamp and put it under a bushel, but on a stand, and it gives light to all in the house.** 16 Let your light so shine before men, that they may see your good works and give glory to your Father who is in heaven.

Cf. Mark 9:50 (§ 132, p. 98)

Luke 14:34–35 (§ 171, p. 121)

34 "Salt is good; but if salt has lost its taste, how shall its saltness be restored?* 35 It is fit neither for the land nor for the dung-hill; men throw it away. He who has ears to hear, let him hear."

11:33 (§ 153, p. 108)

33 "No one after lighting a lamp puts it in a cellar or under a bushel, but on a stand, that those who enter may see the light.

21. WORDS OF JESUS ON THE LAW.
Matt. 5:17–20

17 "Think not that I have come to abolish the law and the prophets; I have come not to abolish them but to fulfil them. 18 For truly, I say to you, till heaven and earth pass away, not an iota, not a dot, will pass from the law until all is accomplished.*** 19 Whoever then relaxes one of the least of these commandments and teaches men so, shall be called least in the kingdom of heaven; but he who does them and teaches them shall be called great in the kingdom of heaven. 20 For I tell you, unless your righteousness exceeds that of the scribes and Pharisees, you will never enter the kingdom of heaven.

* Mark 9:50 (§ 132, p.98): "Salt is good; but if the salt has lost its saltness, how will you season it?"

** Mark 4:21 (§ 94, p.67): And he said to them, "Is a lamp brought in to be put under a bushel, or under a bed, and not on a stand?"

Luke 8:16 (§ 94, p.67): "No one after lighting a lamp covers it with a vessel, or puts it under a bed, but puts it on a stand, that those who enter may see the light."

*** Luke 16:17 (§ 176, p.123): "But it is easier for heaven and earth to pass away, than for one dot of the law to become void." (Cf. Matt. 24:35 = Mark 13:31 = Luke 21:33, § 221, p.158.)

To Matt. 5:14 cf. *Oxyrhynchus Papyrus 1, Logion 7:* Jesus says, "A city built on the top of a high hill and established can neither fall nor be hidden."

To Matt. 5:17 cf. **Gospel of the Ebionites,** (in Epiphanius, *Against Heresies, XXX.16.5):* "I have come to destroy sacrifices; and if you do not stop making sacrifices, the wrath (of God) will not leave you."

Gospel of the Egyptians, (in Clement of Alexandria, *Miscellanies III.9.63):* "I have come to destroy the works of the female." (Cf. also Matt. 19:12, § 187, p. 129.)

22. ON MURDER.
Matt. 5:21-26

21 "You have heard that it was said to the men of old, 'You shall not kill; and whoever kills shall be liable to judgment.' 22 But I say to you that every one who is angry with his brother[i] shall be liable to judgment; whoever insults[j] his brother shall be liable to the council, and whoever says, 'You fool!' shall be liable to the hell[k] of fire. 23 So if you are offering your gift at the altar, and there remember that your brother has something against you, 24 leave your gift there before the altar and go;

first be reconciled to your brother, and then come and offer your gift. 25 Make friends quickly with your accuser, while you are going with him to court, lest your accuser hand you over to the judge, and the judge to the guard, and you be put in prison; 26 truly, I say to you, you will never get out till you have paid the last penny.

12:57-59 (§ 161, p. 115): 57 "And why do you not judge for yourselves what is right? 58 As you go with your accuser before the magistrate, make an effort to settle with him on the way, lest he drag you to the judge, and the judge hand you over to the officer, and the officer put you in prison. 59 I tell you, you will never get out till you have paid the very last copper."

23. ON ADULTERY.
Matt. 5:27-30

27 "You have heard that it was said, 'You shall not commit adultery.' 28 But I say to you that every one who looks at a woman lustfully has already committed adultery with her in his heart. 29 If your right eye causes you to sin, pluck it out and throw it away; it is better that you lose one of your members than that your whole body be thrown into hell.[k] 30 And if your right hand causes you to sin, cut it off and throw it away; it is better that you lose one of your members than that your whole body go into hell.*[k]

* Matt. 18:8-9 (§ 131, p.97):
8 "And if your hand or your foot causes you to sin, cut it off and throw it from you; it is better for you to enter life maimed or lame than with two hands or two feet to be thrown into the eternal fire.

9 And if your eye causes you to sin, pluck it out and throw it from you; it is better for you to enter life with one eye than with two eyes to be thrown into the hell of fire."

Mark 9:43-48 (§ 131, p.97):
43 "And if your hand causes you to sin, cut it off; it is better for you to enter life maimed than with two hands to go to hell, to the unquenchable fire. 45 And if your foot causes you to sin, cut it off; it is better for you to enter life lame than with two feet to be thrown into hell. 47 And if your eye causes you to sin, pluck it out; it is better for you to enter the kingdom of God with one eye than with two eyes to be thrown into hell, 48 where their worm does not die, and the fire is not quenched."

Matt. 5:21—Exodus 20:13 and Deuteronomy 5:17.   5:27—Exodus 20:14 and Deuteronomy 5:18.

[i] text: P[67?] S B vg Justin, Origen; add, *without cause:* D W Θ λ φ 𝕽 it sy^c sy^s sy^p sa bo.   [j] Greek, *says Raca to,* (an obscure term of abuse).   [k] Greek, *Gehenna.*

To Matt. 5:22 cf. **Gospel of the Nazaraeans:** The words, "without cause" are not inserted in some copies, or in the Jewish Gospel.
To Matt. 5:23 cf. **Gospel according to the Hebrews** (in Jerome *Commentary on Ezekiel 18:7*): And in the Gospel according to the Hebrews, which the Nazaraeans are accustomed to read, one of the greatest sins is "To grieve the spirit of one's brother." And, Jerome on Ephesians 5:4 writes: As also we read in the Hebrew Gospel that the Lord spoke to his disciples: "And never," he said, "be joyful except when you look on your brother with love."

24. ON DIVORCE.

Matt. 5:31–32	Matt. 19:9 (§ 187, p. 129)	Mark 10:11–12 (§ 187, p. 129)	Luke 16:18 (§ 176, p. 123)
31 "It was also said, 'Whoever divorces his wife, let him give her a certificate of divorce.' 32 But I say to you that every one who divorces his wife, except on the ground of unchastity, makes her an adulteress; and whoever marries a divorced woman commits adultery.	9 "And I say to you: whoever divorces his wife, except for unchastity,[1] and marries another, commits adultery." m	11 And he said to them, "Whoever divorces his wife and marries another, commits adultery against her; 12 and if she divorces her husband and marries another, she commits adultery."	18 "Every one who divorces his wife and marries another commits adultery, and he who marries a woman divorced from her husband commits adultery."

25. ON SWEARING.

Matt. 5:33–37

(Cf. Matt. 23:16–22, § 210, p. 150)

33 "Again you have heard that it was said to the men of old, 'You shall not swear falsely, but shall perform to the Lord what you have sworn.' 34 But I say to you, Do not swear at all, either by heaven, for it is the throne of God, 35 or by the earth, for it is his footstool, or by Jerusalem, for it is the city of the great King. 36 And do not swear by your head, for you cannot make one hair white or black. 37 Let what you say be simply 'Yes' or 'No'; anything more than this comes from evil.n

26. ON RETALIATION.

Matt. 5:38–42	Luke 6:29–30 (§ 75, p. 55)
38 "You have heard that it was said, 'An eye for an eye and a tooth for a tooth.' 39 But I say to you, Do not resist one who is evil. But if any one strikes you on the right cheek, turn to him the other also; 40 and if any one would sue you and take your coat, let him have your cloak as well; 41 and if any one forces you to go one mile, go with him two miles. 42 Give to him who begs from you, and do not refuse him who would borrow from you.	29 "To him who strikes you on the cheek, offer the other also; and from him who takes away your coat do not withhold even your shirt. 30 Give to every one who begs from you; and of him who takes away your goods do not ask them again."

Matt. 5:31—Deuteronomy 24:1.   5:33—Leviticus 19:12.   5:34–35—Isaiah 66:1.   5:35—Psalm 48:2.   5:38—Exodus 21:24, Deuteronomy 19:21, Leviticus 24:20.

[1] text: S W Θ ℜ vg sy⁸ syᵖ; *except on the ground of unchastity, and marries another, commits adultery* (*against her:* syᶜ): D φ it syᶜ sa; *except on the ground of unchastity, makes her commit adultery:* P²⁵ᵗ B λ bo; *except for unchastity, and marries another, makes her commit adultery:* C.   m text: S D it (some MSS.) syᶜ sy⁸ sa; add, *And whoever marries a divorced woman commits adultery:* P²⁵ B C W Θ λ φ ℜ it (some MSS.) vg syᵖ bo (cf. Matt. 5:32).   n Or, *the evil one.*

27. ON LOVE OF ONE'S ENEMIES.

Matt. 5:43–48

43 "You have heard that it was said, 'You shall love your neighbor and hate your enemy.' 44 But I say to you, Love your enemies and pray for those who persecute you, 45 so that you may be sons of your Father who is in heaven; for he makes his sun rise on the evil and on the good, and sends rain on the just and on the unjust. 46 For if you love those who love you, what reward have you? Do not even the tax collectors do the same? 47 And if you salute only your brethren, what more are you doing than others? Do not even the Gentiles do the same?

48 You, therefore, must be perfect, as your heavenly Father is perfect.

Luke 6:27–28, 32–36 *(§ 75, pp. 55, 56)*

27 "But I say to you that hear, Love your enemies, do good to those who hate you, 28 bless those who curse you, pray for those who abuse you.

32 If you love those who love you, what credit is that to you? For even sinners love those who love them. 33 And if you do good to those who do good to you, what credit is that to you? For even sinners do the same. 34 And if you lend to those from whom you hope to receive, what credit is that to you? Even sinners lend to sinners, to receive as much again. 35 But love your enemies, and do good, and lend, expecting nothing in return; [o] and your reward will be great, and you will be sons of the Most High; for he is kind to the ungrateful and the selfish. 36 Be merciful, even as your Father is merciful."

28. ON ALMSGIVING.

Matt: 6:1–4

1 "Beware of practicing your piety [p] before men in order to be seen by them; for then you will have no reward from your Father who is in heaven.

2 "Thus, when you give alms, sound no trumpet before you, as the hypocrites do in the synagogues and in the streets, that they may be praised by men. Truly, I say to you, they have received their reward. 3 But when you give alms, do not let your left hand know what your right hand is doing, 4 so that your alms may be in secret; and your Father who sees in secret will reward you.[q]

Matt. 5:43—Leviticus 19:18. 5:48—Deuteronomy 18:13.

[o] text: A B D Θ λ ϕ ℜ it vg sa bo; *despairing of no man:* S W sy^s sy^p. [p] text: S B D λ it vg sy^s sy^p; *beware of giving your alms before men:* W Θ ϕ ℜ. [q] text: S B D λ ϕ it (some MSS.) vg sy^c sa bo; add, *openly:* W Θ ℜ it (some MSS.) sy^s sy^p.

To Matt. 5:44 cf. *Oxyrhynchus Papyrus 1224, fol. 2 recto, col 1:* ". . . and pray for your enemies. . . ."
To Matt. 5:46 cf. II Clement 13:4—God said, "It is no credit to you if you love those who love you; but it is a credit to you if you love your enemies and those who hate you."

29. ON PRAYER.
Matt. 6:5–8

5 "And when you pray, you must not be like the hypocrites; for they love to stand and pray in the synagogues and at the street corners, that they may be seen by men. Truly, I say to you, they have received their reward. 6 But when you pray, go into your room and shut the door and pray to your Father who is in secret; and your Father who sees in secret will reward you.ʳ 7 And in praying do not heap up empty phrases as the Gentiles do; for they think that they will be heard for their many words. 8 Do not be like them, for your Father knows what you need before you ask him.

30. THE LORD'S PRAYER.

Matt. 6:9–15

9 "Pray then like this:

Our Father who art in heaven,
Hallowed be thy name.
10 Thy kingdom come,
Thy will be done,
On earth as it is in heaven.
11 Give us this day our daily bread; ˢ
12 And forgive us our debts,
As we also have forgiven our debtors;
13 And lead us not into temptation,
But deliver us from evil ᵗ. ᵘ
14 For if you forgive men their trespasses, your heavenly Father also will forgive you;*
15 but if you do not forgive men their trespasses,ᵛ neither will your Father forgive your trespasses."

11:25–26 (§201, p. 141)

11:25–26 (§ 201, p. 141)

25 "And whenever you stand praying, forgive, if you have anything against any one; so that your Father also who is in heaven may forgive you your trespasses." ʷ

Luke 11:2–4 (§ 146, p.105)

2 And he said to them, "When you pray, say:
"Father,ʳʳ
hallowed be thy name.
Thy kingdom come.

3 Give us each day our daily bread; ˢ
4 and forgive us our sins, for we ourselves forgive everyone who is indebted to us; and lead us not into temptation."

---

* Cf. Matt. 18:35 (§ 136, p.100).

Matt. 6:6—Isaiah 26:20 (Septuagint).   6:8—cf. 6:32.

ʳ text: S B D λ it (some MSS.) vg syᵉ syˢ sa bo; add, *openly:* W Θ φ 𝔎 it (some MSS.) syᵖ.   ʳʳ text: P⁷⁵ S B λ vg syˢ Marcion, Origen; *Our Father who art in heaven:* A C D W Θ φ 𝔎 it syᵉ syᵖ sa bo. Cf. Matt. 6:9. ˢ Or, *our bread for the morrow.*   ᵗ Or, *the evil one.*   ᵘ text: S B D λ it vg bo; add, *for thine is the kingdom and the power and the glory, for ever. Amen:* W Θ φ 𝔎 syᵖ; add, *for thine is the power and the glory for ever. Amen:* sa (Didache omit *Amen*); add, *for thine is the kingdom and the glory for ever. Amen:* syᶜ.   ᵛ text: B W Θ φ 𝔎 syᵉ sa bo (some MSS.); omit: *their trespasses:* S D λ it vg syᵖ bo (some MSS.) Augustine.   ʷ text: S B W syˢ sa bo; add verse 26: *"But if you do not forgive, neither will your Father who is in heaven forgive your trespasses":* A C D Θ λ φ 𝔎 it vg syᵖ Cyprian.

Matt. 6:9–13—Didache 8:2.

To Matt. 6:11 cf. **Gospel of the Nazaraeans** (in Jerome, *Commentary on Matthew 6:11*)—In the so-called Gospel according to the Hebrews, for "bread essential to existence" I found "mahar," which means "of tomorrow"; so the sense is: our bread for tomorrow, that is, of the future, give us this day.

31. WORDS OF JESUS ON FASTING.
Matt. 6:16–18

16 "And when you fast, do not look dismal, like the hypocrites, for they disfigure their faces that their fasting may be seen by men. Truly, I say to you, they have received their reward. [17] But when you fast, anoint your head and wash your face, [18] that your fasting may not be seen by men but by your Father who is in secret; and your Father who sees in secret will reward you.

32. ON TREASURES.

Matt. 6:19–21

19 "Do not lay up for yourselves treasures on earth, where moth and rust [x] consume and where thieves break in and steal, [20] but lay up for yourselves treasures in heaven, where neither moth nor rust [x] consumes and where thieves do not break in and steal. [21] For where your treasure is, there will your heart be also.

Luke 12:33–34 (§ 157, p. 113)

33 "Sell your possessions and give alms;

provide yourselves with purses that do not grow old, with a treasure in the heavens that does not fail, where no thief approaches and no moth destroys. [34] For where your treasure is, there will your heart be also."

33. THE SOUND EYE.

Matt. 6:22–23

22 "The eye is the lamp of the body. So, if your eye is sound, your whole body will be full of light; [23] but if your eye is not sound, your whole body will be full of darkness. If then the light in you is darkness, how great is the darkness!

Luke 11:34–36 (§ 153, p. 109)

34 "Your eye is the lamp of your body; when your eye is sound, your whole body is full of light; but when it is not sound, your body is full of darkness. [35] Therefore be careful lest the light in you be darkness. [36] If then your whole body is full of light, having no part dark, it will be wholly bright, as when a lamp with its rays gives you light."

---

[x] Or, *worm.*

To Matt. 6:16 cf. *Oxyrhynchus Papyrus 1, Logion 2:* Jesus says, "If you do not fast to the world, you shall not find the kingdom of God; and if you do not keep the sabbath, you shall not see the Father."

34. WORDS OF JESUS ON SERVING TWO MASTERS.

Matt. 6:24	Luke 16:13 (§ *174, p. 123*)
24 "No one can serve two masters; for either he will hate the one and love the other, or he will be devoted to the one and despise the other. You cannot serve God and mammon."ˣˣ	13 "No servant can serve two masters; for either he will hate the one and love the other, or he will be devoted to the one and despise the other. You cannot serve God and mammon."ˣˣ

35. ON ANXIETY.

Matt. 6:25–34	Luke 12:22–31 (§ *157, pp. 112–113*)
	22 And he said to his disciples,
25 "Therefore I tell you, do not be anxious about your life, what you shall eat or what you shall drink,ʸ nor about your body, what you shall put on. Is not life more than food, and the body more than clothing? 26 Look at the birds of the air: they neither sow nor reap nor gather into barns, and yet your heavenly Father feeds them. Are you not of more value than they? 27 And which of you by being anxious can add one cubit to his span of life?ᶻ 28 And why are you anxious about clothing?	"Therefore I tell you, do not be anxious about your life, what you shall eat, nor about your body, what you shall put on. 23 For life is more than food, and the body more than clothing. 24 Consider the ravens: they neither sow nor reap, they have neither storehouse nor barn, and yet God feeds them. Of how much more value are you than the birds! 25 And which of you by being anxious can add a cubit to his span of life?ᶻ 26 If then you are not able to do as small a thing as that, why are you anxious about the rest? 27 Consider
Consider the lilies of the field, how they grow; they neither toil nor spin; 29 yet I tell you, even Solomon in all his glory was not arrayed like one of these. 30 But if God so clothes the grass of the field, which today is alive and tomorrow is thrown into the oven, will he not much more clothe you, O men of little faith? 31 Therefore do not be anxious, saying, 'What shall we eat?' or 'What shall we drink?' or 'What shall we wear?' 32 For the Gentiles seek all these things; and your heavenly Father knows that you need them all.	the lilies, how they grow; they neither toil nor spin;ᵃ yet I tell you, even Solomon in all his glory was not arrayed like one of these. 28 But if God so clothes the grass which is alive in the field today and tomorrow is thrown into the oven, how much more will he clothe you, O men of little faith! 29 And do not seek what you are to eat and what you are to drink, nor be of anxious mind. 30 For all the nations of the world seek these things; and your Father knows that you need them.

ˣˣ Mammon is a Semitic word for money or riches.   ʸ text: B W φ it (some MSS.) sa (some MSS.) bo; *what you shall eat and what you shall drink:* Θ 𝕽 syᵖ; omit, *or what you shall drink:* S λ it (some MSS.) vg syᶜ sa (some MSS.).   ᶻ Or, *stature.*   ᵃ text: P⁴⁵ P⁷⁵ S A B W Θ λ φ 𝕽 it (some MSS.) vg syᵖ sa bo; *lilies, how they neither spin nor weave:* D syᶜ syˢ; *how they grow; they neither toil nor spin nor weave:* it (some MSS.).

To Matt. 6:25ff, cf. *Oxyrhynchus Papyrus 655 I a, b:* "(Take no thought) from morning until evening or from evening until morning, either for your food, what you shall eat, or for your clothes, what you shall put on. You are far better than the lilies which grow but do not spin. Having one garment, what do you (lack)? . . . Who could add to your span of life? He, himself, will give you your garment. . . ."

33 But seek first his kingdom and his righteousness, and all these things shall be yours as well.

34 Therefore do not be anxious about to-morrow, for tomorrow will be anxious for itself. Let the day's own trouble be sufficient for the day.

31 Instead, seek his [b] kingdom, and these things shall be yours as well."

36. ON JUDGING.

Matt. 7:1–5

1 "Judge not, that you be not jud-ged. 2 For with the judgment you pronounce you will be judged,

and the measure you give will be the measure you get.* 3 Why do you see the speck that is in your brother's eye, but do not notice the log that is in your own eye? 4 Or how can you say to your brother, 'Let me take the speck out of your eye,' when there is the log in your own eye? 5 You hypocrite, first take the log out of your own eye, and then you will see clearly to take the speck out of your brother's eye.

Luke 6:37–38, 41–42 (§ 76, pp. 56–57)

37 "Judge not, and you will not be jud-ged; condemn not, and you will not be condemned; forgive, and you will be forgiven; 38 give, and it will be given to you; good measure, pressed down, shaken together, running over, will be put into your lap. For the measure you give will be the measure you get back.* 41 Why do you see the speck that is in your brother's eye, but do not notice the log that is in your own eye? 42 Or how can you say to your brother, 'Brother, let me take out the speck that is in your eye,' when you yourself do not see the log that is in your own eye? You hypocrite, first take the log out of your own eye, and then you will see clearly to take out the speck that is in your brother's eye."

37. ON PROFANING THE HOLY.

Matt. 7:6

6 "Do not give dogs what is holy; and do not throw your pearls before swine, lest they trample them underfoot and turn to attack you.

---

* Mark 4:24 (§ 94, p.68): And he said to them, "Take heed what you hear; the measure you give will be the measure you get, and still more will be given you. " (Cf. also Matt. 6:33 and Luke 12:31.)

[b] text: S B D sa bo; *God's:* P⁴⁵ A W Θ λ φ 𝔐 it vg syᶜ syˢ syᵖ; *the kingdom:* P⁷⁵.

To Matt. 6:33 cf. Origen, *On Prayer 2, 2; 14, 1:* "Ask for the great things, and the small things shall be yours as well; and ask for the heavenly things, and the earthly things shall be yours as well." (Cf. also Clement of Alexandria, *Miscellanies,* I.24.158.)

To Matt. 7:1 (also Matt. 5:7, 6:14; Luke 6:31, 37f.) cf. I Clement 13:2: "Be merciful, that you may obtain mercy. Forgive that you may be forgiven. As you do, so shall it be done to you. As you give, so shall it be given to you. As you judge, so shall you be judged. The kindness you show will be shown you. The measure you give will be the measure you get."

To Matt. 7:5 cf. **Gospel of the Nazaraeans:** The Jewish Gospel reads here: "If you be in my bosom and do not the will of my Father who is in heaven, I will cast you away from my bosom."

To Matt. 7:5 and Luke 6:42 cf. *Oxyrhynchus Papyrus 1, Logion 1:* "And then you will see clearly to take out the speck that is in your brother's eye."

To Matt. 7:6 cf. Didache 9:5: "But let no one eat or drink of your Eucharist, except those who have been baptized in the name of the Lord; for concerning this the Lord has said, 'Do not give dogs what is holy.' " Cf. Epiphanius, *Against Heresies, XXIV.5.2.* Cf. also **Gospel of Thomas, Logion 93.**

38. GOD'S ANSWERING OF PRAYER.

Matt. 7:7–11

"7 Ask, and it will be given you; seek, and you will find; knock, and it will be opened to you. 8 For every one who asks receives, and he who seeks finds, and to him who knocks it will be opened. 9 Or what man of you, if his son asks him for bread, will give him a stone? 10 Or if he asks for a fish, will give him a serpent?

11 If you then, who are evil, know how to give good gifts to your children, how much more will your Father who is in heaven give good things to those who ask him!

Luke 11:9–13 (§ 148, p. 106)

9 "And I tell you, Ask, and it will be given you; seek, and you will find; knock, and it will be opened to you. 10 For every one who asks receives, and he who seeks finds, and to him who knocks it will be opened. 11 What father among you, if his son asks for c

a fish, will instead of a fish give him a serpent; 12 or if asks for an egg, will give him a scorpion? 13 If you then, who are evil, know how to give good gifts to your children, how much more will the heavenly Father give the Holy Spirit to those who ask him!"

39. "THE GOLDEN RULE."

Matt. 7:12

12 "So whatever you wish that men would do to you, do so to them; for this is the law and the prophets.

Luke 6:31 (§ 75, p. 56)

31 "And as you wish that men would do to you, do so to them."

40. THE NARROW GATE.

Matt. 7:13–14

13 "Enter by the narrow gate; for the gate is wide and the way is easy,d that leads to destruction, and those who enter by it are many. 14 For the gate is narrow and the way is hard, that leads to life, and those who find it are few.

Luke 13:23–24 (§ 165, p. 117)

23 And some one said to him, "Lord, will those who are saved be few?" And he said to them, 24 "Strive to enter by the narrow door; for many, I tell you, will seek to enter and will not be able."

Matt. 7:12—Tobit 4:15 and Ecclesiasticus 31:15.

c text: P45 P75 B sys sa; add, *bread, will give him a stone; or, if he asks for:* S A C D W Θ λ φ ℜ it vg syc syp bo. d text: B C W Θ λ φ ℜ it (some MSS.) vg syc syp sa bo; *for the way is wide and easy:* S it (some MSS.) Clement, Origen.

To Matt. 7:7 cf. **Gospel according to the Hebrews** (in Clement of Alexandria, *Miscellanies V.14.96*); also cf. *Oxyrhynchus Papyrus 654, Logion 1:* "He who seeks will not give up until he finds; and having found, he will marvel; and having marveled, he will reign; and having reigned, he will rest." Cf. **Gospel of Thomas, Logion 2:** Jesus said, "Let him who seeks not cease seeking until he finds, and when he finds he will be troubled, and when he has been troubled he will marvel and he will reign over the All."

To Matt. 7:12 cf. Didache 1:2: "Whatever you would not have done to yourself, do not do to another."

41. THE TEST OF A GOOD MAN.

Matt. 7:15-20

15 "Beware of false prophets, who come to you in sheep's clothing but inwardly are ravenous wolves. 16 You will know them by their fruits. Are grapes gathered from thorns, or figs from thistles? 17 So, every sound tree bears good fruit, but the bad tree bears evil fruit.* 18 A sound tree cannot bear evil fruit, nor can a bad tree bear good fruit. 19 Every tree that does not bear good fruit is cut down and thrown into the fire.** 20 Thus you will know them by their fruits.

See 12:35 (§ 86, p. 63)

Luke 6:43–45 (§ 77, p. 57)

43 "For no good tree bears bad fruit, nor again does a bad tree bear good fruit; 44 for each tree is known by its own fruit.* For figs are not gathered from thorns, nor are grapes picked from a bramble bush. 45 The good man out of the good treasure of his heart produces good, and the evil man out of his evil treasure produces evil; for out of the abundance of the heart his mouth speaks.

42. WARNING AGAINST SELF-DECEPTION.

Matt. 7:21-23

21 "Not every one who says to me, 'Lord, Lord,' shall enter the kingdom of heaven, but he who does the will of my Father who is in heaven. 22 On that day many will say to me, 'Lord, Lord, did we not prophesy in your name, and cast out demons in your name, and do many mighty works in your name?' 23 And then will I declare to them, 'I never knew you; depart from me, you evildoers.'

Luke 6:46 (§ 77, p. 57)

46 "Why do you call me 'Lord, Lord,' and not do what I tell you?

13:26–27 (§ 165, pp. 117–118)

26 "Then you will begin to say, 'We ate and drank in your presence, and you taught in our streets.' 27 But he will say, 'I tell you, I do not know where you come from; depart from me, all you workers of iniquity.' "

---

* Matt. 12:33-35 (§ 86, p.62-63): 33 "Either make the tree good, and its fruit good; or make the tree bad, and its fruit bad; for the tree is known by its fruit. 34 You brood of vipers! how can you speak good, when you are evil? For out of the abundance of the heart the mouth speaks. 35 The good man out of his good treasure brings forth good, and the evil man out of his evil treasure brings forth evil."

** Cf. Matt. 3:10 and Luke 3:9 (§ 2, p.9).

Matt. 7:23 and Luke 13:27—Psalm 6:8.

To Matt. 7:15 cf. Justin, *Dialogue, 35.3:* For, he says, "Many will come in my name, clothed in sheepskins, but inwardly they are ravenous wolves"; and "there will be divisions and heresies."

To Matt. 7:21 cf. II Clement 4:2: For he says, "Not every one who says to me, 'Lord, Lord,' shall be saved; but he who practices piety."

To Matt. 7:22f. cf. II Clement 4:5: The Lord said, "If you are gathered together with me in my bosom, and do not obey my commandments, I will cast you out and say to you, Depart from me; I do not know where you come from, you evil-doers." (Cf. Luke 13:25ff.).

43. HEARERS AND DOERS OF THE WORD.

Matt. 7:24–27

24 "Every one then who hears these words of mine and does them will be like a wise man who built his house upon the rock; 25 and the rain fell, and the floods came, and the winds blew and beat upon that house, but it did not fall, because it had been founded on the rock. 26 And every one who hears these words of mine and does not do them will be like a foolish man who built his house upon the sand; 27 and the rain fell, and the floods came, and the winds blew and beat against that house, and it fell; and great was the fall of it."

Luke 6:47–49 (§ 78, p. 58)

47 "Every one who comes to me and hears my words and does them, I will show you what he is like: 48 he is like a man building a house, who dug deep, and laid the foundation upon rock; and when a flood arose, the stream broke against that house, and could not shake it, because it had been well built.e

49 But he who hears and does not do them is like a man who built a house on the ground without a foundation; against which the stream broke, and immediately it fell, and the ruin of that house was great."

44. THE END OF THE SERMON.
Matt. 7:28–29

28 And when Jesus finished these sayings, the crowds were astonished at his teaching, 29 for he taught them as one who had authority, and not as their scribes.* | 7:1a (p. 32)

45. THE HEALING OF A LEPER.

Matt. 8:1–4

1 When he came down from the mountain great crowds followed him; 2 and behold, a leper came to him and knelt before him, saying,

Mark 1:40–45
(1:39, § 16, p. 18)

40 And a leper came to him beseeching him, and kneeling said to him,

Luke 5:12–16
(5:1–11, § 17, p. 19)

12 While he was in one of the cities, there came a man a man full of leprosy; and when he saw Jesus, he fell on his face and besought him,

* Mark 1:21-22 (§ 12, p.16): 21 And they went into Capernaum; and immediately on the sabbath he entered the synagogue and taught. 22 And they were astonished at his teaching, for he taught them as one who had authority, and not as the scribes.

Luke 4:31-32 (§ 12, p.16): 31 And he went down to Capernaum, a city of Galilee. And he was teaching them on the sabbath; 32 and they were astonished at his teaching, for his word was with authority.

e text: P75? S B W sa bo; *because it had been founded on the rock:* A C D Θ λ φ ℜ it vg syp; omit phrase: P45? sys.

To § 44 cf. John 7:46: The officers answered, "No man ever spoke like this man!"

"Lord, if you will, you can make me clean."

3 And he stretched out his hand and touched him, saying,   "I will; be clean." And immediately his leprosy was cleansed.

4 And Jesus said to him, "See that you say nothing to anyone; but go, show yourself to the priest, and offer   the gift that Moses commanded, for a proof to the people." f

---

"If you will, you can make me clean." 41 Moved with pity,   he stretched out his hand and touched him, and said to him, "I will; be clean." 42 And immediately the leprosy left him, and he was made clean. 43 And he sternly charged him, and sent him away at once, 44 and said to him, "See that you say nothing to anyone; but go, show yourself to the priest, and offer for your cleansing what Moses commanded, for a proof to the people." f 45 But he went out and began to talk freely about it, and to spread the news, so that Jesus g could no longer openly enter a town, but was out in the country; * and people came to him from every quarter.

(2:1–12, § 52, pp. 35–36)

"Lord, if you will, you can make me clean."

13 And he stretched out his hand, and touched him, saying,   "I will; be clean." And immediately the leprosy left him.

14 And he charged him   to tell no one; but "go and show yourself to the priest, and make an offering for your cleansing, as Moses commanded, for a proof to the people." f 15 But so much the more the report went abroad concerning him; and great multitudes gathered to hear and to be healed of their infirmities. 16 But he withdrew to the wilderness and prayed.*

(5:17–26, § 52, pp. 35–36)

---

46. THE CENTURION'S SERVANT.

Matt. 8:5–13

5 As he entered Capernaum, a centurion came forward to him, beseeching him 6 and saying, "Lord, my servant is lying paralyzed at home, in terrible distress." 7 And he said to him, "I will come and heal him."

Luke 7:1–10 (§ 79, p. 58)

1 After he had ended all his sayings in the hearing of the people he entered Capernaum. 2 Now a centurion had a slave who was dear to him, who was sick and at the point of death. 3 When he heard of Jesus, he sent to him elders of the Jews, asking him to come and heal his slave. 4 And when they came to Jesus, they besought him earnestly, saying, "He is worthy to have you do this for him, 5 for he loves our nation, and he built us our synagogue."

---

* Cf. Mark 1:35 and Luke 4:42 (§ 15, p.18).

Matt. 8:4, Mark 1:44 and Luke 5:14—Leviticus 13:49; 14:2ff.

f Greek, *to them.*   g Greek, *he.*

To § 46, cf. John 4:46-53.

To Matt. 8:2-4 and parallels, cf. *Egerton Papyrus 2:* And behold, a leper, coming to him, said, "Master Jesus, journeying with lepers and eating with them in the inn, I also became a leper. If, therefore, you will, I can be made clean." The Lord then said to him, "I will; be clean." And immediately the leprosy left him, and the Lord said to him, "Go and show yourself to the priests . . . "

8 But the centurion answered him,
"Lord,

    I am not worthy to have
you come under my roof;

    but only
say the word, and my servant will be
healed. 9 For I am a man   under
authority, with soldiers under me;
and I say to one, 'Go,' and he goes,
and to another, 'Come,' and he comes,
and to my slave, 'Do this,' and he
does it." 10 When Jesus heard him, he
marveled, and   said
to those who followed him,
"Truly I say to you, not even[h] in Israel
have I found such faith.

11 "I tell you, many will come from
east and west and sit at table with
    Abraham, Isaac, and Jacob

    in the kingdom of heaven,
12 while the sons of the kingdom will be
thrown into the outer darkness; there
men will weep and gnash their teeth."

13 And to the centurion Jesus said,
"Go; be it done for you as you have
believed." And the servant was healed
at that very moment.[i]

6 And Jesus went with them. When he
was not far from the house, the centurion sent friends to him, saying
to him, "Lord do not trouble yourself, for I am not worthy to have
you come under my roof; 7 therefore I
did not presume to come to you. But
say the word, and let my servant be
healed. 8 For I am a man set under
authority, with soldiers under me:
and I say to one, 'Go,' and he goes;
and to another, 'Come,' and he comes;
and to my slave, 'Do this,' and he
does it." 9 When Jesus heard this he
marveled at him, and turned and said
to the multitude that followed him,
"I tell you, not even in Israel have
I found such faith."

13:28–30 (§ *165, p. 118):* 28 "There you
will weep and gnash your teeth, when
you see Abraham and Isaac and Jacob and
all the prophets in the kingdom of God
and you yourselves thrust out. 29 And
men will come from east and west, and
from north and south, and sit at
table in the kingdom of God. 30 And
behold, some are last who will be
first, and some are first who will be
last."

7:10 And when those who had been sent
returned to the house, they found the
slave well.

47. THE HEALING OF PETER'S MOTHER-IN-LAW.
Matt. 8:14–15 (= *Mark 1:29–31 = Luke 4:38–39, § 13, p. 17*)

14 And when Jesus entered Peter's house, he saw his mother-in-law lying sick with
a fever; 15 he touched her hand, and the fever left her, and she rose and served him. | *1:29–31* | *4:38–39* |

Matt. 8:11 and Luke 13:29—Psalm 107:3.

[h] text: S C Θ φ ℜ it (some MSS.) vg sy^s sy^p; *with no one:* B W λ it (some MSS.) sy^c sa bo.   [i] text: B W
φ ℜ it vg sy^c sy^s sy^p sa bo; *and when the centurion returned to his house in that hour he found the servant well:* S C Θ λ.
Cf. Luke 7:10.

To Matt. 8:14 cf. **Gospel of the Ebionites, p.16.**

48. THE SICK HEALED AT EVENING.

Matt. 8:16–17 (= *Mark 1:32–34 = Luke 4:40–41, § 14, p. 18*)

16 That evening they brought to him many who were possessed with demons; and he cast out the spirits with a word, and healed all who were sick. 17 This was to fulfil what was spoken by the prophet Isaiah, "He took our infirmities and bore our diseases." | *1:32–34* | *4:40–41* |

49. THE NATURE OF DISCIPLESHIP.

Matt. 8:18–22	Luke 9:57–60 (*§ 138, p. 101*)
18 Now when Jesus saw great crowds around him, he gave orders to go over to the other side. *4:35*	
19 And a scribe came up and said to him, "Teacher, I will follow you wherever you go." 20 And Jesus said to him, "Foxes have holes, and birds of the air have nests; but the Son of man has nowhere to lay his head."	57 And as they were going along the road, a man said to him, "I will follow you wherever you go." 58 And Jesus said to him, "Foxes have holes, and birds of the air have nests; but the Son of man has nowhere to lay his head."
21 Another of his disciples said to him, "Lord, let me first go and bury my father." 22 But Jesus said to him, "Follow me, and leave the dead to bury their own dead."	59 To another he said, "Follow me." But he said, "Lord, let me first go and bury my father." 60 But he said to him, "Leave the dead to bury their own dead; but as for you, go and proclaim the kingdom of God."

50. CALMING THE STORM.

Matt. 8:23–27 (= *Mark 4:35–41 = Luke 8:22–25, § 105, pp. 71–72*)

23 And when he got into the boat, his disciples followed him. 24 And behold, there arose a great storm on the sea, so that the boat was being swamped by the waves; but he was asleep. 25 And they went and woke him, saying, "Save, Lord; we are perishing." 26 And he said to them, "Why are you afraid, O men of little faith?" Then he rose and rebuked the winds and the sea; and there was a great calm. 27 And the men marveled, saying, "What sort of man is this, that even winds and sea obey him?" | *4:35–41* | *8:22–25* |

Matt. 8:17—Isaiah 53:4.

51. THE GADARENE DEMONIACS.

Matt. 8:28–34 (= *Mark 5:1–20* = *Luke 8:26–39, § 106, pp. 72–73*)

28 And when he came to the other side, to the country of the Gadarenes,ʲ two demoniacs met him, coming out of the tombs, so fierce that no one could pass that way. ²⁹ And behold, they cried out, "What have you to do with us, O Son of God? Have you come here to torment us before the time?" ³⁰ Now a herd of many swine was feeding at some distance from them. ³¹ And the demons begged him, "If you cast us out, send us away into the herd of swine." ³² And he said to them, "Go." So they came out and went into the swine; and behold, the whole herd rushed down the steep bank into the sea, and perished in the waters. ³³ The herdsmen fled, and going into the city they told everything, and what had happened to the demoniacs. ³⁴ And behold, all the city came out to meet Jesus; and when they saw him, they begged him to leave their neighborhood.

5:1–20 | *8:26–39*

52. THE HEALING OF THE PARALYTIC.

Matt. 9:1–8	Mark 2:1–12 *(1:40–45, § 45, p. 31f.)*	Luke 5:17–26 *(5:12–16, § 45, p. 31f.)*
1 And getting into a boat he crossed over and came to his own city.	1 And when he returned to Capernaum after some days, it was reported that he was at home. ² And many were gathered together, so that there was no longer room for them, not even about the door; and he was preaching the word to them.	17 On one of those days, as he was teaching, there were Pharisees and teachers of the law sitting by, who had come from every village of Galilee and Judea and from Jerusalem; and the power of the Lord was with him to heal.ᵏ
² And behold, they brought to him a paralytic, lying on his bed;	³ And they came, bringing to him a paralytic carried by four men.	18 And behold, men were bringing on a bed a man who was paralyzed, and they sought to bring him in and lay him before Jesus;ˡ 19 but finding no way to bring him in, because of the crowd, they went up on the roof and let him down with his bed through the tiles into the midst before Jesus.
and when Jesus saw their faith he said to the paralytic, "Take heart, my son; your sins are forgiven."	⁴ And when they could not get near him because of the crowd, they removed the roof above him; and when they had made an opening, they let down the pallet on which the paralytic lay. ⁵ And when Jesus saw their faith, he said to the paralytic, "My son, your sins are forgiven."	20 And when he saw their faith he said, "Man, your sins are forgiven you."
³ And behold, some of the scribes said to themselves, "This man is blaspheming."	⁶ Now some of the scribes were sitting there, questioning in their hearts, ⁷ "Why does this man speak thus? It is blasphemy! Who can forgive sins but God alone?"	21 And the scribes and the Pharisees began to question, saying, "Who is this that speaks blasphemies? Who can forgive sins but God only?"

ʲ text: S B C Θ syˢ syᵖ; *Gergesenes:* W λ φ 𝕽 bo; *Gerasenes:* it vg sa.   ᵏ text: S B W sa; *was present to heal them:* A C D Θ λ φ 𝕽 it vg syᵖ bo; *was for healing:* syˢ.   ˡ Greek, *him.*

4 But Jesus, knowing [m] their thoughts, said, "Why do you think evil in your hearts? 5 For which is easier, to say, 'Your sins are forgiven,'[n] or to say, 'Rise and walk'? 6 But that you may know that the Son of man has authority on earth to forgive sins"—he then said to the paralytic— "Rise, take up your bed and go home." 7 And he rose and went home. 8 When the crowds saw it, they were afraid, and they glorified God, who had given such authority to men.

8 And immediately Jesus, perceiving in his spirit that they thus questioned within themselves, said to them, "Why do you question thus in your hearts? 9 Which is easier, to say to the paralytic, 'Your sins are forgiven,' or to say, 'Rise, take up your pallet and walk'? 10 But that you may know that the Son of man has authority on earth to forgive sins"—he said to the paralytic— 11 "I say to you, rise, take up your pallet and go home." 12 And he rose, and immediately took up the pallet and went out before them all; so that they were all amazed and glorified God, saying, "We never saw anything like this!"

22 When Jesus perceived their questionings, he answered them, "Why do you question in your hearts? 23 Which is easier, to say, 'Your sins are forgiven you,' or to say, 'Rise and walk'? 24 But that you may know that the Son of man has authority on earth to forgive sins"— he said to the man who was paralyzed—"I say to you, rise, take up your bed and go home." 25 And immediately he rose before them, and took up that on which he lay, and went home, glorifying God. 26 And amazement seized them all, and they glorified God and were filled with awe, saying, "We have seen strange things today."

53. THE CALL OF LEVI.

Matt. 9:9–13	Mark 2:13–17	Luke 5:27–32
	13 He went out again beside the sea; and all the crowd gathered about him, and he taught them. 14 And as he	27 After this he went out,
9 As Jesus passed on from there, he saw a man called Matthew sitting at the tax office; and he said to him, "Follow me." And he rose and followed him.	passed on, he saw Levi[o] the son of Alphaeus sitting at the tax office, and he said. to him, "Follow me." And he rose and followed him.	and saw a tax collector, named Levi, sitting at the tax office; and he said to him, "Follow me." 28 And he left everything, and rose and followed him.

---

[m] text: B Θ λ sy[p] sa; *seeing:* S C D W φ 𝔑 it vg bo.   [n] text: S B D vg sa bo; *have been forgiven:* C W Θ λ 𝔑 it .   [o] text: S A B C W λ 𝔑 vg sy[p] sa bo: *James:* D Θ φ it. (Cf. Matt. 10:3 and parallels, § 58, p.40.)

To Matt. 9:6-7 and parallels, cf. John 5:8-9: 8 Jesus said to him, "Rise, take up your pallet, and walk." 9 And at once the man was healed, and he took up his pallet and walked.

Matt. 9:10–14

10 And as he sat at table[p] in the house, behold, many tax collectors and sinners came and sat down with Jesus and his disciples.

11 And when the Pharisees saw this, they said to his disciples, "Why does your teacher eat with tax collectors and sinners?" 12 But when he heard it, he said, "Those who are well have no need of a physician, but those who are sick. 13 Go and learn what this means, 'I desire mercy, and not sacrifice.' For I came not to call the righteous, but sinners."

Mark 2:15–18

15 And as he sat at table in his house, many tax collectors and sinners were sitting with Jesus and his disciples; for there were many who followed him. 16 And the scribes of[q] the Pharisees, when they saw that he was eating with sinners and tax collectors, said to his disciples, "Why does he eat[r] with tax collectors and sinners?" 17 And when Jesus heard it, he said to them, "Those who are well have no need of a physician, but those who are sick; I came not to call the righteous, but sinners."

Luke 5:29–33

29 And Levi made him a great feast in his house; and there was a large company of tax collectors and others sitting at table[p] with him. 30 And the Pharisees and their scribes murmured against his disciples, saying, "Why do you eat and drink with tax collectors and sinners?" * 31 And Jesus answered them, "Those who are well have no need of a physician, but those who are sick; 32 I have not come to call the righteous, but sinners to repentance."

54. THE QUESTION ABOUT FASTING.

Matt. 9:14–17

14 Then the disciples of John came to him, saying, "Why do we and the Pharisees fast,[s] but your disciples do not fast?"

Mark 2:18–22

18 Now John's disciples and the Pharisees were fasting; and people came and said to him, "Why do John's disciples and the disciples of the Pharisees fast, but your disciples do not fast?"

Luke 5:33–39

33 And they said to him, "The disciples of John fast often and offer prayers, and so do the disciples of the Pharisees, but yours eat and drink."

---

* To Luke 5:29-30 cf. Luke 15:1-2.

Matt. 9:13 (= 12:7): Hosea 6:6.

[p] Greek, *reclined* (*reclining*). [q] text: S B W; *and:* A C D Θ λ φ 𝔎 it vg sy^{p} sa bo. [r] text: B D W Θ it; *eat and drink:* A λ 𝔎 sy^{p}; *Why does your teacher eat:* S; *Why does your teacher eat and drink:* C φ vg sa bo. [s] text: S B; *fast often:* C D W Θ λ φ 𝔎 it vg sy^{s} sy^{p} sa bo.

To Mark 2:16-17 cf. *Oxyrhynchus Papyrus 1224, fol. 2 verso, col. 2:* When the scribes and the Pharisees and priests saw him, they became indignant, because he reclined in the midst of sinners. But when Jesus heard them, he said, "Those who are well have no need of a physician . . . (but those who are sick)."

To Luke 5:32 cf. Justin, *Apology I.15.8.*—after "to repentance" he adds: "for your heavenly Father prefers the repentance of a sinner to his punishment."

To Mark 2:18 cf. *Didache 8:1:* "Do not fast with the hypocrites, for they fast on the second and fifth days of the week" (i.e., Mondays and Thursdays); "but you should fast on the fourth day and on the day of Preparation" (i.e., Wednesdays and Fridays).

15 And Jesus said to them, "Can the wedding guests mourn as long as the bridegroom is with them?

The days will come, when the bridegroom is taken away from them, and then they will fast.

16 And no one puts a piece of unshrunk cloth on

an old garment, for

the patch tears away from the garment,

and a worse tear is made.

17 Neither is new wine put into old wineskins; if it is, the skins burst,   and the wine is spilled,   and   the   skins are destroyed;   but new wine   is   put   into   fresh wineskins, and so both are preserved."

19 And Jesus said to them, "Can the wedding guests fast while the bridegroom is with them? As long as they have the bridegroom with them, they cannot fast. 20 The days will come, when the bridegroom is taken away from them, and then they will fast in that day.

21 No one sews a piece of unshrunk cloth on

an old garment; if he does, the patch tears away from it, the new from the old, and a worse tear is made.

22 And no one puts new wine   into   old   wineskins; if he does, the   wine will burst the skins, and the wine is lost, and so are the skins; but new wine is for fresh skins."[t]

(2:23–28, § 69, pp. 50–51)

34 And Jesus said to them, "Can you make wedding guests fast while the bridegroom is with them?

35 The days will come, when the bridegroom is taken away from them, and then they will fast in those days."

36 He told them a parable also: "No one tears a piece from a new garment and puts it upon an old garment; if he does, he will tear the new, and the piece from the new will not match the old. 37 And no one puts new wine into old wineskins; if he does, the new wine will burst the skins and it will be spilled, and the skins will be destroyed. 38 But new wine must be put into fresh wineskins. 39 And no one after drinking old wine desires new; for he says, 'The old is good.'"[u]

(6:1–5, § 69, pp. 50–51)

55. JAIRUS' DAUGHTER AND A WOMAN'S FAITH.

Matt. 9:18–26 (= *Mark 5:21–43* = *Luke 8:40–56, § 107, pp. 74–75*)

18 While he was thus speaking to them, behold, a ruler came in and knelt before him, saying, "My daughter has just died; but come and lay your hand on her, and she will live." 19 And Jesus rose and followed him, with his disciples.
20 And behold, a woman who had suffered from a hemorrhage for twelve years came up behind him and touched the fringe of his garment. 21 For she said to herself, "If I only touch his garment, I shall be made well." 22 Jesus turned, and seeing her he said, "Take heart, daughter; your faith has made you well." And instantly the woman was made well.
23 And when Jesus came to the ruler's house, and saw the flute players, and the crowd making a tumult, 24 he said, "Depart; for the girl is not dead but sleeping." And they laughed at him. 25 But when the crowd had been put outside, he went in and took her by the hand, and the girl arose. 26 And the report of this went through all that district.

	5:21–43	8:40–56
		7:50
	5:34	8:48
	10:52	18:42

---

[t] text: S A B C W Θ λ φ 𝕽 vg sy[s] sy[p] sa bo; omit, *but new wine is for fresh skins:* D it.   [u] text: P[4] P[75][r] S B W sy[p] sa bo; *better:* A C Θ λ φ 𝕽 it (some MSS.) vg. Omit v. 39: D it (some MSS.) Marcion, Irenaeus, Eusebius.

To Mark 2:19-20 cf. **Gospel of Thomas, Logia 27 and 104b.**
To Luke 5:39 cf. **Gospel of Thomas, Logion 47b.**

56. TWO BLIND MEN HEALED.

Matt. 9:27–31

(cf. Matt. 20:29–34 = Mark 10:46–52 = Luke 18:35–43, § 193, p. 134)

27 And as Jesus passed on from there, two blind men followed him, crying aloud, "Have mercy on us, Son of David." 28 When he entered the house, the blind men came to him; and Jesus said to them, "Do you believe that I am able to do this?" They said to him, "Yes, Lord." 29 Then he touched their eyes, saying, "According to your faith be it done to you." 30 And their eyes were opened. And Jesus sternly charged them, "See that no one knows it." 31 But they went away and spread his fame through all that district.

57. THE HEALING OF A DUMB DEMONIAC

Matt. 9:32–34

32 As they were going away, behold, a dumb demoniac was brought to him. 33 And when the demon had been cast out, the dumb man spoke; and the crowds marveled, saying, "Never was anything like this seen in Israel." 34 But the Pharisees said, "He casts out demons by the prince of demons." * uu

58. THE SENDING OUT OF THE TWELVE.

Matt. 9:35–10:16	Mark 6:6b (§ 109, p. 76)		Luke 10:1–2 (§ 139, p. 102)
35 And Jesus went about all the cities and villages, teaching in their synagogues and preaching the gospel of the kingdom, and healing every disease and every infirmity.**	And he went about among the villages teaching.	*Luke 8:1 (§ 84, p. 60)*	1 After this the Lord appointed seventy others, and sent them on ahead of him, two by two, into every town and place where he himself was about to come.
36 When he saw the crowds, he had compassion for them, because they were harassed and helpless, like sheep without a shepherd.	6:34 (§ 112, p. 79) .. As he landed he saw a great throng, and he had compassion on them, because they were like sheep without a shepherd; . . .		
37 Then he said to his disciples, "The harvest is plentiful, but the laborers are few;			2 And he said to them, "The harvest is plentiful, but the laborers are few;

* Matt. 12:22-24 (§ 85, p.61): 22 Then a blind and dumb demoniac was brought to him, and he healed him, so that the dumb man spoke and saw. 23 And all the people were amazed, and said, "Can this be the Son of David?" 24 But when the Pharisees heard it they said, "It is only by Beelzebul, the prince of demons, that this man casts out demons."	Mark 3:22(§ 85,p.61): And the scribes who came down from Jerusalem said, "He is possessed by Beelzebul, and by the prince of demons he casts out the demons."	Luke 11:14-15 (§ 149, p.106) 14 Now he was casting out a demon that was dumb; when the demon had gone out, the dumb man spoke, and the people marveled. 15 But some of them said, "He casts out demons by Beelzebul, the prince of demons";

** Matt. 4:23 (§ 16, p.18). And he went about all Galilee, teaching in their synagogues and preaching the gospel of the kingdom and healing every disease and every infirmity among the people.

Matt. 9:36—Numbers 27:17, I Kings 22:17.

uu text: S B C λ φ ℜ it (some MSS.) vg syᵖ sa bo; omit verse 34: D it (some MSS.) syˢ Diatessaron.

To Matt. 9:37 cf. John 4:35—"Do you not say, 'There are yet four months, then comes the harvest'? I tell you, lift up your eyes, and see how the fields are already white for harvest."

38 pray therefore the Lord of the harvest to send out laborers into his harvest."

pray therefore the Lord of the harvest to send out laborers into his harvest."
(For v. 3 see parallel to Matt. 10:16, p. 42)

10:1 And he called to him his twelve disciples and gave them authority over unclean spirits, to cast them out, and to heal every disease and every infirmity.

6:7 *(§ 109, p. 77):* And he called to him the twelve, and began to send them out two by two, and gave them authority over the unclean spirits.

Luke 9:1 *(§ 109, p. 77):* And he called the twelve together and gave them power and authority over all demons and to cure diseases,

3:13–19 *(§ 72, p. 54):*
13 And he went up on the mountain, and called to him those whom he desired; and they came to him.
14 And he appointed twelve,[v] to be with him, and to be sent out to preach **15** and have authority to cast out demons:

2 The names of the twelve apostles are these: first, Simon, who is called Peter, and Andrew his brother; James the son of Zebedee, and John his brother;

16 Simon[vv] whom he surnamed Peter; **17** James the son of Zebedee and John the brother of James, whom he surnamed Boanerges, that is, sons of thunder;

6:13–16 *(§ 72, p. 54):*

and chose from them twelve, whom he named apostles;
14 Simon, whom he named Peter, and Andrew his brother, and James and John, and Philip, and Bartholomew, **15** and Matthew, and Thomas, and James the son of Alphaeus, and Simon who was called the Zealot, **16** and Judas the son of James, and Judas Iscariot, who became a traitor.

Acts 1:13 And when they had entered, they went up to the upper room, where they were staying, Peter and John and James and Andrew,

Philip and Thomas, Bartholomew and Matthew, James the son of Alphaeus and Simon the Zealot and Judas the son of James.

3 Philip and Bartholomew; Thomas and Matthew the tax collector; James the son of Alphaeus, and Thaddaeus;[w] **4** Simon the Cananaean, and

18 Andrew, and Philip, and Bartholomew, and Matthew, and Thomas, and James the son of Alphaeus. and Thaddaeus,[ww] and Simon the Cananaean. **19** and

Judas Iscariot, who betrayed him.

Judas Iscariot, who betrayed him.

---

[v] text: A D λ ℜ it vg sy^s sy^p; add, *whom also he named apostles:* S B C? W Θ φ sa bo.   [vv] text: A D λ φ ℜ it sy^s sy^p sa bo; *demons.* **16** *So he appointed the twelve: Simon:* S B C.   [w] text: S B φ it (some MSS.) vg sa bo; *Lebbaeus:* D; *Lebbaeus called Thaddaeus:* C? W Θ λ ℜ sy^p; *Judas Zelotes:* it (some MSS.); add, *Judas the son of James* after "Cananaean" in v. 4: sy^s.   [ww] text: S A B C Θ λ φ ℜ it (some MSS.) vg sy^s sy^p sa bo; *Lebbaeus:* D it (some MSS.).

To Matt. 10:2 and parallels, cf. John 1:42: He brought him to Jesus. Jesus looked at him, and said, "So you are Simon the son of John? You shall be called Cephas" (which means Peter).

5 These twelve Jesus sent out, charging them, "Go nowhere among the Gentiles, and enter no town of the Samaritans, 6 but go rather to the lost sheep of the house of Israel.* 7 And preach as you go, saying, 'The kingdom of heaven is at hand.' 8 Heal the sick, raise the dead, cleanse lepers, cast out demons. You received without paying, give without pay.

9 "Take no gold, nor silver, nor copper in your belts, 10 no bag for your journey, nor two tunics, nor sandals, nor a staff; for the laborer deserves his food.

11 "And whatever town or village you enter, find out who is worthy in it, and stay with him until you depart. 12 As you enter the house, salute it. 13 And if the house is worthy, let your peace come upon it; but if it is not worthy, let your peace return to you.

6:8-11 *(§ 109, p. 77):*
8 He charged them to take nothing for their journey except a staff; no bread, no bag, no money in their belts; 9 but to wear sandals and not put on two tunics.

10 And he said to them, "Where you enter a house,
　　　　stay there
until you leave the place.

9:2-5 *(§ 109, p. 77):*
2 And he sent them out to preach the kingdom of God and to heal.

see v. 9 below

3 And he said to them, "Take nothing for your journey, no staff, nor bag, nor bread, nor money;

and do not have two tunics.

4 And whatever house you enter,
　　　　stay there,
and from there depart.

Luke 10:4 "Carry no purse, no bag, no sandals; and salute no one on the road.

5 "Whatever house you enter, first say, 'Peace be to this house!' 6 And if a son of peace is there, your peace shall rest upon him; but if not, it shall return to you. 7 And remain in the same house, eating and drinking what they provide, for the laborer deserves his wages; do not go from house to house. 8 Whenever you enter a town and they receive you, eat what is set before you;

---

* Matt. 15:24 (§ 116, p.84): He answered, "I was sent only to the lost sheep of the house of Israel."

To Matt. 10:10 cf. I Timothy 5:18—For the scripture says, . . . "The laborer deserves his wages (S: food)." Also cf. Didache 13:1 and I Corinthians 9:14—In the same way, the Lord commanded that those who proclaim the gospel should get their living by the gospel.

			9 heal the sick in it and say to them, 'The kingdom of God has come near you.'
14 "And if any one will not receive you or listen to your words, shake off the dust from your feet as you leave that house or town.	11 "And if any place will not receive you and they refuse to hear you, when you leave, shake off the dust that is on your feet for a testimony against them."	5 "And wherever they do not receive you, when you leave that town, shake off the dust from your feet as a testimony against them."	10 "But whenever you enter a town and they do not receive you, go into its streets and say, 11 'Even the dust of your town that clings to our feet, we wipe off against you; neverthe-less know this, that the kingdom of God has come near.'
15 "Truly, I say to you, it shall be more tolerable on the day of judgment for the land of Sodom and Gom-orrah than for that town.			12 I tell you, it shall be more tolerable on that day for Sodom than for that town.
16 "Behold, I send you out as sheep in the midst of wolves; so be wise as serpents and innocent as doves.			3 "Go your way; behold, I send you out as lambs in the midst of wolves."

To Matt. 10:16 cf. II Clement 5:2-4: For the Lord said, "You will be as lambs in the midst of wolves." But Peter answered him, "Suppose, then, the wolves tear the lambs?" Jesus answered Peter, "Let not the lambs fear the wolves after their death; and you, fear not those who kill you and can do no more to you. But fear him who, after your death, has power over soul and body, to cast them into the hell of fire."x

Cf. also **Gospel of the Nazaraeans**—The Jewish Gospel: [wise] more than serpents.

x Greek, *Gehenna*.

59. THE FATE OF THE DISCIPLES.
Matt. 10:17–25 *

17 "Beware of men; for they will deliver you up to councils, and flog you in their synagogues, 18 and you will be dragged before governors and kings for my sake, to bear testimony before them and the Gentiles. 19 When they deliver you up, do not be anxious how you are to speak or what you are to say; for what you are to say will be given to you in that hour; 20 for it is not you who speak, but the Spirit of your Father speaking through you.** 21 Brother will deliver up brother to death, and the father his child, and children will rise against parents and have them put to death; 22 and you will be hated by all for my name's sake. But he who endures to the end will be saved. 23 When they persecute you in one town, flee to the next; for truly, I say to you, you will not have gone through all the towns of Israel, before the Son of man comes.

* Matt. 24:9, 13 (§ 215, pp.154-155): 9 "Then they will deliver you up to tribulation, and put you to death; and you will be hated by all nations for my name's sake. 13 But he who endures to the end will be saved."	Mark 13:9-13 (§ 215, pp.154-155): 9 "But take heed to yourselves; for they will deliver you up to councils; and you will be beaten in synagogues; and you will stand before governors and kings for my sake, to bear testimony before them. 10 And the gospel must first be preached to all nations. 11 And when they bring you to trial and deliver you up, do not be anxious beforehand what you are to say; but say whatever is given you in that hour, for it is not you who speak, but the Holy Spirit. ** 12 And brother will deliver up brother to death, and the father his child, and children will rise against parents and have them put to death; 13 and you will be hated by all for my name's sake. But he who endures to the end will be saved."	Luke 21:12-17, 19 (§ 215 pp.154-155): 12 "But before all this they will lay their hands on you and persecute you, delivering you up to the synagogues and prisons, and you will be brought before kings and governors for my name's sake. 13 This will be a time for you to bear testimony. 14 Settle it therefore in your minds, not to meditate beforehand how to answer; 15 for I will give you a mouth and wisdom, which none of your adversaries will be able to withstand or contradict. 16 You will be delivered up even by parents and brothers and kinsmen and friends, and some of you they will put to death; 17 you will be hated by all for my name's sake. (v. 18, see Matt. 10:30) 19 By your endurance you will gain your lives."

** Luke 12:11-12 (§ 155. p. 112): 11 "And when they bring you before the synagogues and the rulers and the authorities, do not be anxious how or what you are to answer or what you are to say; 12 for the Holy Spirit will teach you in that very hour what you ought to say."

Matt. 10:21—cf. v. 35, and Micah 7:6.

Matt. 10:19-20—cf. John 14:26: "But the Counselor, the Holy Spirit, whom the Father will send in my name, he will teach you all things, and bring to your remembrance all that I have said to you."

24 "A disciple is not above his teacher, nor a servant[y] above his master; 25 it is enough for the disciple to be like his teacher,* and the servant[y] like his master. If they have called the master of the house Beelzebul, how much more will they malign those of his household.

60. EXHORTATION TO FEARLESS CONFESSION.

Matt. 10:26–33

26 "So have no fear of them; for nothing is covered that will not be revealed, or hidden that will not be known.**

27 What I tell you in the dark, utter in the light; and what you hear whispered, proclaim upon the housetops.

28 "And do not fear those who kill the body but cannot kill the soul;

rather fear him who can destroy both soul and body in hell.[z]

29 "Are not two sparrows sold for a penny? And not one of them will fall to the ground without your Father's will. 30 But even the hairs of your head are all numbered.*** 31 Fear not, therefore; you are of more value than many sparrows.

Luke 12:2–9 (§ 155, p. 111)

2 "Nothing is covered up that will not be revealed, or hidden that will not be known.** 3 Therefore whatever you have said in the dark shall be heard in the light, and what you have whispered in private rooms shall be proclaimed upon the housetops.

4 "I tell you, my friends, do not fear those who kill the body, and after that have no more that they can do. 5 But I will warn you whom to fear: fear him who, after he has killed, has power to cast into hell;[z] yes, I tell you, fear him!

6 "Are not five sparrows sold for two pennies? And not one of them is forgotten before God. 7 Why, even the hairs of your head are all numbered.*** Fear not; you are of more value than many sparrows.

---

* Luke 6:40 (§ 76, p.57): "A disciple is not above his teacher, but every one when he is fully taught will be like his teacher."

** Mark 4:22 (§ 94, p.68): "For there is nothing hid, except to be made manifest; nor is anything secret, except to come to light."

Luke 8:17 (§ 94, p.68): "For nothing is hid that shall not be made manifest, nor anything secret that shall not be known and come to light."

*** Luke 21:18 (§ 215, p.155): "But not a hair of your head will perish."

---

[y] Or, slave.   [z] Greek, Gehenna.

To Matt. 10:24, cf. John 13:16—"Truly, truly, I say to you, a servant is not greater than his master; nor is he who is sent greater than he who sent him." Also cf. John 15:20—"Remember the word that I said to you, 'A servant is not greater than his master.' "

To Matt. 10:26 cf. *Oxyrhynchus Papyrus 654, Logion 4:* Jesus says, "Everything that is not before you, and what is hid from you will be revealed to you. For there is nothing hid which will not be revealed; nor buried, which will not be raised." Cf. **Gospel of Thomas, Logia 5 and 6.**

To Matt. 10:28 cf. II Clement 5:2-4, p.42.

³² "So every one who acknowledges me before men, I also will acknowledge before my Father who is in heaven; ³³ but whoever denies me before men, I also will deny before my Father who is in heaven.*

⁸ "And I tell you, every one who acknowledges me before men, the Son of man also will acknowledge before the angels of God; ⁹ but he who denies me before men will be denied before the angels of God." *

61. DIVISION IN HOUSEHOLDS.

Matt. 10:34–36

³⁴ "Do not think that I have come to bring peace on earth; I have not come to bring peace, but a sword.

³⁵ "For I have come to set a
man against his father,
and a daughter
against her mother,
and a daughter-in-law
against her mother-in-law; ³⁶ and a man's foes will be those of his own household.

Luke 12:51–53 (§ *160, p. 115*)

⁵¹ "Do you think that I have come to give peace on earth? No, I tell you, but rather division; ⁵² for henceforth in one house there will be five divided, three against two and two against three; ⁵³ they will be divided, father against son and son against father, mother against daughter and daughter against her mother, mother-in-law against her daughter-in-law and daughter-in-law against her mother-in-law."

62. CONDITIONS OF DISCIPLESHIP.

Matt. 10:37–39

³⁷ "He who loves father or mother more than me is not worthy of me; and he who loves son or daughter more than me is not worthy of me;

³⁸ and he who does not take his cross and follow me is not worthy of me.

Luke 14:26–27 (§ *171, p. 120*)

²⁶ "If any one comes to me and does not hate his own father and mother and wife and children and brothers and sisters, yes, and even his own life, he cannot be my disciple. ²⁷ Whoever does not bear his own cross and come after me, cannot be my disciple."

---

* Mark 8:38 (§ 123, p.90): "For whoever is ashamed of me and of my words in this adulterous and sinful generation, of him will the Son of man also be ashamed, when he comes in the glory of his Father with the holy angels."

Luke 9:26 (§ 123, p.90): "For whoever is ashamed of me and of my words,
of him will the Son of man be ashamed when he comes in his glory and the glory of the Father and of the holy angels."

Matt. 10:35-36 = Luke 12:53—Micah 7:6; cf. also Matt. 10:21.
Matt. 10:37-38 = Luke 14:26-27—cf. **Gospel of Thomas, Logia 55 and 101.**
Logion 55 reads: Jesus said, "Whoever does not hate his father and his mother will not be able to be a disciple to me, and (whoever does not) hate his brothers and his sisters and (does not) take up his cross in my way will not be worthy of me."

[39] He who finds his life will lose it, and he who loses his life for my sake will find it.*	17:33 (*§ 184, p. 126*) "Whoever seeks to gain his life will lose it, but whoever loses his life will preserve it." *

63. END OF THE DISCOURSE.
Matt. 10:40–11:1

40 "He who receives you receives me, and he who receives me receives him who sent me.** [41] He who receives a prophet because he is a prophet shall receive a prophet's reward, and he who receives a righteous man because he is a righteous man shall receive a righteous man's reward. [42] And whoever gives to one of these little ones even a cup of cold water because he is a disciple, truly, I say to you, he shall not lose his reward." ***

11:1 And when Jesus had finished instructing his twelve disciples, he went on from there to teach and preach in their cities.

---

* Matt. 16:24-25 (§ 123, p.90):
[24] Then Jesus told his disciples, "If any man would come after me, let him deny himself and take up his cross and follow me. [25] For whoever would save his life will lose it, and whoever loses his life for my sake will find it."

Mark 8:34-35 (§ 123, p.90):
[34] And he called to him the multitude with his disciples, and said to them, "If any man would come after me, let him deny himself and take up his cross and follow me. [35] For whoever would save his life will lose it; and whoever loses his life for my sake and the gospel's will save it."

Luke 9:23-24 (§ 123, p.90):
[23] And he said to all, "If any man would come after me, let him deny himself and take up his cross daily and follow me. [24] For whoever would save his life will lose it; and whoever loses his life for my sake, he will save it."

** Matt. 18:5 (§ 129, p.96): "Whoever receives one such child in my name receives me."

Mark 9:37 (§ 129, p.96): "Whoever receives one such child in my name receives me; and whoever receives me, receives not me but him who sent me."

Luke 9:48 (§ 129, p.96): "Whoever receives this child in my name receives me, and whoever receives me receives him who sent me."

Luke 10:16 (§ 139, p.103): "He who hears you hears me, and he who rejects you rejects me, and he who rejects me rejects him who sent me."

*** Mark 9:41 (§ 130, p.96): "For truly, I say to you, whoever gives you a cup of water to drink because you bear the name of Christ, will by no means lose his reward."

Matt. 10:39—John 12:25—"He who loves his life loses it, and he who hates his life in this world will keep it for eternal life."

Matt. 10:40—John 12:44-45: [44] And Jesus cried out and said, "He who believes in me, believes not in me but in him who sent me. [45] And he who sees me sees him who sent me." Also John 13:20—"Truly, truly, I say to you, he who receives any one whom I send receives me; and he who receives me receives him who sent me."

64. JOHN'S QUESTION TO JESUS.

Matt. 11:2–6

2 Now when John heard in prison about the deeds of the Christ,

he sent word by his disciples ³ and said to him, "Are you he who is to come, or shall we look for another?"

⁴ And Jesus answered them, "Go and tell John what you hear and see: ⁵ the blind receive their sight and the lame walk, lepers are cleansed and the deaf hear, and the dead are raised up, and the poor have good news preached to them. ⁶ And blessed is he who takes no offense at me."

Luke 7:18–23 (*§ 81, p. 59*)

18 The disciples of John told him of all these things. ¹⁹ And John, calling to him two of his disciples, sent them to the Lord, saying, "Are you he who is to come, or shall we look for another?" ²⁰ And when the men had come to him, they said, "John the Baptist has sent us to you, saying, 'Are you he who is to come, or shall we look for another?'" ²¹ In that hour he cured many of diseases and plagues and evil spirits, and on many that were blind he bestowed sight. ²² And he answered them, "Go and tell John what you have seen and heard: the blind receive their sight, the lame walk, lepers are cleansed, and the deaf hear, the dead are raised up, the poor have good news preached to them. ²³ And blessed is he who takes no offense at me."

65. JESUS' WORDS ABOUT JOHN.

Matt. 11:7–19

7 As they went away, Jesus began to speak to the crowds concerning John: "What did you go out into the wilderness to behold? A reed shaken by the wind? ⁸ Why then did you go out? To see a man[a] clothed in soft raiment? Behold, those who wear soft raiment are in kings' houses. ⁹ Why then did you go out? To see a prophet?[b] Yes, I tell you, and more than a prophet.

Luke 7:24–35 (*§ 82, p. 59*)

24 When the messengers of John had gone, he began to speak to the crowds concerning John: "What did you go out into the wilderness to behold? A reed shaken by the winds? ²⁵ What then did you go out to see? A man clothed in soft clothing? Behold, those who are gorgeously appareled and live in luxury are in kings' courts. ²⁶ What then did you go out to see? A prophet? Yes, I tell you, and more than a prophet.

Matt. 11:5 = Luke 7:22—Isaiah 29:18-19; 35:5-6; 61:1. Cf. also Luke 4:18.

---

[a] Or, *What then did you go out to see? A man . . .* B? C D Θ λ φ 𝔐 it vg syᶜ syˢ syᵖ sa.   [b] text: S W bo; *What then did you go out to see? A prophet?:*

10 This is he of whom it is written,

'Behold, I send my messenger before thy face,

who shall prepare thy way before thee.'

11 Truly, I say to you, among those born of women there has risen no one greater than John the Baptist; yet he who is least in the kingdom of heaven is greater than he.

Cf. Matt. 21:32 (§ 203, p. 142)

12 "From the days of John the Baptist until now the kingdom of heaven has suffered violence,[c] and men of violence take it by force. **13** For all the prophets and the law prophesied until John; **14** and if you are willing to accept it, he is Elijah who is to come. **15** He who has ears to hear,[d] let him hear.

16 "But to what shall I compare this generation?

It is like children sitting in the market places and calling to their playmates,

17 'We piped to you, and you did not dance;

we wailed, and you did not mourn.'

18 For John   came neither eating nor drinking,   and they say, 'He has a demon'; **19** the Son of man came eating and drinking, and they say, 'Behold, a glutton and a drunkard, a friend of tax collectors and sinners!'

Yet wisdom is justified by   her deeds."[e]

1:2
(p. 8)

Cf. 9:13
(p. 92)

27 This is he of whom it is written,

'Behold, I send my messenger before thy face,

who shall prepare thy way before thee.'

28 I tell you,   among those born of women   none is greater than John;   yet he who is least in the kingdom of God is greater than he."

29 (When they heard this all the people and the tax collectors justified God, having been baptized with the baptism of John; **30** but the Pharisees and the lawyers rejected the purpose of God for themselves, not having been baptized by him.)

16:16 (§ 176, p. 123): "The law and the prophets were until John; since then the good news of the kingdom of God is preached, and every one enters it violently."

7:31 "To what then shall I compare the men of this generation, and what are they like? **32** They are like children sitting in the market place and calling to one another,

'We piped to you, and you did not dance;

we wailed, and you did not weep.'

33 For John the Baptist has come eating no bread and drinking no wine; and you say, 'He has a demon.' **34** The Son of man has come eating and drinking; and you say, 'Behold, a glutton and a drunkard, a friend of tax collectors and sinners!' **35** Yet wisdom is justified by all her children."

Matt. 11:10 = Luke 7:27—Malachi 3:1.   Matt. 11:14—Malachi 4:5

[c] Or, *has been coming violently.*   [d] text: S C W Θ λ φ ℜ it vg sy[c] sy[p] sa bo; omit, *to hear:* B D sy[s].
[e] text: S B W φ sy[p] bo; *children* (Luke 7:35) C D Θ ʌ ℜ it vg sy[c] sy[s] sa.

To Matt. 11:11 cf. **Gospel of Thomas, Logion 46:** Jesus said, "From Adam to John the Baptist, no one born of woman is grester than John the Baptist, so that his eyes will not (. . .). But I have said that anyone among you who becomes as a child will know the kingdom, and will become greater than John."

To Matt. 11:12 cf. **Gospel of the Nazaraeans:** The Jewish Gospel has: [the kingdom of heaven] is plundered.

66. WOES ON THE CITIES OF GALILEE.

Matt. 11:20–24	Luke 10:13–15 (§ *139, p. 103*)
20 Then he began to upbraid the cities where most of his mighty works had been done, because they did not repent. 21 "Woe to you, Chorazin! woe to you, Bethsaida! for if the mighty works done in you had been done in Tyre and Sidon, they would have repented long ago in sackcloth and ashes. 22 But I tell you, it shall be more tolerable on the day of judgment for Tyre and Sidon than for you. 23 And you, Capernaum, will you be exalted to heaven? You shall be brought down to Hades. For if the mighty works done in you had been done in Sodom, it would have remained until this day. 24 But I tell you that it shall be more tolerable on the day of judgment for the land of Sodom than for you."	13 "Woe to you, Chorazin! woe to you, Bethsaida! for if the mighty works done in you had been done in Tyre and Sidon, they would have repented long ago, sitting in sackcloth and ashes. 14 But it shall be more tolerable in the judgment for Tyre and Sidon than for you. 15 And you, Capernaum, will you be exalted to heaven? You shall be brought down to Hades. *Cf. 10:12 (§ 139, p. 102)*

67. JESUS' THANKSGIVING TO THE FATHER.

Matt. 11:25–27	Luke 10:21–22 (§ *141, pp. 103–104*)
25 At that time Jesus declared, "I thank thee, Father, Lord of heaven and earth, that thou hast hidden these things from the wise and understanding and revealed them to babes; 26 yea, Father, for such was thy gracious will.[f] 27 "All things have been delivered to me by my Father; and no one knows the Son except the Father, and no one knows the Father except the Son and any one to whom the Son chooses to reveal him.	21 In that same hour he rejoiced in the Holy Spirit and said, "I thank thee, Father, Lord of heaven and earth, that thou hast hidden these things from the wise and understanding and revealed them to babes; yea, Father, for such was thy gracious will.[f] 22 "All things have been delivered to me by my Father; and no one knows who the Son is except the Father, or who the Father is except the Son and any one to whom the Son chooses to reveal him."

Matt. 11:23 = Luke 10:15—Isaiah 14:13, 15.

---

[f] Or, *so it was well-pleasing before thee.*

To Matt. 11:27 and Luke 10:22 cf. John 3:35—"The Father loves the Son, and has given all things into his hand." And John 7:29—"I know him, for I come from him, and he sent me." Cf. also John 10:14-15; 17:2

To Matt. 11:25 cf. **Gospel of the Nazaraeans:** The Jewish Gospel has: I am grateful to thee.

68. COMFORT FOR THE HEAVY-LADEN.
Matt. 11:28–30

28 "Come to me, all who labor and are heavy laden, and I will give you rest. 29 Take my yoke upon you, and learn from me; for I am gentle and lowly in heart, and you will find rest for your souls. 30 For my yoke is easy, and my burden is light."

69. PLUCKING HEADS OF GRAIN ON THE SABBATH.

Matt. 12:1-8	Mark 2:23–28 (2:18–22, § 54, p. 37f.)	Luke 6:1–5 (5:33–39, § 54, p. 37f.)
1 At that time Jesus went through the grainfields on the sabbath; his disciples were hungry, and they began to pluck heads of grain and to eat. 2 But when the Pharisees saw it, they said to him, "Look, your disciples are doing what is not lawful to do on the sabbath." 3 He said to them, "Have you not read what David did, when he was hungry, and those who were with him: 4 how he entered the house of God and ate the bread of the Presence, which it was not lawful for him to eat nor for those who were with him, but only for the priests?	23 One sabbath he was going through the grainfields; and as they made their way his disciples began to pluck heads of grain. 24 And the Pharisees said to him, "Look, why are they doing what is not lawful on the sabbath?" 25 And he said to them, "Have you never read what David did, when he was in need and was hungry, he and those who were with him: 26 how he entered the house of God, when Abiathar was high priest,h and ate the bread of the Presence, which it is not lawful for any but the priests to eat, and also gave it to those who were with him?"	1 On a sabbath,g while he was going through the grainfields, his disciples plucked and ate some heads of grain, rubbing them in their hands. 2 But some of the Pharisees said, "Why are you doing what is not lawful to do on the sabbath?" 3 And Jesus answered, "Have you not read what David did when he was hungry, he and those who were with him: 4 how he entered the house of God, and took and ate the bread of the Presence, which it is not lawful for any but the priests to eat, and also gave it to those with him?"

Matt. 11:28-29—Ecclesiasticus 51:23-27.   11:29—Jeremiah 6:16.   12:1 and parallels—Deuteronomy 23:25.   12:2 and parallels—Exodus 20:10 and Deuteronomy 5:14.   12:3f and parallels—I Samuel 21:1-7.   12:4b and parallels—Leviticus 24:7-9.

g text: P4 P757 S B W λ it (some MSS.) syp sa bo; *on the second first sabbath* (*on the second sabbath after the first*): A C D Θ φ ℜ it (some MSS.) vg.   h text: S A B C Θ λ φ ℜ it (some MSS.) vg syp sa bo; omit, *when Abiathar was high priest:* D W it (some MSS.) sys.

To Mark 2:24 and parallels cf. John 5:10—So the Jews said to the man who was cured, "It is the sabbath, it is not lawful for you to carry your pallet."

To Matt. 11:29 cf. **Gospel according to the Hebrews** (in Clement of Alexandria, *Miscellanies II.9.45*)—He who has marveled shall reign, and he who has reigned shall rest.

He who seeks will not give up until he finds; and having found, he will marvel; and having marveled, he will reign; and having reigned, he will rest. *Ibid. V.14.96.* Also *Oxyrhynchus Papyrus 654, Logion 1.* Cf. also **Gospel of Thomas, Logion 2** (see note to Matt. 7:7, p. 29).

5 Or have you not read in the law how on the sabbath the priests in the temple profane the sabbath, and are guiltless? 6 I tell you, something greater than the temple is here. 7 And if you had known what this means, 'I desire mercy, and not sacrifice,' you would not have condemned the guiltless.

8 For the Son of man is lord of the sabbath."

27 And he said to them, "The sabbath was made for man, not man for the sabbath;[1] 28 so the Son of man is lord even of the sabbath."

5 And he said to them,

"The Son of man is lord of the sabbath."[1]

70. THE HEALING OF THE MAN WITH THE WITHERED HAND.

Matt. 12:9–14	Mark 3:1–6	Luke 6:6–11
9 And he went on from there and entered their synagogue. 10 And behold, there was a man with a withered hand. And they asked him, "Is it lawful to heal on the sabbath?" so that they might accuse him.	1 Again he entered the synagogue, and a man was there who had a withered hand. 2 And they watched him, to see whether he would heal him on the sabbath, so that they might accuse him. 3 And he said to the man who had the withered hand, "Come here."	6 On another sabbath, when he entered the synagogue and taught, a man was there whose right hand was withered. 7 And the scribes and the Pharisees watched him, to see whether he would heal on the sabbath, so that they might find an accusation against him. 8 But he knew their thoughts, and he said to the man who had the withered hand, "Come and stand here." And he rose and stood there.

Matt. 12:5—Numbers 28:9-10.   12:7 (= Matt. 9:13): Hosea 6:6.

[1] text: S A B C Θ λ φ ℜ vg syᵖ sa bo; omit v.27: D it; omit v.27b: W syˢ. For Luke 6:5 D reads: On the same day, seeing some one working on the sabbath, he said to him, "Man, if indeed you know what you are doing, you are blessed; but if you do not know, you are cursed and a transgressor of the law."

To Mark 2:27-28 cf. **Gospel of Thomas, Logion 27b:** Jesus said, "If you do not keep the sabbath as sabbath you will not see the Father."

To Matt. 12:10 cf. **Gospel of the Nazaraeans** (in Jerome, *Commentary on Matthew 12:13*)—In the Gospel which the Nazarenes and the Ebionites use, which we have recently translated from Hebrew to Greek, and which most people call the authentic [Gospel] of Matthew, the man who had the withered hand is described as a mason who begged for help in the following words: "I was a mason, earning a living with my hands; I beg you, Jesus, restore my health to me, so that I need not beg for my food in shame."

11 He said to them, "What man of you, if he has one sheep and it falls into a pit on the sabbath, will not lay hold of it and lift it out? 12 Of how much more value is a man than a sheep! *

So it is lawful to do good on the sabbath."

13 Then he said to the man, "Stretch out your hand." And the man stretched it out, and it was restored, whole like the other. 14 But the Pharisees went out and took counsel against him, how to destroy him.

4 And he said to them, "Is it lawful on the sabbath to do good or to do harm, to save life or to kill?" But they were silent.** 5 And he looked around at them with anger, grieved at their hardness of heart, and said to the man, "Stretch out your hand." He stretched it out, and his hand was restored. 6 The Pharisees went out, and immediately held counsel with the Herodians against him, how to destroy him.

14:5 (§ 168, p. 119):
5 And he said to them, "Which of you, having a son or an ox that has fallen into a well, will not immediately pull him out on a sabbath day?" *

6:9 And Jesus said to them, "I ask you, is it lawful on the sabbath to do good or to do harm, to save life or to destroy it?" ** 10 And he looked around on them all,

and said to him, "Stretch out your hand." And he did so, and his hand was restored. 11 But they were filled with fury and discussed with one another what they might do to Jesus.

The Call of the Twelve.

(Luke 6:12–16 = Mark 3:13–19, § 72, p. 54)

---

* Luke 13:15-16 (§ 163, p.116): 15 Then the Lord answered him, "You hypocrites! Does not each of you on the sabbath untie his ox or his ass from the manger, and lead it away to water it? 16 And ought not this woman, a daughter of Abraham whom Satan bound for eighteen years, be loosed from this bond on the sabbath day?"

** Luke 14:3 (§ 168, p.119): And Jesus spoke to the lawyers and Pharisees, saying, "Is it lawful to heal on the sabbath, or not?" But they were silent.

71. JESUS HEALS THE MULTITUDES.

Matt. 12:15–21	Mark 3:7–12	Luke 6:17–19
15 Jesus, aware of this, withdrew from there. And many followed him,	7 Jesus withdrew with his disciples to the sea, and a great multitude from Galilee followed; also from Judea 8 and Jerusalem and Idumea and from beyond the Jordan and from about Tyre and Sidon a great multitude, hearing all that he did, came to him. 9 And he told his disciples to have a boat ready for him because of the crowd, lest they should crush him; 10 for he had healed many, so that all who had diseases pressed upon him to touch him.* 11 And whenever the unclean spirits beheld him,** they fell down before him and cried out, "You are the Son of God." 12 And he strictly ordered them not to make him known.	17 And he came down with them and stood on a level place, with a great crowd of his disciples and a great multitude of people from all Judea and Jerusalem and the seacoast of Tyre and Sidon, who came to hear him and to be healed of their diseases·
4:25 (§ 16, p. 19): And great crowds followed him from Galilee and the Decapolis and Jerusalem and Judea and from beyond the Jordan.		
12:15 b and he healed them all,		18 and those who were troubled with unclean spirits were cured. 19 And all the crowd sought to touch him,* for power came forth from him and healed them all.
16 and ordered them not to make him known. 17 This was to fulfil what was spoken by the prophet Isaiah: 18 "Behold, my servant whom I have chosen, my beloved with whom my soul is well pleased. I will put my Spirit upon him, and he shall proclaim justice to the Gentiles. 19 He will not wrangle or cry aloud, nor will any one hear his voice in the streets; 20 he will not break a bruised reed or quench a smoldering wick, till he brings justice to victory; 21 and in his name will the Gentiles hope."		*4:41 (§ 14, p. 18):* And demons also came out of many, crying, "You are the Son of God!" But he rebuked them and would not allow them to speak, because they knew that he was the Christ.
(12:22, § 85, p. 61)		

---

* Matt. 14:36 (§ 114, p.81): And besought him that they might only touch a fringe of his garment; and as many as touched it were made well.

Mark 6:56 (§ 114, p.81): And besought him that they might touch even the fringe of his garment; and as many as touched it were made well.

** Matt. 4:24 (§ 16, p.19): So his fame spread throughout all Syria, and they brought him all the sick, those afflicted with various diseases and pains, demoniacs, epileptics, and paralytics, and he healed them.

Matt. 12:18-21—Isaiah 42:1-4.

72. THE CALL OF THE TWELVE.

Matt. 10:1–4 (§ 58, p. 40)	Mark 3:13–19	Luke 6:12–16
5:1 (§ 18, p. 20)	13 And he went up on the mountain,	12 In these days he went out to the mountain to pray; and all night he continued in prayer to God. 13 And when it was day, he called his disciples, and chose from them twelve, whom he named apostles;
1 And he called to him his twelve disciples and gave them authority over unclean spirits, to cast them out, and to heal every disease and every infirmity.	and called to him those whom he desired; and they came to him. 14 And he appointed twelve[j] to be with him, and to be sent out to preach 15 and have authority to cast out demons:* 16 Simon[jj] whom he surnamed Peter; 17 James the son of Zebedee and John the brother of James, whom he surnamed Boanerges, that is, sons of thunder; 18 Andrew, and Philip, and Bartholomew, and Matthew, and Thomas, and	
2 The names of the twelve apostles are these: first Simon, who is called Peter, and Andrew his brother; James the son of Zebedee, and John his brother, 3 Philip and Bartholomew; Thomas and Matthew the tax collector; James the son of Alphaeus, and Thaddaeus;[l] 4 Simon the Cananaean, and Judas Iscariot,		14 Simon, whom he named Peter, and Andrew his brother, and James and John, and Philip, and Bartholomew, 15 and Matthew, and Thomas, and James the son of Alphaeus, and Simon who was called the Zealot, 16 and Judas the son of James, and Judas Iscariot, who became a traitor.
who betrayed him.	James the son of Alphaeus, and Thaddaeus,[k] and Simon the Cananaean, 19 and Judas Iscariot,	
	who betrayed him	
	(3:19b–22, § 85, p. 61)	*(6:17–19, §71, p. 53)*

---

* Mark 6:7 (§ 109, p.77): And he called to him the twelve, and began to send them out two by two, and gave them authority over the unclean spirits.

Luke 9:1-2 (§ 109, p.77): 1 And he called the twelve together and gave them power and authority over all demons and to cure diseases, 2 and he sent them out to preach the kingdom of God and to heal.

---

[j] text: A D λ 𝕽 it vg sy[s] sy[p]; add, *whom also he named apostles:* S B C? W Θ φ sa bo.   [jj] text: A D λ φ 𝕽 it vg sy[s] sy[p] sa bo; *demons.* 16 *So he appointed the twelve: Simon:* S B C.   [k] text: S A B C Θ λ φ 𝕽 it (some MSS.) vg sy[s] sy[p] sa bo; *Lebbaeus:* D it (some MSS.).   [l] text: S B φ it (some MSS.) vg sa bo; *Lebbaeus:* D; *Lebbaeus called Thaddaeus:* C? W Θ λ 𝕽 sy[p]; *Judas Zelotes;* it (some MSS.); add, *Judas the son of James* after "Cananaean" in v.4: sy[s].

To Luke 6:14a and parallels cf. John 1:42—Jesus looked at him, and said, "So you are Simon the son of John? You shall be called Cephas" (which means Peter).

The Sermon on the Plain

Luke 6:20–49

73. THE BEATITUDES.

Matt. 5:3, 4, 6, 11, 12 (§ *19, p. 20*)

3 "Blessed are the poor in spirit, for theirs is the kingdom of heaven. 4 Blessed are those who mourn, for they shall be comforted. 6 Blessed are those who hunger and thirst for righteousness, for they shall be satisfied. 11 Blessed are you when men revile you and persecute you and utter all kinds of evil against you falsely on my account. 12 Rejoice and be glad, for your reward is great in heaven, for so men persecuted the prophets who were before you."

Luke 6:20–23

20 And he lifted up his eyes on his disciples, and said: "Blessed are you poor, for yours is the kingdom of God.

21 Blessed are you that hunger now, for you shall be satisfied. Blessed are you that weep now, for you shall laugh. 22 Blessed are you when men hate you, and when they exclude you and revile you, and cast out your name as evil, on account of the Son of man! 23 Rejoice in that day, and leap for joy, for behold, your reward is great in heaven; for so their fathers did to the prophets.

74. THE WOES
Luke 6:24–26

24 "But woe to you that are rich, for you have received your consolation. 25 Woe to you that are full now, for you shall hunger. Woe to you that laugh now, for you shall mourn and weep. 26 Woe to you, when all men speak well of you, for so their fathers did to the false prophets.

75. ON LOVE OF ONE'S ENEMIES.

Matt. 5:39–42, 44–48 (§ *26, 27, p. 23–24*)

44 "But I say to you,   Love your enemies

         and pray for those who persecute you.

39 But I say to you, Do not resist one who is evil. But if any one strikes you on the right cheek, turn to him the other also; 40 and if any one would sue you and take your coat, let him have your cloak as well; 41 and if any one forces you to go one mile, go with him two miles. 42 Give to him who begs from you, and do not refuse him who would borrow from you."

Luke 6:27–36

27 "But I say to you that hear, Love your enemies, do good to those who hate you, 28 bless those who curse you, pray for those who abuse you.

29 To him who strikes you on the   cheek, offer the other also; and from him who takes away your coat do not withhold even your shirt.

30 Give to every one who begs from you; and of him who takes away your goods do not ask them again.

7:12 (§ 39, p. 29): "So whatever you wish that men would do to you, do so to them; for this is the law and the prophets."

5:46 "For if you love those who love you, what reward have you? Do not even the tax collectors do the same? **47** And if you salute only your brethren, what more are you doing than others? Do not even the Gentiles do the same?"

5:45 ". . . so that you may be sons of your Father who is in heaven; for he makes his sun rise on the evil and on the good, and sends rain on the just and on the unjust. **48** You, therefore, must be perfect, as your heavenly Father is perfect."

31 "And as you wish that men would do to you, do so to them.

32 If you love those who love you, what credit is that to you? For even sinners love those who love them. **33** And if you do good to those who do good to you, what credit is that to you? For even sinners do the same. **34** And if you lend to those from whom you hope to receive, what credit is that to you? Even sinners lend to sinners, to receive as much again. **35** But love your enemies, and do good, and lend, expecting nothing in return;^m and your reward will be great, and you will be sons of the Most High; for he is kind to the ungrateful and the selfish.

36 Be merciful, even as your Father is merciful.

76. ON JUDGING.

Matt. 7:1–5 (§ 36, p. 28)

1 "Judge not, that you be not judged. **2** For with the judgment you pronounce you will be judged,

and the measure you give will be the measure you get." *

15:14 (§ 115, p. 83): "Let them alone; they are blind guides. And if a blind man leads a blind man, both will fall into a pit."

Luke 6:37–42

37 "Judge not, and you will not be judged; condemn not, and you will not be condemned; forgive, and you will be forgiven; **38** give, and it will be given to you; good measure, pressed down, shaken together, running over, will be put into your lap. For the measure you give will be the measure you get back." *

39 He also told them a parable: "Can a blind man lead a blind man? Will they not both fall into a pit?

---

* Mark 4:24 (§ 94, p.68): And he said to them, "Take heed what you hear; the measure you give will be the measure you get, and still more will be given you."

^m text: A B D Θ λ φ ℜ it vg sa bo; *despairing of no man:* S W sy^s sy^p.

To Luke 6:32 cf. II Clement 13:4—God said, "It is no credit to you if you love those who love you; but it is a credit to you if you love your enemies and those who hate you."

10:24–25 (§ 59, p. 44): ²⁴ "A disciple is not above his teacher, nor a servant above his master; ²⁵ it is enough for the disciple to be like his teacher, and the servant like his master."	⁴⁰ A disciple is not above his teacher, but every one when he is fully taught will be like his teacher.
7:3 "Why do you see the speck that is in your brother's eye, but do not notice the log that is in your own eye? ⁴ Or how can you say to your brother, 'Let me take the speck out of your eye,' when there is the log in your own eye? ⁵ You hypocrite, first take the log out of your own eye, and then you will see clearly to take the speck out of your brother's eye."	⁴¹ "Why do you see the speck that is in your brother's eye, but do not notice the log that is in your own eye? ⁴² Or how can you say to your brother, 'Brother, let me take out the speck that is in your eye,' when you yourself do not see the log that is in your own eye? You hypocrite, first take the log out of your own eye, and then you will see clearly to take out the speck that is in your brother's eye.

77. A TEST OF GOODNESS.

Matt. 7:16–21 *(§ 41, p. 30)*	Matt. 12:33–35 *(§ 86, pp. 62–63)*	Luke 6:43–46
¹⁶ "You will know them by their fruits. Are grapes gathered from thorns, or figs from thistles? ¹⁷ So, every sound tree bears good fruit, but the bad tree bears evil fruit. ¹⁸ A sound tree cannot bear evil fruit, nor can a bad tree bear good fruit. ¹⁹ Every tree that does not bear good fruit is cut down and thrown into the fire. ²⁰ Thus you will know them by their fruits.	³³ "Either make the tree good, and its fruit good; or make the tree bad, and its fruit bad; for the tree is known by its fruit. ³⁴ You brood of vipers! how can you speak good, when you are evil? For out of the abundance of the heart the mouth speaks.	⁴³ "For no good tree bears bad fruit, nor again does a bad tree bear good fruit; ⁴⁴ for each tree is known by its own fruit. For figs are not gathered from thorns, nor are grapes picked from a bramble bush.
	³⁵ "The good man out of his good treasure brings forth good, and the evil man out of his evil treasure brings forth evil."	⁴⁵ "The good man out of the good treasure of his heart produces good, and the evil man out of his evil treasure produces evil; for out of the abundance of the heart his mouth speaks.
²¹ "Not every one who says to me, 'Lord Lord,' shall enter the kingdom of heaven, but he who does the will of my Father who is in heaven."		⁴⁶ "Why do you call me 'Lord, Lord,' and not do what I tell you?

To Luke 6:40 cf. John 13:16 and 15:20—"A servant is not greater than his master."

78. HEARERS AND DOERS OF THE WORD.

Matt. 7:24–27 (§ 43, p. 31)	Luke 6:47–49
24 "Every one then who hears these words of mine and does them will be like a wise man who built his house upon the rock; 25 and the rain fell, and the floods came, and the winds blew and beat upon that house, but it did not fall, because it had been founded on the rock. 26 And every one who hears these words of mine and does not do them will be like a foolish man who built his house upon the sand; 27 and the rain fell, and and floods came, and the winds blew and beat against that house, and it fell; and great was the fall of it."	47 "Every one who comes to me and hears my words and does them, I will show you what he is like: 48 he is like a man building a house, who dug deep, and laid the foundation upon rock; and when a flood arose, the stream broke against that house, and could not shake it, because it had been well built.[n] 49 But he who hears and does not do them is like a man who built a house on the ground without a foundation; against which the stream broke, and immediately it fell, and the ruin of that house was great."

79. THE CENTURION'S SLAVE.
Luke 7:1–10 (=Matt. 8:5–13, § 46, p. 32)

7:28a
(p. 31)

8:5–13
(p. 32f.)

1 After he had ended all his sayings in the hearing of the people he entered Capernaum. 2 Now a centurion had a slave who was dear[o] to him, who was sick and at the point of death. 3 When he heard of Jesus, he sent to him elders of the Jews, asking him to come and heal his slave. 4 And when they came to Jesus, they besought him earnestly, saying, "He is worthy to have you do this for him, 5 for he loves our nation, and he built us our synagogue." 6 And Jesus went with them. When he was not far from the house, the centurion sent friends to him, saying to him, "Lord, do not trouble yourself, for I am not worthy to have you come under my roof; 7 therefore I did not presume to come to you. But say the word, and let my servant be healed. 8 For I am a man set under authority, with soldiers under me: and I say to one, 'Go,' and he goes; and to another, 'Come,' and he comes; and to my slave, 'Do this,' and he does it." 9 When Jesus heard this he marveled at him, and turned and said to the multitude that followed him, "I tell you, not even in Israel have I found such faith." 10 And when those who had been sent returned to the house, they found the slave well.

80. THE WIDOW'S SON AT NAIN.
Luke 7:11–17

11 Soon afterward[p] he went to a city called Nain, and his disciples and a great crowd went with him. 12 As he drew near to the gate of the city, behold, a man who had died was being carried out, the only son of his mother, and she was a widow; and a large crowd from the city was with her. 13 And when the Lord saw her, he had compassion on her and said to her, "Do not weep." 14 And he came and touched the bier, and the bearers stood still. And he said, "Young man, I say to you, arise." 15 And the

---

[n] text: P75? S B W sa bo; *founded on the rock:* A C D Θ λ φ ℜ it vg sy[p]; omit phrase: P45? sy[s].   [o] Or, *valuable.*   [p] text: P75 A B Θ φ ℜ it (some MSS.) vg sy[s] sa; *next day:* S C D W it (some MSS.) sy[p] bo.

To § 79 cf. John 4:46–54.

dead man sat up, and began to speak. And he gave him to his mother. ¹⁶ Fear seized them all; and they glorified God, saying, "A great prophet has arisen among us!" and "God has visited his people!" ¹⁷ And this report concerning him spread through the whole of Judea and all the surrounding country.

81. JOHN'S QUESTION TO JESUS.

Luke 7:18–23 (=Matt. 11:2–6, § 64, p. 47)

11:2–6
(p. 47)

18 The disciples of John told him of all these things. ¹⁹ And John, calling to him two of his disciples, sent them to the Lord, saying, "Are you he who is to come, or shall we look for another?" ²⁰ And when the men had come to him, they said, "John the Baptist has sent us to you, saying, 'Are you he who is to come, or shall we look for another?' " ²¹ In that hour he cured many of diseases and plagues and evil spirits, and on many that were blind he bestowed sight. ²² And he answered them, "Go and tell John what you have seen and heard: the blind receive their sight, the lame walk, lepers are cleansed, and the deaf hear, the dead are raised up, the poor have good news preached to them. ²³ And blessed is he who takes no offense at me."

82. JESUS' WORDS ABOUT JOHN.
Luke 7:24–35 (=Matt. 11:7–19, § 65, p. 47)

11:7–19
(p. 47f.)

1:2
(p. 8)

24 When the messengers of John had gone, he began to speak to the crowds concerning John: "What did you go out into the wilderness to behold? A reed shaken by the wind? ²⁵ What then did you go out to see? A man clothed in soft clothing? Behold, those who are gorgeously appareled and live in luxury are in kings' courts. ²⁶ What then did you go out to see? A prophet? Yes, I tell you, and more than a prophet. ²⁷ This is he of whom it is written, 'Behold, I send my messenger before thy face, who shall prepare thy way before thee.' ²⁸ I tell you, among those born of women none is greater than John; yet he who is least in the kingdom of God is greater than he." ²⁹ (When they heard this all the people and the tax collectors justified God, having been baptized with the baptism of John; ³⁰ but the Pharisees and the lawyers rejected the purpose of God for themselves, not having been baptized by him.)* ³¹ "To what then shall I compare the men of this generation, and what are they like? ³² They are like children sitting in the market place and calling to one another, 'We piped to you, and you did not dance; we wailed, and you did not weep.' ³³ For John the Baptist has come eating no bread and drinking no wine; and you say, 'He has a demon.' ³⁴ The Son of man has come eating and drinking; and you say, 'Behold, a glutton and a drunkard, a friend of tax collectors and sinners!' ³⁵ Yet wisdom is justified by all her children."

* Matt. 21:32 (§ 203, p.142): "For John came to you in the way of righteousness, and you did not believe him, but the tax collectors and the harlots believed him; and even when you saw it, you did not afterward repent and believe him."

Luke 7:15—I Kings 17:23.   Luke 7:22 (= Matt. 11:5)—Isaiah 29:18-19; 35:5-6; 61:1.   Luke 7:27 (= Matt. 11:10)—Malachi 3:1.

To Luke 7:28 cf. **Gospel of Thomas, Logion 46** (see note to Matt. 11:11, p.48).

83. THE WOMAN WITH THE OINTMENT.
Luke 7:36–50
(Cf. Matt. 26:6–13 = Mark 14:3–9, § 232, p. 163)

36 One of the Pharisees asked him to eat with him, and he went into the Pharisee's house, and took his place at table. 37 And behold, a woman of the city, who was a sinner, when she learned that he was at table in the Pharisee's house, brought an alabaster flask of ointment, 38 and standing behind him at his feet, weeping, she began to wet his feet with her tears, and wiped them with the hair of her head, and kissed his feet, and anointed them with the ointment. 39 Now when the Pharisee who had invited him saw it, he said to himself, "If this man were a prophet, he would have known who and what sort of woman this is who is touching him, for she is a sinner." 40 And Jesus answering said to him, "Simon, I have something to say to you." And he answered, "What is it, Teacher?" 41 "A certain creditor had two debtors; one owed five hundred denarii,q and the other fifty. 42 When they could not pay, he forgave them both. Now which of them will love him more?" 43 Simon answered, "The one, I suppose, to whom he forgave more." And he said to him "You have judged rightly." 44 Then turning toward the woman he said to Simon, "Do you see this woman? I entered your house, you gave me no water for my feet, but she has wet my feet with her tears and wiped them with her hair. 45 You gave me no kiss, but from the time I came in she has not ceased to kiss my feet. 46 You did not anoint my head with oil, but she has anointed my feet with ointment. 47 Therefore I tell you, her sins, which are many, are forgiven, for she loved much; but he who is forgiven little, loves little." 48 And he said to her, "Your sins are forgiven." 49 Then those who were at table with him began to say among themselves, "Who is this, who even forgives sins?" 50 And he said to the woman, "Your faith has saved you; go in peace."

(left margin references: 9:22 | 5:34 10:52)

84. THE MINISTERING WOMEN.
Luke 8:1–3

1 Soon afterward he went on through cities and villages, preaching and bringing the good news of the kingdom of God. And the twelve were with him, 2 and also some women who had been healed of evil spirits and infirmities: Mary, called Magdalene, from whom seven demons had gone out, 3 and Joanna, the wife of Chuza, Herod's steward, and Susanna, and many others, who provided for them r out of their means.
(8:4–8, § 90, p. 65)

(left margin references: 4:23 (p. 18) | 9:35 16:9 | (p. 39) (p. 191) | 27:55 15:41 | (§ 250, p. 184))

Luke 7:50—I Samuel 1:17.

q The denarius was a day's wage for a laborer.   r text: B D W Θ φ ℜ it (some MSS.) vg (some MSS.) syᶜ syˢ syᵖ;
him: S A λ it (some MSS.) vg (some MSS.) sa bo.

To § 83 cf. John 12:1-8.

85. ACCUSATIONS AGAINST JESUS.

Matt. 12:22–24 *(Matt. 12:15-21, § 71, p. 53)*	Mark 3:19 b–22 *(3:13-19, § 72, p. 54)*	Luke 11:14-16 *(§ 149, p. 106)*
	19b Then he went home; 20 and the crowd came together again, so that they could not even eat. 21 And when his family heard it, they went out to seize him, for people were saying, "He is beside himself."	
22 Then a blind and dumb demoniac was brought to him, and he healed him, so that the dumb man spoke and saw. 23 And all the people were amazed,* and said, "Can this be the Son of David?" 24 But when the Pharisees heard it they said, "It is only by Beelzebul, the prince of demons, that this man casts out demons."**	22 And the scribes who came down from Jerusalem said, "He is possessed by Beelzebul, and by the prince of demons he casts out the demons."	14 Now he was casting out a demon that was dumb; when the demon had gone out, the dumb man spoke, and the people marveled.* 15 But some of them said, "He casts out demons by Beelzebul the prince of demons";** 16 while others, to test him, sought from him a sign from heaven.

86. A HOUSE DIVIDED.

Matt. 12:25–37	Mark 3:23–30	Luke 11:17-23 *(§ 149, p. 107):*
25 Knowing their thoughts, he said to them, "Every kingdom divided against itself is laid waste, and no city or house divided against itself will stand; 26 and if Satan casts out Satan, he is divided against himself; how then will his kingdom stand?	23 And he called them to him, and said to them in parables, "How can Satan cast out Satan? 24 If a kingdom is divided against itself, that kingdom cannot stand. 25 And if a house is divided against itself, that house will not be able to stand. 26 And if Satan has risen up against himself and is divided, he cannot stand, but is coming to an end.	17 But he, knowing their thoughts, said to them, "Every kingdom divided against itself is laid waste, and a divided household falls. 18 And if Satan also is divided against himself, how will his kingdom stand?

---

* Cf. Matt. 9:32-34 (§ 57, p.39.)

** Matt. 9:34 (§ 57, p.39): But the Pharisees said, **"He casts out demons by the prince of demons."**

To Mark 3:22 cf. John 7:20; 8:48, 52—"You have a demon!" Also 10:20—"He has a demon."

27 And if I cast out demons by Beelzebul, by whom do your sons cast them out? Therefore they shall be your judges. 28 But if it is by the Spirit of God that I cast out demons, then the kingdom of God has come upon you.

29 Or how can one enter a strong man's house and plunder his goods, unless he first binds the strong man? Then indeed he may plunder his house.

30 He who is not with me is against me,* and he who does not gather with me scatters.

31 "Therefore I tell you, every sin and blasphemy will be forgiven men, but the blasphemy against the Spirit will not be forgiven. 32 And whoever says a word against the Son of man will be forgiven; but whoever speaks against the Holy Spirit will not be forgiven; either in this age or in the age to come.

33 "Either make the tree good, and its fruit good; or make the tree bad, and its fruit bad; for the tree is known by its fruit.**

---

27 But no one can enter a strong man's house and plunder his goods, unless he first binds the strong man; then indeed he may plunder his house.

28 Truly, I say to you, all sins will be forgiven the sons of men, and whatever blasphemies they utter;

29 but whoever blasphemes against the Holy Spirit never has ⁸ forgiveness, but is guilty of an eternal sin"
—30 for they had said, "He has an unclean spirit."
(3:31–35, § 89, p. 64)

For you say that I cast out demons by Beelzebul. 19 And if I cast out demons by Beelzebul, by whom do your sons cast them out? Therefore they shall be your judges. 20 But if it is by the finger of God that I cast out demons, then the kingdom of God has come upon you.

21 When a strong man, fully armed, guards his own palace, his goods are in peace; 22 but when one stronger than he assails him and overcomes him, he takes away his armor in which he trusted, and divides his spoil. 23 He who is not with me is against me,* and he who does not gather with me scatters."

12:10 (§ 155, p. 111):
"And every one who speaks a word against the Son of man will be forgiven; but he who blasphemes against the Holy Spirit will not be forgiven."

6:43–45 (§ 77, p. 57)
43 "For no good tree bears bad fruit, nor again does a bad tree bear good fruit; 44 for each tree is known by its own fruit.**

---

* Mark 9:40 (§ 130, p.96): "For he that is not against us is for us."

Luke 9:50 (§ 130, p.96): "For he that is not against you is for you."

** Matt. 7:16-20 (§ 41, p.30): 16 "You will know them by their fruits. Are grapes gathered from thorns, or figs from thistles? 17 So, every sound tree bears good fruit, but the bad tree bears evil fruit. 18 A sound tree cannot bear evil fruit, nor can a bad tree bear good fruit. 19 Every tree that does not bear good fruit is cut down and thrown into the fire. 20 Thus you will know them by their fruits."

⁸ text: S A B C φ 𝔐 vg sy^p sa bo; *has not:* D W Θ λ it sy^s?.

34 "You brood of vipers! how can you speak good when you are evil? For out of the abundance of the heart the mouth speaks.

35 "The good man out of his good treasure brings forth good, and the evil man out of his evil treasure brings forth evil.

36 "I tell you, on the day of judgment men will render account for every careless word they utter; 37 for by your words you will be justified, and by your words you will be condemned."

45 "The good man out of the good treasure of his heart produces good, and the evil man out of his evil treasure produces evil; for out of the abundance of the heart his mouth speaks."

87. AGAINST SEEKING FOR SIGNS.

Matt. 12:38–42

38 Then some of the scribes and Pharisees said to him, "Teacher, we wish to see a sign from you." 39 But he answered them, "An evil and adulterous generation seeks for a sign; but no sign shall be given to it except the sign of the prophet Jonah.* 40 For as Jonah was three days and three nights in the belly of the whale, so will the Son of man be three days and three nights in the heart of the earth. 41 The men of Nineveh will arise at the judgment with this generation and condemn it; for they repented at the preaching of Jonah, and behold, something greater than Jonah is here. 42 The queen of the South will arise at the judgment with   this generation and condemn it; for she came from the ends of the earth to hear the wisdom of Solomon, and behold, something greater than Solomon is here.

Luke 11:29–32 (§ 152, p. 108)

29 When the crowds were increasing, he began to say,

"This generation is an evil generation; it seeks a sign, but no sign shall be given to it except the sign of Jonah.* 30 For as Jonah became a sign to the men of Nineveh, so will the Son of man be to this generation.

32 The men of Nineveh will arise at the judgment with this generation and condemn it; for they repented at the preaching of Jonah, and behold, something greater than Jonah is here. 31 The queen of the South will arise at the judgment with the men of this generation and condemn them; for she came from the ends of the earth to hear the wisdom of Solomon, and behold, something greater than Solomon is here."

* Matt. 16:1, 2, 4 (§ 119, p.86): 1 And the Pharisees and Sadducees came, and to test him they asked him to show them a sign from heaven. 2 He answered them, 4 "An evil and adulterous generation seeks for a sign, but no sign shall be given to it except the sign of Jonah."

Mark 8:11-12 (§ 119, p.86): 11 The Pharisees came and began to argue with him, seeking from him a sign from heaven, to test him. 12 And he sighed deeply in his spirit, and said, "Why does this generation seek a sign? Truly, I say to you, no sign shall be given to this generation."

Matt. 12:40—Jonah 1:17   Matt. 12:41 = Luke 11:32—Jonah 3:5.   Matt. 12:42 = Luke 11:31—I Kings 10:1ff.

To Matt. 12:40b cf. **Gospel of the Nazaraeans:** The Jewish Gospel does not have: three days and three nights.

88. THE RETURN OF THE EVIL SPIRIT.

Matt. 12:43–45

43 "When the unclean spirit has gone out of a man, he passes through water-less places seeking rest, but he finds none. 44 Then he says, 'I will return to my house from which I came.' And when he comes he finds it empty, swept, and put in order. 45 Then he goes and brings with him seven other spirits more evil than himself, and they enter and dwell there, and the last state of that man becomes worse than the first. So shall it be also with this evil generation."

Luke 11:24–26 (§ *150, p. 107*)

24 "When the unclean spirit has gone out of a man, he passes through water-less places seeking rest; and finding none he says, 'I will return to my house from which I came.' 25 And when he comes he finds it   swept and put in order. 26 Then he goes and brings   seven other spirits more evil than himself, and they enter and dwell there; and the last state of that man becomes worse than the first."

89. JESUS' TRUE RELATIVES.

Matt. 12:46–50

46 While he was still speak-ing to the people, behold, his mother and his brothers stood outside, asking to speak to him.[t]

48 But he replied to the man who told him, "Who is my mother, and who are my brothers?" 49 And stretching out his hand toward his disciples, he said, "Here are my mother and my brothers! 50 For whoever does the will of my Father in heaven is my brother, and sis-ter, and mother."

Mark 3:31–35

(*3:23–30, § 86, pp. 61–62*)

31 And his mother and his brothers came; and standing outside they sent to him and called him. 32 And a crowd was sitting about him; and they said to him, "Your mother and your brothers[u] are outside, asking for you." 33 And he replied,

"Who are my mother and my brothers?" 34 And looking around on those who sat about him,   he said, "Here are my mother and my brothers! 35 Whoever does the will of God   is my brother, and sis-ter, and mother."

Luke 8:19–21

(*§ 104, p. 71*)

19 Then his mother and his brothers came to him, but they could not reach him for the crowd.

20 And he was told, "Your mother and your brothers are standing outside, desiring to see you." 21 But he said to them,

"My mother and my brothers are those who hear the word of God and do it."

---

[t] text: S B syᶜ syˢ sa; add verse 47: *Some one told him, "Your mother and your brothers are standing outside, asking to speak to you"*: C D W Θ λ φ 𝕽 it vg syᵖ bo.   [u] text: S B C W Θ λ φ 𝕽 it (some MSS.) vg syˢ syᵖ sa bo; add, *and your sisters:* A D it (some MSS.).

To Matt. 12.50 and parallels cf. John 15:14—"You are my friends if you do what I command you."

To Matt. 12:47–50 cf. **Gospel of the Ebionites** (in Epiphanius, *Against Heresies, XXX.14.5*)—Moreover they deny that he was a man, apparently on the basis of the word which the Savior spoke when it was announced to him, "Behold, your mother and your brothers stand without"—namely: "Who are my mother and brothers?" And stretching out his hand toward his disciples he said, "These who do the will of my Father are my brothers and mother and sisters."

90. THE PARABLE OF THE SOWER.

Matt. 13:1–9	Mark 4:1–9	Luke 8:4–8
1 That same day Jesus went out of the house and sat beside the sea. 2 And great crowds gathered about him, so that he got into a boat and sat there; and the whole crowd stood on the beach. 3 And he told them many things in parables, saying: "A sower went out to sow. 4 And as he sowed, some seeds fell along the path, and the birds came and devoured them. 5 Other seeds fell on rocky ground, where they had not much soil, and immediately they sprang up, since they had no depth of soil, 6 but when the sun rose they were scorched; and since they had no root they withered away.	1 Again he began to teach beside the sea. And a very large crowd gathered about him, so that he got into a boat and sat in it on the sea; and the whole crowd was beside the sea on the land. 2 And he taught them many things in parables, and in his teaching he said to them: 3 "Listen! A sower went out to sow. 4 And as he sowed, some seed fell along the path, and the birds came and devoured it. 5 Other seed fell on rocky ground, where it had not much soil, and immediately it sprang up, since it had no depth of soil; 6 and when the sun rose it was scorched, and since it had no root it withered away.	*(8:1–3, § 84, p. 60)* 4 And when a great crowd came together and people from town after town came to him, *cf. 5:1–3 (§ 17, p. 19)* he said in a parable: 5 "A sower went out to sow his seed; and as he sowed, some fell along the path, and was trodden under foot, and the birds of the air devoured it. 6 And some fell on the rock; and as it grew up, it withered away, because it had no moisture.
7 Other seeds fell upon thorns, and the thorns grew up and choked them. 8 Other seeds fell on good soil and brought forth grain, some a hundred-fold, some sixty, some thirty.	7 Other seed fell among thorns and the thorns grew up and choked it, and it yielded no grain. 8 And other seeds fell into good soil and brought forth grain, growing up and increasing and yielding thirty-fold and sixtyfold and a hundredfold." 9 And he said,	7 And some fell among thorns; and the thorns grew with it and choked it. 8 And some fell into good soil and grew and yielded a hundredfold." As he said this, he called out, "He who has ears to hear, let him hear."
9 He who has ears,[v] let him hear."	"He who has ears to hear, let him hear."	

[v] text: S B it (some MSS.) sy[s]; add, *to hear:* C D W Θ λ φ ℜ it (some MSS.) vg sy[c] sy[p] sa bo.

91. THE REASON FOR SPEAKING IN PARABLES.

Matt. 13:10–15	Mark 4:10–12	Luke 8:9–10
10 Then the disciples came and said to him, "Why do you speak to them in parables?" 11 And he answered them, "To you it has been given to know the secrets of the kingdom of heaven, but to them it has not been given.	10 And when he was alone, those who were about him with the twelve asked him concerning the parables. 11 And he said to them, "To you has been given the secret of the kingdom of God,	9 And when his disciples asked him what this parable meant, 10 he said, "To you it has been given to know the secrets of the kingdom of God;
12 "For to him who has will more be given, and he will have abundance; but from him who has not, even what he has will be taken away. 13 This is why I speak to them in parables, because seeing they do not see, and hearing they do not hear, nor do they understand.	*4:25 (§ 94, p. 68)* but for those outside everything is in parables; 12 so that they may indeed see but not perceive, and may indeed hear but not understand; lest they should turn again, and be forgiven."	*8:18b (§ 94, p. 68)* but for others they are in parables, so that seeing they may not see, and hearing they may not understand."
14 "With them indeed is fulfilled the prophecy of Isaiah which says:		

'You shall indeed hear but
  never understand,
and you shall indeed see
  but never perceive.
15 For this people's heart has
  grown dull,
and their ears are heavy
  of hearing ,
and their eyes they have
  closed,
lest they should perceive
  with their eyes,
and hear with their ears,
and understand with their
  heart,
and turn for me to heal
  them.'

92. THE BLESSEDNESS OF THE DISCIPLES.

Matt. 13:16–17	Luke 10:23–24 *(§ 142, p. 104)*
16 "But blessed are your eyes, for they see, and your ears, for they hear. 17 Truly, I say to you, many prophets and righteous men longed to see what you see, and did not see it, and to hear what you hear, and did not hear it.	23 Then turning to the disciples he said privately, "Blessed are the eyes which see what you see! 24 For I tell you that many prophets and kings desired to see what you see, and did not see it, and to hear what you hear, and did not hear it."

Matt. 13:13 and parallels—Isaiah 6:9-10.   Matt. 13:14-15—Isaiah 6:9-10.

To Matt. 13:14-15 cf. John 12:40.

To Matt. 13:11 cf. Clement of Alexandria, *Miscellanies* V.10.63,7: Not grudgingly did the Lord declare in a certain gospel, "My secret is for me and the sons of my house."

93. THE INTERPRETATION OF THE PARABLE OF THE SOWER.

Matt. 13:18-23	Mark 4:13-20	Luke 8:11-15
18 "Hear then the parable of the sower.	13 And he said to them, "Do you not understand this parable? How then will you understand all the parables? 14 The sower sows the word. 15 And these	11 "Now the parable is this: The seed is the word of God.
19 When any one hears the word of the kingdom and does not understand it, the evil one comes and snatches away what is sown in his heart; this is what was sown along the path. 20 As for what was sown on rocky ground, this is he who hears the word and immediately receives it with joy; 21 yet he has no root in himself, but endures for a while, and when tribulation or persecution arises on account of the word, immediately he falls away.w 22 As for what was sown among thorns, this is he who hears the word, but the cares of the world and the delight in riches	are the ones along the path, where the word is sown; when they hear, Satan immediately comes and takes away the word which is sown in them. 16 And these in like manner are the ones sown upon rocky ground, who, when they hear the word, immediately receive it with joy; 17 and they have no root in themselves, but endure for a while; then, when tribulation or persecution arises on account of the word, immediately they fall away.w 18 And others are the ones sown among thorns; they are those who hear the word, 19 but the cares of the world, and the delight in riches, and the desire for other things, enter	12 The ones along the path are those who have heard; then the devil comes and takes away the word from their hearts, that they may not believe and be saved. 13 And the ones on the rock are those who, when they hear the word, receive it with joy; but these have no root, they believe for a while and in time of temptation fall away. 14 And as for what fell among the thorns, they are those who hear, but as they go on their way they are choked by the cares and riches and pleasures of life, and their fruit
choke the word, and it proves unfruitful. 23 As for what was sown on good soil, this is he who hears the word and understands it; he indeed bears fruit, and yields, in one case a hundredfold, in another sixty, and in another thirty."	in and choke the word, and it proves unfruitful. 20 But those that were sown upon the good soil are the ones who hear the word and accept it and bear fruit, thirtyfold and sixty-fold and a hundredfold."	does not mature. 15 And as for that in the good soil, they are those who, hearing the word, hold it fast in an honest and good heart, and bring forth fruit with patience."

94. THE PURPOSE OF PARABLES.

Matt. 13:12 (§ 91, p. 66)	Mark 4:21-25	Luke 8:16-18
	21 And he said to them, "Is a lamp brought inx to be put under a bushel, or under a bed, and not on a stand?*	16 "No one after lighting a lamp covers it with a vessel, or puts it under a bed, but puts it on a stand, that those who enter may see the light.*

---

* Matt. 5:15 (§ 20, p.21): "Nor do men light a lamp and put it under a bushel, but on a stand, and it gives light to all in the house."

Luke 11:33 (§ 153, p.108): "No one after lighting a lamp puts it in a cellar or under a bushel, but on a stand, that those who enter may see the light."

---

w Or, *stumble (stumbles)*.   x text: S A B C Θ λ 𝕽 it (some MSS.) vg syᵖ; *lighted*: D W φ it (some MSS.) sa bo·

	22 For there is nothing hid, except to be made manifest; nor is anything secret, except to come to light.* 23 If any man has ears to hear, let him hear."	17 For nothing is hid that shall not be made manifest, nor anything secret that shall not be known and come to light.*
	24 And he said to them, "Take heed what you hear; the measure you give will be the measure you get,** and still more will	18 Take heed then how you hear;
12 "For to him who has will more be given, and he will have abundance; but from him who has not, even what he has will be taken away." ***	be given you. 25 For to him who has will more be given; and from him who has not, even what he has will be taken away." ***	for to him who has will more be given, and from him who has not, even what he thinks that he has will be taken away." ***

(8:19–21, § 104, p. 71)

95. THE PARABLE OF THE SEED GROWING SECRETLY.
Mark 4:26–29

26 And he said, "The kingdom of God is as if a man should scatter seed upon the ground, 27 and should sleep and rise night and day, and the seed should sprout and grow, he knows not how. 28 The earth produces of itself, first the blade, then the ear, then the full grain in the ear. 29 But when the grain is ripe, at once he puts in the sickle, because the harvest has come."

---

* Matt. 10:26 (§ 60, p.44): "Nothing is covered up that will not be revealed, or hidden that will not be known."

** Matt. 7:2 (§ 36, p.28): "For with the judgment you pronounce you will be judged, and the measure you give will be the measure you get."

*** Matt. 25:29 (§ 228, p.161): "For to every one who has will more be given, and he will have abundance; but from him who has not, even what he has will be taken away."

Mark 4:29—Joel 3:13.

Luke 12:2 (§ 155, p.111): "Nothing is covered up that will not be revealed, or hidden that will not be known."

Luke 6:38 (§ 76, p.56): "For the measure you give will be the measure you get back."

Luke 19:26 (§ 195, p.136): "I tell you, that to every one who has will more be given; but from him who has not, even what he has will be taken away "

96. THE PARABLE OF THE WEEDS.
Matt. 13:24–30

24 Another parable he put before them, saying, "The kingdom of heaven may be compared to a man who sowed good seed in his field; 25 but while men were sleeping, his enemy came and sowed weeds among the wheat, and went away. 26 So when the plants came up and bore grain, then the weeds appeared also. 27 And the servants^y of the householder came and said to him, 'Sir, did you not sow good seed in your field? How then has it weeds?' 28 He said to them, 'An enemy has done this.' The servants^y said to him, 'Then do you want us to go and gather them?' 29 But he said, 'No; lest in gathering the weeds you root up the wheat along with them. 30 Let both grow together until the harvest; and at harvest time I will tell the reapers, Gather the weeds first and bind them in bundles to be burned, but gather the wheat into my barn.' "

97. THE PARABLE OF THE MUSTARD SEED.

Matt. 13:31–32	Mark 4:30–32	Luke 13:18–19 (§ *164, p. 117*)
31 Another parable he put before them, saying, "The kingdom of heaven is like a grain of mustard seed which a man took and sowed in his field; 32 it is the smallest of all seeds, but when it has grown it is the greatest of shrubs and becomes a tree, so that the birds of the air come and make nests in its branches."	30 And he said, "With what can we compare the kingdom of God, or what parable shall we use for it? 31 It is like a grain of mustard seed, which, when sown upon the ground, is the smallest of all the seeds on earth; 32 yet when it is sown it grows up and becomes the greatest of all shrubs, and puts forth large branches, so that the birds of the air can make nests in its shade."	18 He said therefore, "What is the kingdom of God like? And to what shall I compare it? 19 It is like a grain of mustard seed which a man took and sowed in his garden; and it grew and became a tree, and the birds of the air made nests in its branches."

98. THE PARABLE OF THE LEAVEN.

Matt. 13:33	Luke 13:20–21 (§ *164, p. 117*)
33 He told them another parable. "The kingdom of heaven is like leaven which a woman took and hid in three measures of flour, till it was all leavened."	20 And again he said, "To what shall I compare the kingdom of God? 21 It is like leaven which a woman took and hid in three measures of flour, till it was all leavened."

Matt. 13:32 and parallels—Daniel 4:21.

y Or, *slaves.*

99. JESUS' USE OF PARABLES.

Matt. 13:34–35	Mark 4:33–34
34 All this Jesus said to the crowds in parables; indeed he said nothing to them without a parable.	33 With many such parables he spoke the word to them, as they were able to hear it; 34 he did not speak to them without a parable, but privately to his own disciples he explained everything. *(4:35, § 105, p. 71)*
35 This was to fulfil what was spoken by the prophet: z "I will open my mouth in parables, I will utter what has been hidden since the foundation of the world."	

100. THE INTERPRETATION OF THE PARABLE OF THE WEEDS.
Matt. 13:36–43

36 Then he left the crowds and went into the house. And his disciples came to him, saying, "Explain to us the parable of the weeds of the field." 37 He answered, "He who sows the good seed is the Son of man; 38 the field is the world, and the good seed means the sons of the kingdom; the weeds are the sons of the evil one, 39 and the enemy who sowed them is the devil; the harvest is the close of the age, and the reapers are angels. 40 Just as the weeds are gathered and burned with fire, so will it be at the close of the age. 41 The Son of man will send his angels, and they will gather out of his kingdom all causes of sin and all evil-doers, 42 and throw them into the furnace of fire; there men will weep and gnash their teeth. 43 Then the righteous will shine like the sun in the kingdom of their Father. He who has ears, let him hear.

101. THE PARABLES OF THE HIDDEN TREASURE AND OF THE PEARL.
Matt. 13:44–46

44 "The kingdom of heaven is like treasure hidden in a field, which a man found and covered up; then in his joy he goes and sells all that ᵃ he has and buys that field.
45 "Again, the kingdom of heaven is like a merchant in search of fine pearls, 46 who, on finding one pearl of great value, went and sold all that he had and bought it.

Matt. 13:35—Psalm 78:2.   Matt. 13:41—Zephaniah 1:3.   Matt. 13:43—Daniel 12:3.

ᶻ text: B C D W 𝔐 it vg syᶜ syˢ syᵖ sa bo; *the prophet Isaiah:* S Θ λ φ.   ᵃ text: S C D W Θ λ φ 𝔐 it vg syᶜ syˢ syᵖ sa; *what:* B bo Origen.

To Matt. 13:44 cf. **Gospel of Thomas, Logion 109:** Jesus said, "The kingdom is like a man who had a treasure hidden in his field, and did not know it. And when he died he left it to his son, who also knew nothing about it, and accepted the field, and sold it. And the buyer went, and while he was plowing he found the treasure. And he began to lend at interest to whomever he wished."

102. THE PARABLE OF THE NET.
Matt. 13:47–50

47 "Again, the kingdom of heaven is like a net which was thrown into the sea and gathered fish of every kind; 48 when it was full, men drew it ashore and sat down and sorted the good into vessels but threw away the bad. 49 So it will be at the close of the age. The angels will come out and separate the evil from the righteous, 50 and throw them into the furnace of fire; there men will weep and gnash their teeth.

103. THE PARABLE OF THE HOUSEHOLDER.
Matt. 13:51–52

51 "Have you understood all this?" They said to him, "Yes.' 52 And he said to them, "Therefore every scribe who has been trained for the kingdom of heaven is like a householder who brings out of his treasure what is new and what is old."

(13:53–58, § 108, p. 76)

104. JESUS' TRUE RELATIVES.
Luke 8:19–21 (= Matt. 12:46–50 = Mark 3:31–35, § 89, p. 64.)

19 Then his mother and his brothers came to him, but they could not reach him for the crowd. 20 And he was told, "Your mother and your brothers are standing outside, desiring to see you." 21 But he said to them, "My mother and my brothers are those who hear the word of God and do it."

105. THE STILLING OF THE STORM.

Matt. 8:18 (§ 49, p. 34)	Mark 4:35–41 (4:33–34, § 99, p. 70)	Luke 8:22–25
Now when Jesus saw great crowds around him, he gave orders to go over to the other side. 8:23–27 (§ 50, p. 34): 23 And when he got into the boat, his disciples followed him. 24 And behold there arose a great storm on the sea, so that the boat was being swamped by the waves; but he was asleep. 25 And they went and woke him, saying, "Save, Lord; we are perishing." 26 And he said to them, "Why are you afraid, O men of little faith?" Then he rose and rebuked the winds and the sea; and there was a great calm.	35 On that day, when evening had come, he said to them, "Let us go across to the other side." 36 And leaving the crowd, they took him with them in the boat, just as he was. And other boats were with him. 37 And a great storm of wind arose, and the waves beat into the boat, so that the boat was already filling. 38 But he was in the stern, asleep on the cushion; and they woke him and said to him, "Teacher, do you not care if we perish?" 39 And he awoke and rebuked the wind, and said to the sea, "Peace! Be still!" And the wind ceased, and there was a great calm.	22 One day he got into a boat with his disciples, and he said to them, "Let us go across to the other side of the lake." So they set out, 23 and as they sailed he fell asleep. And a storm of wind came down on the lake, and they were filling with water, and were in danger. 24 And they went and woke him, saying, "Master, Master, we are perishing!" And he awoke and rebuked the wind and the raging waves; and they ceased, and there was a calm.

To Luke 8:21 cf. John 15:14—"You are my friends if you do what I command you."

27 And the men marveled, saying, "What sort of man is this, that even winds and sea obey him?"	40 He said to them, "Why are you afraid? Have you no faith?b" 41 And they were filled with awe, and said to one another, "Who then is this, that even wind and sea obey him?"	25 He said to them, "Where is your faith?" And they were afraid, and they marveled, saying to one another, "Who then is this, that he commands even wind and water, and they obey him?"

106. THE GERASENE DEMONIAC.

Matt. 8:28–34 (§ *51, p. 35*)	Mark 5:1–20	Luke 8:26–39
28 And when he came to the other side, to the country of the Gadarenes,c two demoniacs met him, coming out of the tombs, so fierce that no one could pass that way.	1 They came to the other side of the sea, to the country of the Gerasenes.d 2 And when he had come out of the boat, there met him out of the tombs a man with an unclean spirit, 3 who lived among the tombs; and no one could bind him any more, even with a chain; 4 for he had often been bound with fetters and chains, but the chains he wrenched apart, and the fetters he broke in pieces; and no one had the strength to subdue him. 5 Night and day among the tombs and on the mountains he was always crying out, and bruising himself with stones. 6 And when he saw Jesus from afar, he ran and worshiped him; 7 and crying out with a loud voice, he said, "What have you to do with me, Jesus, Son of the Most High God? I adjure you by God, do not torment me." 8 For he had said to him, "Come out of the man, you unclean spirit!"	26 Then they arrived at the country of the Gerasenes,e which is opposite Galilee. 27 And as he stepped out on land, there met him a man from the city who had demons; for a long time he had worn no clothes, and he lived not in a house but among the tombs.
29 And behold, they cried out, "What have you to do with us, O Son of God? Have you come here to torment us before the time?"		28 When he saw Jesus, he cried out and fell down before him, and said with a loud voice, "What have you to do with me, Jesus, Son of the Most High God? I beseech you, do not torment me." 29 For he had commanded the unclean spirit to come out of the man. (For many a time it had seized him; he was kept under guard, and bound with chains and fetters, but he broke the bonds and was driven by the demon into the desert.)
	9 And Jesusf asked him, "What is your name?" He replied, "My name is Legion; for we are many."	30 Jesus then asked him, "What is your name?" And he said, "Legion"; for many demons had entered him.

b text: S B D Θ it vg sa bo; *Why are you so very afraid? Why have you no faith?:* A C 𝔐 syp; *Why are you so very afraid? Have you no faith?:* P45? λ φ.   c text: S B C Θ sys syp; *Gerasenes:* it vg sa; *Gergesenes:* W λ φ 𝔐 bo.
d text: S B D it vg sa; *Gadarenes:* A C φ 𝔐 syp; *Gergesenes:* Θ λ sys bo; *Gergustenes:* W.   e text: P75 B D it vg sa; *Gadarenes:* A W φ 𝔐 syc sys syp; *Gergesenes:* S Θ λ bo.   f Greek: *he*.

30 Now a herd of many swine was feeding at some distance from them. 31 And the demons begged him, "If you cast us out, send us away into the herd of swine." 32 And he said to them, "Go." So they came out and went into the swine; and behold, the whole herd rushed down the steep bank into the sea, and perished in the waters.

33 The herdsmen
fled,
and going into the city they told everything, and what had happened to the demoniacs.

34 And behold, all the city came out to meet Jesus; and when they saw him,

they begged him to leave their neighborhood.

---

10 And he begged him eagerly not to send them out of the country.

11 Now a great herd of swine was feeding there on the hillside; 12 and they begged him, "Send us to the swine, let us enter them." 13 So he gave them leave. And the unclean spirits came out, and entered the swine;   and the herd, numbering about two thousand, rushed down the steep bank into the sea, and were drowned in the sea.

14 The herdsmen
fled
and told it in the city and in the country. And people came to see what it was that had happened. 15 And they came to Jesus, and saw the demoniac sitting there, clothed and in his right mind, the man who had had the legion; and they were afraid. 16 And those who had seen it told what had happened to the demoniac and to the swine.

17 And they began

to beg Jesus[g] to depart from their neighborhood.
18 And as he was getting into the boat, the man who had been possessed with demons begged him that he might be with him. 19 But he refused, and said to him, "Go home to your friends, and tell them how much the Lord has done for you, and how he has had mercy on you." 20 And he went away and began to proclaim in the Decapolis how much Jesus had done for him; and all men marveled.

---

31 And they begged him not to command them to depart into the abyss.

32 Now a large herd of swine was feeding there on the hillside;   and they begged him
to let them
enter these. So he gave them leave. 33 Then the demons came out of the man and entered the swine,   and the herd

rushed down the steep bank into the lake and were drowned.

34 When the herdsmen saw what had happened, they fled, and told it in the city and in the country. 35 Then people went out to see what had happened, and they came to Jesus, and found the man from whom the demons had gone, sitting at the feet of Jesus, clothed and in his right mind; and they were afraid. 36 And those who had seen it told them how he who had been possessed with demons was healed.

37 Then all the people of the surrounding country of the Gerasenes[h] asked him to depart from them; for they were seized with great fear; so he got into the boat and returned. 38 The man from whom the demons had gone begged   that he might be with him; but he sent   him   away,   saying, 39 "Return to your home, and declare   how   much   God has done for you."

And
he went away,   proclaiming throughout the whole city how much Jesus had done for him.

---

g Greek, him.   h text: P75 B C D it vg sa; Gergesenes: S Θ λ φ bo; Gadarenes: A W 𝕽 syᶜ syˢ syᵖ.

107. JAIRUS' DAUGHTER AND A WOMAN'S FAITH.

Matt. 9:18–26 (§ 55, p. 38)	Mark 5:21–43	Luke 8:40–56
18 While he was thus speaking to them,	21 And when Jesus had crossed again in the boat to the other side, a great crowd gathered about him; and he was beside the sea. 22 Then came one of the rulers of the synagogue, Jairus by name; and seeing him, he fell at his feet, 23 and besought him, saying, "My little daughter is at the point of death. Come and lay your hands on her, so that she may be made well, and live." 24 And he went with him. And a great crowd followed him and pressed round him.	40 Now when Jesus returned, the crowd welcomed him, for they were all waiting for him. 41 And there came a man named Jairus, who was a ruler of the synagogue; and falling at Jesus' feet he besought him to come to his house, 42 for he had an only daughter, about twelve years of age, and she was dying. As he went, the people pressed round him.
behold, a ruler came in and knelt before him, saying, "My daughter has just died; but come and lay your hand on her, and she will live." 19 And Jesus rose and followed him, with his disciples.		
20 And behold, a woman who had suffered from a hemorrhage for twelve years	25 And there was a woman who had had a flow of blood for twelve years, 26 and who had suffered much under many physicians, and had spent all that she had, and was no better but rather grew worse. 27 She had heard the reports about Jesus, and came up behind him in the	43 And a woman who had had a flow of blood for twelve years[i] and could not be healed by any one,
came up behind him and touched the fringe of his garment. 21 For she said to herself, "If I only touch his garment, I shall be made well."	crowd and touched his garment. 28 For she said, "If I touch even his garments, I shall be made well." 29 And immediately the hemorrhage ceased; and she felt in her body that she was healed of her disease. 30 And Jesus, perceiving in himself that power had gone forth from him, immediately turned about in the crowd, and said, "Who touched my garments?" 31 And his disciples said to him, "You see the crowd pressing around you, and yet you say, 'Who touched me?'" 32 And he looked around to see who had done it. 33 But the woman, knowing what had been done to her, came in fear and trembling and fell down before him, and told him the whole truth.	44 came up behind him, and touched the fringe of his garment; and immediately her flow of blood ceased. 45 And Jesus said, "Who was it that touched me?" When all denied it, Peter[j] said, "Master, the multitudes surround you and press upon you!" 46 But Jesus said, "Some one touched me; for I perceive that power has gone forth from me." 47 And when the woman saw that she was not hidden, she came trembling, and falling down before him declared in the presence of all the people why she had touched him, and how she had been immediately healed.

---

i text: P75 B D sys sa; add, *who had spent all her living upon physicians:* S A C W Θ λ φ 𝔐 it vg sye syp bo.
j text: P75 B sye sys sa; add, *and those who were with him:* S A C D W Θ λ φ 𝔐 it vg syp bo.

22 Jesus turned, and seeing her he said, "Take heart, daughter; your faith has made you well." And instantly the woman was made well.

34 And he said to her, "Daughter, your faith has made you well; go in peace, and be healed of your disease."

48 And he said to her, "Daughter, your faith has made you well; go in peace."

35 While he was still speaking, there came from the ruler's house some who said, "Your daughter is dead. Why trouble the Teacher any further? 36 But ignoring[k] what they said, Jesus said to the ruler of the synagogue, "Do not fear, only believe." 37 And he allowed no one to follow him except Peter and James and John the brother of James.

49 While he was still speaking, a man from the ruler's house came and said, "Your daughter is dead; do not trouble the Teacher any more." 50 But Jesus on hearing this answered him,

"Do not fear; only believe, and she shall be well."

23 And when Jesus came to the ruler's house, and saw the flute players, and the crowd making a tumult, 24 he said,

38 When they came to the house of the ruler of the synagogue, he saw a tumult, and people weeping and wailing loudly. 39 And when he had entered, he said to them, "Why do you make a tumult and weep?

51 And when he came to the house, he permitted no one to enter with him, except Peter and John and James, and the father and mother of the child. 52 And all were weeping and bewailing her; but he said,

"Depart; for the girl is not dead but sleeping." And they laughed at him. 25 But when the crowd had been put outside,

The child is not dead but sleeping." 40 And they laughed at him. But he put them all outside, and took the child's father and mother and those who were with him, and went in where the child was. 41 Taking her by the hand he said to her, "Talitha cumi"; which means, "Little girl, I say to you, arise."

"Do not weep; for she is not dead but sleeping." 53 And they laughed at him, knowing that she was dead.

he went in and took her by the hand,

42 And immediately the girl got up and walked (she was twelve years of age), and they were immediately overcome with amazement. 43 And he strictly charged them that no one should know this, and told them to give her something to eat.

54 But taking her by the hand he called, saying,

"Child, arise." 55 And her spirit returned, and she got up at once; and he directed that something should be given her to eat. 56 And her parents were amazed; but he charged them to tell no one what had happened.

and the girl arose.

26 And the report of this went through all that district.

---

k Or, *overhearing;* text: S B W; *hearing:* A C D Θ λ φ 𝕽 it vg sa bo.

108. JESUS IS REJECTED AT NAZARETH.

Matt. 13:53–58 *(13:51–52, § 103, p. 71)*	Mark 6:1–6a	
53 And when Jesus had finished these parables, he went away from there, 54 and coming to his own country he taught them in their synagogue, so that they were astonished, and said, "Where did this man get this wisdom and these mighty works? 55 Is not this the carpenter's son? Is not his mother called Mary? And are not his brothers James and Joseph and Simon and Judas? 56 And are not all his sisters with us? Where then did this man get all this?" 57 And they took offense[1] at him. But Jesus said to them, "A prophet is not without honor except in his own country and in his own house." 58 And he did not do many mighty works there, because of their unbelief.	1 He went away from there and came to his own country; and his disciples followed him. 2 And on the sabbath he began to teach in the synagogue; and many who heard him were astonished, saying, "Where did this man get all this? What is the wisdom given to him? What mighty works are wrought by his hands! 3 Is not this the carpenter, the son of Mary and brother of James and Joses and Judas and Simon, and are not his sisters here with us?" And they took offense[1] at him. 4 And Jesus said to them, "A prophet is not without honor, except in his own country, and among his own kin, and in his own house." 5 And he could do no mighty work there, except that he laid his hands upon a few sick people and healed them. 6 And he marveled because of their unbelief.	*4:16–30* *(§ 10,* *p. 14ff.)* *4:22* *4:24*

109. THE SENDING OUT OF THE TWELVE.

Matt. 9:35; 10:1, 9–11, 14 *(§ 58, p. 39ff.)*	Mark 6:6b–13	Luke 9:1–6 *(Cf. 10:1–12, § 139, p. 102)*
9:35 And Jesus went about all the cities and villages, teaching in their synagogues and preaching the gospel of the kingdom, and healing every disease and every infirmity.	6b And he went about among the villages teaching.	

To Matt. 13:54 cf. John 7:15—The Jews marveled at it, saying, "How is it that this man has learning, when he has never studied?"

To Matt. 13:55 cf. John 6:42—They said, "Is not this Jesus, the son of Joseph, whose father and mother we know? How does he now say, 'I have come down from heaven'?"

To Matt. 13:57 cf. John 4:44—For Jesus himself testified that a prophet has no honor in his own country.

To Matt. 13:58 cf. John 7:5—For even his brothers did not believe in him.

[1] Or, *stumbled.*

10:1 And he called to him his twelve disciples and gave them authority over unclean spirits, to cast them out, and to heal every disease and every infirmity.

9 Take no gold, nor silver, nor copper in your belts, 10 no bag for your journey, nor two tunics, nor sandals, nor a staff; for the laborer deserves his food.
11 And whatever town or village you enter, find out who is worthy in it, and stay with him until you depart.   14 And if any one will not receive you or listen to your words, shake off the dust from your feet as you leave that house or town."

7 And he called to him the twelve, and began to send them out two by two, and gave them authority over the unclean spirits.*

8 He charged them to take nothing for their journey except a staff; no bread, no bag, no money in their belts; 9 but to wear sandals and not put on two tunics.
10 And he said to them, "Where you enter a house, stay there until you leave the place. 11 And if any place will not receive you and they refuse to hear you, when you leave, shake off the dust that is on your feet for a testimony against them." 12 So they went out and preached that men should repent. 13 And they cast out many demons, and anointed with oil many that were sick and healed them.

1 And he called the twelve together and gave them power and authority over all demons and to cure diseases, 2 and he sent them out to preach the kingdom of God and to heal.* 3 And he said to them, "Take nothing for your journey, no staff, nor bag, nor bread, nor money; and do not have two tunics.

4 And whatever house you enter,

stay there, and from there depart.   5 And wherever they do not receive you, when you leave that town shake off the dust from your feet as a testimony against them." 6 And they departed and went through the villages, preaching the gospel and healing everywhere.

110. HEROD THINKS JESUS IS JOHN, RISEN.

Matt. 14:1–2	**Mark 6:14–16**	**Luke 9:7–9**
1 At that time Herod the tetrarch heard about the fame of Jesus; 2 and he said to his servants, "This is John the Baptist, he has been raised from the dead; that is why these powers are at work in him."	14 King Herod heard of it; for Jesus'[m] name had become known. Some[n] said, "John the baptizer has been raised from the dead; that is why these powers are at work in him." 15 But others said, "It is Elijah." And others said, "It is a prophet, like one of the prophets of old." 16 But when Herod heard of it he said, "John, whom I beheaded, has been raised."	7 Now Herod the tetrarch heard of all that was done, and he was perplexed, because it was said by some that John had been raised from the dead, 8 by some that Elijah had appeared, and by others that one of the old prophets had risen. 9 Herod said, "John I beheaded; but who is this about whom I hear such things?" And he sought to see him.

* Mark 3:14-15 (§ 72, p.54): 14 And he appointed twelve, to be with him, and to be sent out to preach 15 and have authority to cast out demons.

m Greek, *his*.   n text: B D W it (some MSS.); *he said:* S A C Θ λ φ 𝕽 it (some MSS.) vg sy^s sy^h sa bo.

111. THE DEATH OF JOHN.

Matt. 14:3–12	Mark 6:17–29
3 For Herod had seized John and bound him and put him in prison, for the sake of Herodias, his brother Philip's wife; ° 4 because John said to him, "It is not lawful for you to have her." *	17 For Herod had sent and seized John, and bound him in prison for the sake of Herodias, his brother Philip's wife; because he had married her. 18 For John said to Herod, "It is not lawful for you to have your brother's wife." *
5 And though he wanted to put him to death, he feared the people, because they held him to be a prophet.	19 And Herodias had a grudge against him, and wanted to kill him. But she could not, 20 for Herod feared John, knowing that he was a righteous and holy man, and kept him safe. When he heard him, he was much perplexed; and yet he heard him gladly.
6 But when Herod's birthday came, the daughter of Herodias danced before the company, and pleased Herod,	21 But an opportunity came when Herod on his birthday gave a banquet for his courtiers and officers and the leading men of Galilee. 22 For when Herodias' daughter came in and danced, she pleased Herod and his guests; and the king said to the girl, "Ask me for whatever you wish, and I will grant it."
7 so that he promised with an oath to give her whatever she might ask. 8 Prompted by her mother,	23 And he vowed to her, "Whatever you ask me, I will give you, even half of my kingdom." 24 And she went out, and said to her mother, "What shall I ask?" And she said, "The head of John the baptizer."
she said, "Give me the head of John the Baptist here on a platter." 9 And the king was sorry; but because of his oaths and his guests	25 And she came in immediately with haste to the king, and asked, saying, "I want you to give me at once the head of John the Baptist on a platter." 26 And the king was exceedingly sorry; but because of his oaths and his guests he did not want to break his word to her. 27 And
he commanded it to be given; 10 he sent and had John beheaded in prison, 11 and his head was brought on a platter and given to the girl, and she brought it to her mother. 12 And his disciples came and took the body and buried it; and they went and told Jesus.	immediately the king sent a soldier of the guard and gave orders to bring his head. He went and beheaded him in the prison, 28 and brought his head on a platter, and gave it to the girl; and the girl gave it to her mother. 29 When his disciples heard of it, they came and took his body, and laid it in a tomb.

* Luke 3:19-20 (§ 5, p.10): 19 But Herod the tetrarch, who had been reproved by him for Herodias, his brother's wife, and for all the evil things that Herod had done, 20 added this to them all, that he shut up John in prison.

Mark 6:18—Leviticus 18:16; 20:21.

° text: S B C W Θ λ φ 𝔎 it (some MSS.) sy^c sy^s sy^p sa bo; *his brother's wife:* D it (some MSS.) vg.

112. THE RETURN OF THE TWELVE, AND
THE FEEDING OF THE FIVE THOUSAND.
(Cf. Matt. 15:32–39 = Mark 8:1–10, § 118, p. 85)

Matt. 14:13–21	Mark 6:30–44	Luke 9:10–17
	30 The apostles returned to Jesus, and told him all that they had done and taught.	10 On their return the apostles told him what they had done.*
13 Now when Jesus heard this,	31 And he said to them, "Come away by yourselves to a lonely place, and rest a while." For many were coming and going, and they had no leisure even to eat.	
he withdrew from there in a boat to a lonely place apart. But when the crowds heard it, they followed him on foot from the towns.	32 And they went away in the boat to a lonely place by themselves. 33 Now many saw them going, and knew them, and they ran there on foot from all the towns, and got there ahead of them.	And he took them and withdrew apart to a city called Bethsaida. 11 When the crowds learned it, they followed him;
14 As he went ashore he saw a great throng;**	34 As he went ashore he saw a great throng, and he had compassion on them, because they were like sheep without a shepherd;** and he began to teach them many things.	and he welcomed them and spoke to them of the kingdom of God,
and he had compassion on them, and healed their sick.		and cured those who had need of healing.
15 When it was evening, the disciples came to him and said, "This is a lonely place, and the day is now over; send the crowds away to go into the villages and buy food for themselves."	35 And when it grew late, his disciples came to him and said, "This is a lonely place, and the hour is now late; 36 send them away, to go into the country and villages round about and buy themselves something to eat."	12 Now the day began to wear away; and the twelve came and said to him, "Send the crowd away, to go into the villages and country round about, to lodge and get provisions; for we are here in a lonely place."
16 Jesus said, "They need not go away; you give them something to eat." 17 They said to him,	37 But he answered them, "You give them something to eat." And they said to him, "Shall we go and buy two hundred denarii ᴾ worth of bread, and give it to them to eat?" 38 And he said to them, "How many loaves have you? Go and see." And when they had found out, they said, "Five, and two fish."	13 But he said to them, "You give them something to eat." They said,
"We have only five loaves here and two fish."		"We have no more than five loaves and two fish — unless we are to go and buy food for all these people."

---

* Luke 10:17 (§ 140, p.103): The seventy returned with joy, saying, "Lord, even the demons are subject to us in your name!"
** Matt. 9:36 (§ 58, p.39): When he saw the crowds, he had compassion for them, because they were harassed and helpless, like sheep without a shepherd.

Mark 6:34—Numbers 27:17, I Kings 22:17.

ᴾ The denarius was a day's wage for a laborer.

To § 112 cf. John 6:1-13.

18 And he said, "Bring them here to me." 19 Then he ordered the crowds to sit down on the grass;

and taking the five loaves and the two fish he looked up to heaven, and blessed, and broke and gave the loaves to the disciples, and the disciples gave them to the crowds.

20 And they all ate and were satisfied. And they took up twelve baskets full of the broken pieces left over. 21 And those who ate were about five thousand men, besides women and children.

39 Then he commanded them all to sit down by companies upon the green grass. 40 So they sat down in groups, by hundreds and by fifties. 41 And taking the five loaves and the two fish he looked up to heaven, and blessed, and broke the loaves, and gave them to the disciples to set before the people; and he divided the two fish among them all. 42 And they all ate and were satisfied. 43 And they took up twelve baskets full of broken pieces and of the fish. 44 And those who ate the loaves were five thousand men.

14 For there were about five thousand men. And he said to his disciples, "Make them sit down in companies, about fifty each." 15 And they did so, and made them all sit down. 16 And taking the five loaves and the two fish he looked up to heaven, and blessed and broke them, and gave them to the disciples to set before the crowd.

17 And all ate and were satisfied. And they took up what was left over, twelve baskets of broken pieces.

(9:18–22, § 122, pp. 88–89)

113. THE WALKING ON THE WATER.

Matt. 14:22–33

22 Then he made the disciples get into the boat and go before him to the other side, while he dismissed the crowds. 23 And after he had dismissed the crowds, he went up on the mountain by himself to pray. **When evening came, he was there alone,** 24 but the boat by this time was many furlongs distant from the land,q beaten by the waves; for the wind was against them. 25 And in the fourth watch of the night he came to them, walking on the sea. 26 But when the disciples saw him walking on the sea, they were terrified, saying, "It is a ghost!" And they cried out for fear. 27 But immediately he spoke to them, saying, "Take heart, it is I; have no fear."

Mark 6:45–52

45 Immediately he made his disciples get into the boat and go before him to the other side, to Bethsaida, while he dismissed the crowd. 46 And after he had taken leave of them, he went up on the mountain to pray. 47 And when evening came, the boat was out on the sea, and he was alone on the land. 48 And he saw that they were making headway painfully. for the wind was against them. And about the fourth watch of the night he came to them, walking on the sea. He meant to pass by them, 49 but when they saw him walking on the sea, they thought it was a ghost, and cried out; 50 for they all saw himr and were terrified. But immediately he spoke to them and said, "Take heart, it is I; have no fear."

---

q text: B Θ φ syᶜ syᵖ sa bo; omit: *many furlongs distant from the land*, and insert: *out on the sea:* S C D W λ 𝔑 it vg.　　ʳ text: P⁴⁵ᵗ S A B W λ φ 𝔑 vg syˢ syᵖ sa bo; omit: *for they saw him* and put *all* at end of v.49: D Θ it.

To § 113 cf. John 6:15–21.

28 And Peter answered him, "Lord, if it is you, bid me come to you on the water." 29 He said, "Come." So Peter got out of the boat and walked on the water and came to Jesus; 30 but when he saw the wind,ˢ he was afraid, and beginning to sink he cried out, "Lord, save me." 31 Jesus immediately reached out his hand and caught him, saying to him, "O man of little faith, why did you doubt?" 32 And when they got into the boat, the wind ceased. 33 And those in the boat worshiped him, saying, "Truly you are the Son of God."

51 And he got into the boat with them and the wind ceased. And they were utterly astounded, 52 for they did not understand about the loaves, but their hearts were hardened.

114. HEALINGS AT GENNESARET.

Matt. 14:34–36	Mark 6:53–56
34 And when they had crossed over, they came to land at Gennesaret.	53 And when they had crossed over, they came to land at Gennesaret, and moored to the shore. 54 And when they got out of the boat, immediately the people recognized him, 55 and ran about the whole neighborhood and began to bring sick people on their pallets to any place where they heard he was. 56 And wherever he came, in villages, cities, or country, they laid the sick in the market places,
35 And when the men of that place recognized him, they sent round to all that region and brought to him all that were sick,	
36 and besought him that they might only touch the fringe of his garment; and as many as touched it were made well.✻	and besought him that they might touch even the fringe of his garment; and as many as touched it were made well.✻

✻ Matt. 4:24 (§ 16, p.19): So his fame spread throughout all Syria, and they brought him all the sick, those afflicted with various diseases and pains, demoniacs, epileptics, and paralytics, and he healed them.

Mark 3:10 (§ 71, p.53): For he had healed many, so that all who had diseases pressed upon him to touch him. Cf. also 1:32f. (§ 14, p.18).

Luke 6:18-19 (§ 71 p.53): 18 And those who were troubled with unclean spirits were cured. 19 And all the crowd sought to touch him, for power came forth from him and healed them all. Cf. also 4:40f. (§ 14, p.18).

ˢ text: S B sa bo; *strong wind:* C D Θ λ φ ℜ it vg syᶜ syˢ syᵖ; *very strong wind:* W.

115. WHAT DEFILES A MAN.

Matt. 15:1–20	Mark 7:1–23
1 Then Pharisees and scribes came to Jesus from Jerusalem	1 Now when the Pharisees gathered together to him, with some of the scribes, who had come from Jerusalem,[2] they saw that some of his disciples ate with hands defiled, that is, unwashed. [3] (For the Pharisees, and all the Jews, do not eat unless they wash[t] their hands, observing the tradition of the elders; [4] and when they come from the market place, they do not eat unless they purify [u] themselves;[uu] and there are many other traditions which they observe, the washing of cups and pots and vessels of bronze.)[v] [5] And the Pharisees and the scribes asked him, "Why do your disciples not live[w] according to the tradition of the elders, but eat with hands defiled?"
and said, [2] "Why do your disciples transgress the tradition of the elders? For they do not wash their hands when they eat." [3] He answered them, "And why do you transgress the commandment of God for the sake of your tradition? [4] For God commanded, 'Honor your father and your mother,' and, 'He who speaks evil of father or mother, let him surely die.' [5] But you say, 'If any one tells his father or his mother, What you would have gained from me is given to God,[x] he need not honor his father.' [6] So, for the sake of your tradition, you have made void the word[y] of God. [7] You hypocrites! Well did Isaiah prophesy of you, when he said:	*See vv. 9-13*
[8] 'This people honors me with their lips, but their heart is far from me; [9] in vain do they worship me, teaching as doctrines the precepts of men.' "	[6] And he said to them, "Well did Isaiah prophesy of you hypocrites, as it is written, 'This people honors me with their lips, but their heart is far from me; [7] in vain do they worship me, teaching as doctrines the precepts of men.' [8] You leave the commandment of God, and hold fast the tradition of men." [9] And he said to them, "You have a fine way of rejecting the commandment of God, in order to keep your tradition! [10] For Moses said, 'Honor your father and your mother'; and 'He who speaks evil of father or mother, let him surely die';
Cf. vv. 3–6.	

Matt. 15:4 = Mark 7:10—Exodus 20:12, Deuteronomy 5:16, Exodus 21:17, Leviticus 20:9. Matt. 15:8-9 = Mark 7:6-7—Isaiah 29:13.

[t] Or, *carefully wash;* text: A B D Θ λ φ ℜ it; *frequently wash:* S W vg sy^p bo; no adverb: sy^s sa.   [u] text: S B sa; *baptize:* A D W Θ λ φ ℜ it vg sy^s sy^p bo.   [uu] perhaps the meaning is: *they do not eat anything from the market unless they purify it.*   [v] text: P^45? S B bo; add, *and beds:* A D W Θ λ φℜit vg sy^p sa; omit, *and vessels of bronze and beds;* sy^s.   [w] Greek, *walk.*   [x] Or, *an offering.*   [y] text: B D Θ it (some MSS.) sy^c sy^s sy^p sa bo Origen; *law:* S C φ; *commandment:* W λ ℜ it (some MSS.) vg.

To Matt. 15:5 cf. **Gospel of the Nazaraeans:** The Jewish Gospel has: Corban is what you should gain from us.

11 but you say, 'If a man tells his father or his mother, What you would have gained from me is Corban' (that is, given to God)ᶻ — 12 then you no longer permit him to do anything for his father or mother, 13 thus making void the word of God through your tradition which you hand on. And many such things you do."

10 And he called the people to him and said to them, "Hear and understand:
11 not what goes into the mouth defiles a man, but what comes out of the mouth, this defiles a man."
12 Then the disciples came and said to him, "Do you know that the Pharisees were offended when they heard this saying?"
13 He answered, "Every plant which my heavenly Father has not planted will be rooted up. 14 Let them alone; they are blind guides. And if a blind man leads a blind man, both will fall into a pit." *
15 But Peter said to him, "Explain the parable to us."
16 And he said,
"Are you also still without understanding? 17 Do you not see that whatever goes into the mouth
passes into the stomach, and so passes on?ᵇ

18 But what comes out of the mouth proceeds from the heart, and this defiles a man.
19 For out of the heart
come evil thoughts,
murder, adultery, fornication, theft, false witness, slander.
20 These are what defile a man; but to eat with unwashed hands does not defile a man."

14 And he called the people to him again, and said to them, "Hear me, all of you, and understand: 15 there is nothing outside a man which by going into him can defile him; but the things which come out of a man are what defile him." ᵃ

17 And when he had entered the house, and left the people, his disciples asked him about the parable. 18 And he said to them, "Then are you also without understanding? Do you not see that whatever goes into a man from outside cannot defile him, 19 since it enters, not his heart but his stomach, and so passes on?" ᵇ (Thus he declared all foods clean.) 20 And he said
"What comes out of a man is what defiles a man.
21 For from within, out of the heart of man, come evil thoughts, fornication, theft, murder, adultery, 22 coveting, wickedness, deceit, licentiousness, envy, slander, pride, foolishness. 23 All these evil things come from within, and they defile a man."

---

* Luke 6:39 (§ 76, p.56): He also told them a parable: "Can a blind man lead a blind man? Will they not both fall into a pit?"

ᶻ Or, an offering.   ᵃ text: S B bo (some MSS.); add verse 16: *If any man has ears to hear, let him hear:* A D W Θ λ φ ℜ it vg syˢ syᵖ sa bo (some MSS.).   ᵇ Or, *is evacuated.*

116. THE SYROPHOENICIAN WOMAN.

Matt. 15:21–28	Mark 7:24–30
21 And Jesus went away from there and withdrew to the district of Tyre and Sidon.	24 And from there he arose and went away to the region of Tyre and Sidon.[c] And he entered a house and would not have any one know it; yet he could not be hid. 25 But immediately a woman
22 And behold, a Canaanite woman from that region came out and cried, "Have mercy on me, O Lord, Son of David; my daughter is severely possessed by a demon." 23 But he did not answer her a word. And his disciples came and begged him, saying, "Send her away, for she is crying after us." 24 He answered, "I was sent only to the lost sheep of the house of Israel." 25 But she came and knelt before him, saying,	whose little daughter was possessed by an unclean spirit,
"Lord, help me."	heard of him, and came and fell down at his feet. 26 Now the woman was a Greek, a Syrophoenician by birth. And she begged him to cast the demon out of her daughter. 27 And he said to her,
26 And he answered, "It is not fair to take the children's bread and throw it to the dogs." 27 She said, "Yes, Lord, yet even the dogs eat the crumbs that fall from their masters' table." 28 Then Jesus answered her, "O woman, great is your faith! Be it done for you as you desire." And her daughter was healed instantly.	"Let the children first be fed, for it is not right to take the children's bread and throw it to the dogs." 28 But she answered him, "Yes, Lord; yet even the dogs under the table eat the children's crumbs." 29 And he said to her, "For this saying you may go your way; the demon has left your daughter." 30 And she went home, and found the child lying in bed, and the demon gone.

117. THE HEALING OF MANY SICK PERSONS (*Matt.*), OF THE DEAF MUTE (*Mark*).

Matt. 15:29–31	Mark 7:31–37
29 And Jesus went on from there and passed along the Sea of Galilee. And he went up on the mountain, and sat down there. 30 And great crowds came to him, bringing with them the lame, the maimed, the blind, the dumb, and many others, and they put them at his feet, and he healed them,	31 Then he returned from the region of Tyre, and went through Sidon to the Sea of Galilee, through the region of the Decapolis. 32 And they brought to him a man who was deaf and had an impediment in his speech; and they besought him to lay his hand upon him. 33 And taking him aside from the multitude privately, he put his fingers into his ears, and he spat and touched his tongue; 34 and looking up to heaven, he sighed, and said to him, "Ephphatha," that is, "Be opened."

[c] text: S A B λ φ 𝕽 it (some MSS.) vg sy[p] sa bo; omit, *and Sidon:* D W Θ it (some MSS.) sy[s].

35 And his ears were opened, his tongue was released, and he spoke plainly. 36 And he charged them to tell no one; but the more he charged them, the more zealously they proclaimed it. 37 And they were astonished beyond measure, saying, "He has done all things well; he even makes the deaf hear and the dumb speak."

31 so that the crowd wondered, when they saw the dumb speaking, the maimed whole, the lame walking, and the blind seeing; and they glorified the God of Israel.

118. THE FEEDING OF THE FOUR THOUSAND.

(Cf. Matt. 14:13–21 = Mark 6:30–44 = Luke 9:10–17, § 112, pp.79–80)

Matt. 15:32–39	Mark 8:1–10
32 Then Jesus called his disciples to him and said, "I have compassion on the crowd, because they have been with me now three days, and have nothing to eat; and I am unwilling to send them away hungry lest they faint on the way."	1 In those days, when again a great crowd had gathered, and they had nothing to eat, he called his disciples to him, and said to them, 2 "I have compassion on the crowd, because they have been with me now three days, and have nothing to eat; 3 and if I send them away hungry to their homes, they will faint on the way; and some of them have come a long way."
33 And the disciples said to him, "Where are we to get bread enough in the desert to feed so great a crowd?" 34 And Jesus said to them, "How many loaves have you?" They said, "Seven, and a few small fish." 35 And commanding the crowd to sit down on the ground, 36 he took the seven loaves and the fish, and having given thanks he broke them and gave them to the disciples, and the disciples gave them to the crowds.	4 And his disciples answered him, "How can one feed these men with bread here in the desert?" 5 And he asked them, "How many loaves have you?" They said, "Seven." 6 And he commanded the crowd to sit down on the ground; and he took the seven loaves, and having given thanks he broke them and gave them to his disciples to set before the people; and they set them before the crowd. 7 And they had a few small fish; and having blessed them, he commanded that these also should be set before them. 8 And they ate, and were satisfied; and they took up the broken pieces left over, seven baskets full. 9 And there were about four thousand people.
37 And they all ate and were satisfied; and they took up seven baskets full of the broken pieces left over. 38 Those who ate were four thousand men, besides women and children. 39 And sending away the crowds, he got into the boat and went to the region of Magadan.	10 And he sent them away; and immediately he got into the boat with his disciples, and went to the district of Dalmanutha.[e]

e text: S A B C 𝔑 vg syᵖ sa bo; *Dalmounai:* W; *Melegada:* D; *Magdala:* Θ λ φ; *Magedan:* it syˢ.

119. THE PHARISEES SEEK A SIGN.

Matt. 16:1-4	Matt. 12:38-39 (§ 87, p. 63)	Mark 8:11-13	Luke 11:29 (§ 152, p. 108)
1 And the Pharisees and Sadducees came, and to test him they asked him to show them a sign from heaven. 2 He answered them,[f] "When it is evening, you say, 'It will be fair weather; for the sky is red.' 3 And in the morning, 'It will be stormy today, for the sky is red and threatening.' You know how to interpret the appearance of the sky, but you cannot interpret the signs of the times.	38 Then some of the scribes and Pharisees said to him, "Teacher, we wish to see a sign from you." 39 But he answered them,	11 The Pharisees came and began to argue with him, seeking from him a sign from heaven, to test him. 12 And he sighed deeply in his spirit, and said,	29 When the crowds were increasing, he began to say, 11:16 (§ 149, p. 106): while others, to try him, sought from him a sign from heaven. 12:54-56 (§ 160, p. 115): 54 He also said to the multitudes, "When you see a cloud rising in the west, you say at once, 'A shower is coming'; and so it happens. 55 And when you see the south wind blowing, you say, 'There will be scorching heat'; and it happens. 56 You hypocrites! You know how to interpret the appearance of earth and sky; but why do you not know how to interpret the present time?"
4 "An evil and adulterous generation seeks for a sign, but no sign shall be given to it except the sign of Jonah." So he left them and departed.	"An evil and adulterous generation seeks for a sign; but no sign shall be given to it except the sign of the prophet Jonah."	"Why does this generation seek a sign? Truly, I say to you, no sign shall be given to this generation." 13 And he left them, and getting into the boat again he departed to the other side.	11:29 "This generation is an evil generation; it seeks a sign, but no sign shall be given to it except the sign of Jonah."

---

[f] text: C D W Θ λ 𝕽 it vg sy^p bo (some MSS.); the following words to the end of verse 3 are omitted: S B φ sy^c sy^s sa bo (some MSS.).

To Matt. 16:1 cf. John 6:30—So they said to him, "Then what sign do you do, that we may see, and believe you? What work do you perform?"

To Matt. 16:2 cf. **Gospel of the Nazaraeans:** What is marked with an asterisk [i.e., from "When it is evening" to the end of v. 3] is not found in other manuscripts, and it is not found in the Jewish Gospel.

120. A DISCOURSE ON LEAVEN.

Matt. 16:5–12	Mark 8:14–21	Luke 12:1 (§ *154, p. 110*)

5 When the disciples reached the other side, they had forgotten to bring any bread. 6 Jesus said to them,
 	
"Take heed and beware of the leaven of the Pharisees and Sadducees."
7 And they discussed it among themselves, saying, "We brought no bread." 8 But Jesus, aware of this, said, "O men of little faith, why do you discuss among yourselves the fact that you have no bread? 9 Do you not yet perceive?
 	
                              Do you not remember the five loaves of the five thousand, and how many baskets   you gathered?
10 Or the seven loaves of the four thousand, and how many baskets you gathered?
 	
11 How is it that you fail to perceive that I did not speak about bread? Beware of the leaven of the Pharisees and Sadducees."   12 Then they understood that he did not tell them to beware of the leaven of bread, but of the teaching of the Pharisees and Sadducees.
	14 Now they had forgotten to bring bread; and they had only one loaf with them in the boat. 15 And he cautioned them, saying,
	"Take heed, beware of the leaven of the Pharisees and the leaven of Herod."ᵍ
	16 And they discussed it with one another, saying, "We have no bread." 17 And being aware of it, Jesus said to them,
	      "Why do you discuss
	
	                 the fact that you have no bread? Do you not yet perceive or understand? Are your hearts hardened? 18 Having eyes do you not see, and having ears do you not hear? And do you not remember? 19 When I broke the five loaves for the five thousand, how many baskets full of broken pieces did you take up?" They said to him, "Twelve." 20 "And the seven for the four thousand, how many baskets full of broken pieces did you take up?" And they said to him, "Seven." 21 And he said to them, "Do you not yet understand?"
		1 In the meantime, when so many thousands of the multitude had gathered together that they trod upon one another, he began to say to his disciples first, "Beware of the leaven of the Pharisees, which is hypocrisy."

Mark 8:18—Jeremiah 5:21, Ezekiel 12:2.

ᵍ text: S A B C D 𝕽 it vg syˢ syᵖ bo; *the Herodians:* P⁴⁵ W Θ λ φ sa.

Matt. 16:9—Matt. 14:19-21.

121. THE BLIND MAN OF BETHSAIDA.
Mark 8:22–26

22 And they came to Bethsaida. And some people brought to him a blind man, and begged him to touch him. 23 And he took the blind man by the hand, and led him out of the village; and when he had spit on his eyes and laid his hands upon him, he asked him, "Do you see anything?" 24 And he looked up and said, "I see men; but they look like trees, walking." 25 Then again he laid his hands upon his eyes; and he looked intently and was restored, and saw everything clearly. 26 And he sent him away to his home, saying, "Do not even enter the village."[h]

122. THE CONFESSION AT CAESAREA PHILIPPI AND THE
FIRST PREDICTION OF THE PASSION.

Matt. 16:13–23	Mark 8:27–33	Luke 9:18–22
		(9:10–17, § 112, pp. 79–80)
13 Now when Jesus came into the district of Caesarea Philippi, he asked his disciples, "Who do men say that the Son of man is?"[i] 14 And they said, "Some say John the Baptist, others say Elijah, and others Jeremiah or one of the prophets." 15 He said to them, "But who do you say that I am?" 16 Simon Peter replied, "You are the Christ, the Son of the living God."	27 And Jesus went on with his disciples, to the villages of Caesarea Philippi; and on the way he asked his disciples, "Who do men say that I am?" 28 And they told him, "John the Baptist; and others say, Elijah; and others one of the prophets." 29 And he asked them, "But who do you say that I am?" Peter answered him, "You are the Christ."	18 Now it happened that as he was praying alone the disciples were with him;[j] and he asked them, "Who do the people say that I am?" 19 And they answered, "John the Baptist; but others say, Elijah; and others that one of the old prophets has risen." 20 And he said to them, "But who do you say that I am?" And Peter answered, "The Christ of God."

[h] text: S B W λ sy[s] sa bo; add, *and tell no one in the village:* A C 𝕽 sy[p]; *saying, "Go into your house and tell no one in the village":* D; *saying, "Go into your house and if you enter the village tell no one":* it vg.   [i] text: S B vg sa bo; *Who do men say that I, the Son of man, am?:* C D W Θ λ φ 𝕽 it sy[c] sy[s] sy[p] Irenaeus.   [j] *met him:* B.

To § 121 cf. John 9:1-7.
To Matt. 16:16 cf. John 6:68-69: 68 Simon Peter answered him, "Lord, to whom shall we go? You have the words of eternal life; 69 and we have believed, and have come to know, that you are the Holy One of God."

17 And Jesus answered him, "Blessed are you, Simon Bar-Jona! For flesh and blood has not revealed this to you, but my Father who is in heaven. 18 And I tell you, you are Peter,[k] and on this rock[l] I will build my church, and the powers of death[m] shall not prevail against it. 19 I will give you the keys of the kingdom of heaven, and whatever you bind on earth shall be bound in heaven, and whatever you loose on earth shall be loosed in heaven." *

20 Then he strictly charged the disciples to tell no one that he was the Christ.	30 And he charged them to tell no one about him.	21 But he charged and command-ed them to tell this to no one,
21 From that time Jesus[n] began to show his disciples that he must go to Jerusalem and suffer many things ˊfrom the elders and chief priests and scribes, and be killed, and on the third day be raised.	31 And he began to teach them that the Son of man must suffer many things, and be rejected by the elders and the chief priests and the scribes, and be killed, and after three days rise again.	22 saying, "The Son of man must suffer many things, and be rejected by the elders and chief priests and scribes, and be killed, and on the third day be raised."
22 And Peter took him and began to rebuke him, saying, "God forbid, Lord! This shall never happen to you." 23 But he turned and said to Peter, "Get behind me, Satan! You are a hindrance[o] to me; for you are not on the side of God, but of men."	32 And he said this plainly. And Peter took him, and began to rebuke him. 33 But turning and seeing his disciples, he rebuked Peter, and said, "Get behind me, Satan! For you are not on the side of God, but of men."	

* Matt. 18:18 (§ 134, p.99): "Truly, I say to you, whatever you bind on earth shall be bound in heaven and whatever you loose on earth shall be loosed in heaven." Cf. John 20:23.

[k] Greek, Petros. [l] Greek, petra. [m] Greek, the gates of Hades. [n] text: C D W Θ λ φ ℜ it vg sy[o] sy[p] sa; add, Christ: S B bo; omit both names: Irenaeus, Origen. [o] Greek, stumbling block.

To Matt. 16:19 cf. John 20:22-23: 22 And when he had said this, he breathed on them, and said to them, "Receive the Holy Spirit. 23 If you forgive the sins of any, they are forgiven; if you retain the sins of any, they are retained."

To Matt. 16:17 cf. **Gospel of the Nazaraeans:** The Jewish Gospel has: "son of John" [for "Bar-Jona"].

123. THE CONDITIONS OF DISCIPLESHIP.

Matt. 16:24–28	Mark 8:34–9:1	Luke 9:23–27
24 Then Jesus told his disciples, "If any man would come after me, let him deny himself and take up his cross and follow me. 25 For whoever would save his life will lose it, and whoever loses his life for my sake will find it.*	34 And he called to him the multitude with his disciples, and said to them, "If any man would come after me, let him deny himself and take up his cross and follow me. 35 For whoever would save his life will lose it; and whoever loses his life for my sake and the gospel's will save it.* p	23 And he said to all, "If any man would come after me, let him deny himself and take up his cross daily and follow me. 24 For whoever would save his life will lose it; and whoever loses his life for my sake, he will save it.*
26 For what will it profit a man, if he gains the whole world and forfeits his life? Or what shall a man give in return for his life?	36 For what does it profit a man, to gain the whole world and forfeit his life? 37 For what can a man give in return for his life? 38 For whoever is ashamed of me and of my words in this adulterous and sinful generation, of him will the Son of man also be ashamed,**	25 For what does it profit a man if he gains the whole world and loses or forfeits himself? 26 For whoever is ashamed of me and of my words, of him will the Son of man be ashamed
27 For the Son of man is to come with his angels in the glory of his Father, and then he will repay every man for what he has done.	when he comes in the glory of his Father with the holy angels."	when he comes in his glory and the glory of the Father and of the holy angels.
28 Truly, I say to you, there are some standing here who will not taste death before they see the Son of man coming in his kingdom."	9:1 And he said to them, "Truly, I say to you, there are some standing here who will not taste death before they see that the kingdom of God has come with power."	27 But I tell you truly, there are some standing here who will not taste death before they see the kingdom of God."

* Matt. 10:38-39 (§ 62, pp.45-46):
38 "And he who does not take his cross and follow me is not worthy of me. 39 He who finds his life will lose it, and he who loses his life for my sake will find it."

** Matt. 10:33 (§ 60, p.45): "But whoever denies me before men, I also will deny before my Father who is in heaven."

Matt. 16:27—Psalm 62:12.

Luke 14:27 (§ 171, p.120): "Whoever does not bear his own cross and come after me, cannot be my disciple."

17:33 (§ 184, p.126): "Whoever seeks to gain his life will lose it, but whoever loses his life will preserve it."

Luke 12:9 (§ 155, p.111): "But he who denies me before men will be denied before the angels of God."

p text: S A B C W Θ λ φ 𝔐 it (some MSS.) vg syp sa bo; *whoever loses his life for the gospel's sake will save it:* P45 D it (some MSS.) sys.

To Matt. 16:25 and parallels cf. John 12:25—"He who loves his life loses it, and he who hates his life in this world will keep it for eternal life."

124. THE TRANSFIGURATION.

Matt. 17:1–8	Mark 9:2–8	Luke 9:28–36
1 And after six days Jesus took with him Peter and James and John his brother, and led them up a high mountain apart. 2 And he was transfigured before them, and his face shone like the sun, and his garments became white as light.	2 And after six days Jesus took with him Peter and James and John, and led them up a high mountain apart by themselves; and he was transfigured before them, 3 and his garments became glistening, intensely white,q as no fuller on earth could bleach them.	28 Now about eight days after these sayings he took with him Peter and John and James, and went up on the mountain to pray. 29 And as he was praying, the appearance of his countenance was altered, and his raiment became dazzling white.
3 And behold, there appeared to them Moses and Elijah, talking with him.	4 And there appeared to them Elijah with Moses; and they were talking to Jesus.	30 And behold, two men talked with him, Moses and Elijah, 31 who appeared in glory and spoke of his departure, which he was to accomplish at Jerusalem. 32 Now Peter and those who were with him were heavy with sleep, and when they wakened they saw his glory and the two men who stood with him.
4 And Peter said to Jesus, "Lord, it is well that we are here; if you wish, I will make three booths here, one for you and one for Moses and one for Elijah."	5 And Peter said to Jesus, "Master,r it is well that we are here; let us make three booths, one for you and one for Moses and one for Elijah." 6 For he did not know what to say, for they were exceedingly afraid.	33 And as the men were parting from him, Peter said to Jesus, "Master, it is well that we are here; let us make three booths, one for you and one for Moses and one for Elijah"— not knowing what he said.
5 He was still speaking, when lo, a bright cloud overshadowed them, and a voice from the cloud said, "This is my beloved Son,s with whom I am well pleased; listen to him." 6 When the disciples heard this, they fell on their faces, and were filled with awe. 7 But Jesus came and touched them, saying, "Rise, and have no fear." 8 And when they lifted up their eyes, they saw no one but Jesus only.	7 And a cloud overshadowed them, and a voice came out of the cloud, "This is my beloved Son;s listen to him."	34 And as he said this, a cloud came and overshadowed them; and they were afraid as they entered the cloud. 35 And a voice came out of the cloud, saying, "This is my Son, my Chosen;t listen to him!"
	8 And suddenly looking around they no longer saw any one with them but Jesus only.	36 And when the voice had spoken, Jesus was found alone. And they kept silence and told no one in those days anything of what they had seen.

To Matt. 17:5 and parallels cf. Matt. 3:17.

q text: P45 S B C W Θ λ sa; *white as snow:* A D φ ℜ it vg sys syp bo.   r Or, *Rabbi.*   s Or, *my Son, my* (or, *the*) *Beloved.*   t text: P45 P75 S B Θ λ it (some MSS.) sys sa bo; *my Beloved:* A C W φ ℜ it (some MSS.) vg sye syp; *my Beloved, with whom I am well pleased:* D.

To Luke 9:32 cf. John 1:14b—We have beheld his glory, glory as of the only Son from the Father.

125. THE COMING OF ELIJAH.

Matt. 17:9–13	Mark 9:9–13	*see*
9 And as they were coming down the mountain, Jesus commanded them, "Tell no one the vision, until the Son of man is raised from the dead."	9 And as they were coming down the mountain, he charged them to tell no one what they had seen, until the Son of man should have risen from the dead. 10 So they kept the matter to themselves, questioning what the rising from the dead meant. 11 And they asked him,	*below* v. 37
10 And the disciples asked him, "Then why do the scribes say that first Elijah must come?" 11 He replied, "Elijah does come, and he is to restore all things;	"Why do the scribes say that first Elijah must come?" 12 And he said to them, "Elijah does come first to restore all things; and how is it written of the Son of man, that he should suffer many things and be treated with contempt? 13 But I tell you that Elijah has come, and they did to him whatever they pleased, as it is written of him."	
v. 12 b		
12 but I tell you that Elijah has already come, and they did not know him, but did to him whatever they pleased. So also the Son of man will suffer at their hands." 13 Then the disciples understood that he was speaking to them of John the Baptist.		

126. AN EPILEPTIC BOY HEALED.

Matt. 17:14–21	Mark 9:14–29	Luke 9:37–43a
see above v. 9	*see above v. 9*	37 On the next day, when they had come **down from the mountain, a great crowd met** him.
14 And when they came to the crowd,	14 And when they came to the disciples, they saw a great crowd about them, and scribes arguing with them. 15 And immediately all the crowd, when they saw him, were greatly amazed, and ran up to him and greeted him. 16 And he asked them, "What are you discussing with them?" 17 And one of the crowd answered him, "Teacher, I brought my son to you, for he has a dumb spirit; 18 and wherever it seizes him, it dashes him down; and he foams and grinds his teeth and becomes rigid;	
a man came up to him and kneeling before him said, 15 "Lord, have mercy upon my son, for he is an epileptic and he suffers terribly; for often he falls into the fire, and often into the water.		38 And behold, a man from the crowd cried, "Teacher, I beg you to look upon my son, for he is my only child; 39 and behold, a spirit seizes him, and he suddenly cries out; it convulses him till he foams, and shatters him, and will hardly leave him.
	see below v. 22	

Matt. 17:10-11 = Mark 9:11-12—Malachi 4:5-6.   Matt. 17:12 = Mark 9:13—I Kings 19:2, 10.
Mark 9:12b—Psalm 22:6, Isaiah 53:3.

16 And I brought him to your disciples, and they could not heal him." 17 And Jesus answered, "O faithless and perverse generation, how long am I to be with you? How long am I to bear with you? Bring him here to me."	and I asked your disciples to cast it out, and they were not able." 19 And he answered them, "O faithless generation, how long am I to be with you? How long am I to bear with you? Bring him to me." 20 And they brought the boy to him; and when the spirit saw him, immediately it convulsed the boy, and he fell on the ground and rolled about, foaming at the mouth. 21 And Jesus^u asked his father, "How long has he had this?" And he said, "From childhood. 22 And it has often cast him into the fire and into the water, to destroy him; but if you can do anything, have pity on us and help us." 23 And Jesus said to him, "If you can! All things are possible to him who believes." 24 Immediately the father of the child cried out^v and said, "I believe; help my unbelief!" 25 And when Jesus saw that a crowd came running together, he rebuked the unclean spirit, saying to it, "You dumb and deaf spirit, I command you, come out of him, and never enter him again." 26 And after crying out and convulsing him terribly, it came out, and the boy was like a corpse; so that most of them said, "He is dead." 27 But Jesus took him by the hand and lifted him up, and he arose.	40 And I begged your disciples to cast it out, but they could not." 41 Jesus answered, "O faithless and perverse generation, how long am I to be with you and bear with you? Bring your son here." 42 While he was coming, the demon tore him and convulsed him.
See above v. 15		
18 And Jesus rebuked him,		But Jesus rebuked the unclean spirit,
and the demon came out of him,		
and the boy was cured instantly.		and healed the boy and gave him back to his father. 43 And all were astonished at the majesty of God.
19 Then the disciples came to Jesus privately and said, "Why could we not cast it out?"	28 And when he had entered the house, his disciples asked him privately, "Why could we not cast it out?"	

^u Greek, *he.*   ^v text: P⁴⁵ S A B C W sy⁸ sa bo; add, *with tears:* D Θ λ φ 𝔐 it vg sy^p.

To Matt. 17:17 cf. John 14:9—Jesus said to him, "Have I been with you so long, and yet you do not know me, Philip? He who has seen me has seen the Father; how can you say, 'Show us the Father'?"

20 He said to them, "Because of your little faith. For truly, I say to you, if you have faith as a grain of mustard seed, you will say to this mountain, 'Move from here to there,' and it will move; and nothing will be impossible to you." * w

29 And he said to them, "This kind cannot be driven out by anything but prayer." x

17:6 (§ *180, p. 125*): And the Lord said,

"If you had faith as a grain of mustard seed, you could say to this sycamine tree, 'Be rooted up, and be planted in the sea,' and it would obey you." *

127. THE SECOND PREDICTION OF THE PASSION.

Matt. 17:22–23	Mark 9:30–32	Luke 9:43b–45
22 As they were gathering y in Galilee, Jesus said to them,	30 They went on from there and passed through Galilee. And he would not have any one know it; 31 for he was teaching his disciples, saying to them, "The	43b But while they were all marveling at everything he did, he said to his disciples, 44 "Let these words sink into your ears; for the
"The Son of man is to be delivered into the hands of men, 23 and they will kill him,	Son of man will be delivered into the hands of men, and they will kill him; and when he is killed, after three days he will rise." 32 But they did not understand the saying,	Son of man is to be delivered into the hands of men."
and he will be raised on the third day."		45 But they did not understand this saying, and it was concealed from them, that they should not perceive it;
And they were greatly distressed.	and they were afraid to ask him.	and they were afraid to ask him about this saying.

128. THE TEMPLE TAX.

Matt. 17:24–27

24 When they came to Capernaum, the collectors of the half-shekel tax went up to Peter and said, "Does not your teacher pay the tax?" 25 He said, "Yes." And when he came home, Jesus spoke to him first, saying, "What do you think, Simon? From whom do kings of the earth take toll or tribute? From their sons or from others?" 26 And when he said, "From others," Jesus said to him, "Then the sons are free. 27 However, not to give offense to them, go to the sea and cast a hook, and take the first fish that comes up, and when you open its mouth you will find a shekel; take that and give it to them for me and for yourself."

---

* Matt. 21:21 (§ 201, pp.140-141): And Jesus answered them, "Truly, I say to you, if you have faith and never doubt, you will not only do what has been done to the fig tree, but even if you say to this mountain, 'Be taken up and cast into the sea,' it will be done."

Matt. 17:24—Exodus 30:13.

Mark 11:22-23 (§ 201, pp.140-141): 22 And Jesus answered them, "Have faith in God. 23 Truly, I say to you, whoever says to this mountain, 'Be taken up and cast into the sea,' and does not doubt in his heart, but believes that what he says will come to pass, it will be done for him."

---

w text: S. B Θ syᶜ syˢ sa bo; add verse 21: *But this kind does not come out except by prayer and fasting:* C D W λ φ𝕽 it vg syᵖ Origen. Cf. also Mark 9:29.   x text: S B Clement; add, *and fasting:* P⁴⁵? A C D W Θ λ φ𝕽 it vg syˢ syᵖ sa bo.   y text: S B λ it vg; *living:* C D W Θ φ 𝕽 syᶜ syˢ syᵖ sa bo.

To Mark 9:30 cf. John 7:1—After this Jesus went about in Galilee; he would not go about in Judea, because the Jews sought to kill him.

129. THE DISPUTE ABOUT GREATNESS.

Matt. 18:1–5	**Mark 9:33–37**	**Luke 9:46–48**
	33 And they came to Capernaum; and when he was in the house he asked them, "What were you discussing on the way?"	
1 At that time the disciples came to Jesus, saying, "Who is greatest in the kingdom of heaven?" *	34 But they were silent; for on the way they had discussed with one another who was the greatest. 35 And he sat down and called the twelve; and he said to them, "If any one would be first, he must be last of all	46 And an argument arose among them as to which of them was the greatest. 47 But when Jesus perceived the thought of their hearts,
		see 9:48b *
2 And calling to him a child, he put him in the midst of them, 3 and said,	and servant of all." * 36 And he took a child, and put him in the midst of them; and taking him in his arms, he said to them,	he took a child and put him by his side, 48 and said to them,
	10:15 (*§ 188, p. 130*):	18:17 (*§ 188, p. 130*):
"Truly, I say to you, unless you turn and become like children, you will never enter the kingdom of heaven. 4 Whoever humbles himself like this child, he is the greatest in the kingdom of heaven.**	"Truly, I say to you, whoever does not receive the kingdom of God like a child shall not enter it."	"Truly, I say to you, whoever does not receive the kingdom of God like a child shall not enter it."
* Matt. 20:26-27 (§ 192, p.133): 26 "It shall not be so among you; but whoever would be great among you must be your servant, 27 and whoever would be first among you must be your slave." 23:11 (§ 210, p.149): "He who is greatest among you shall be your servant."	Mark 10:43-44 (§ 192, p.133): 43 "But it shall not be so among you; but whoever would be great among you must be your servant, 44 and whoever would be first among you must be slave of all."	Luke 22:26 (§ 237b, p.167): "But not so with you; rather let the greatest among you become as the youngest, and the leader as one who serves."
** Matt. 23:12 (§ 210, p. 149): "Whoever exalts himself will be humbled, and whoever humbles himself will be exalted."		Luke 14:11 (§ 169, p.119): "For whoever exalts himself will be humbled, and he who humbles himself will be exalted." Luke 18:14 (§ 186, p.127): "For every one who exalts himself will be humbled, but he who humbles himself will be exalted."

To Matt. 18:3 cf. John 3:3, 5—3 Jesus answered him, "Truly, truly, I say to you, unless one is born anew, he cannot see the kingdom of God." . . . 5 Jesus answered, "Truly, truly, I say to you, unless one is born of water and the Spirit, he cannot enter the kingdom of God."

To Matt. 18:3 cf. Acts of Philip 34—"Unless you change your 'down' to 'up' (and 'up' to 'down' and ''right' to 'left') and 'left' to 'right', you shall not enter my kingdom (of heaven)."

5 "Whoever receives one such child in my name receives me." *	9:37 "Whoever receives one such child in my name receives me; and whoever receives me, receives not me but him who sent me." * *see 9:35b*	9:48 "Whoever receives this child in my name receives me, and whoever receives me receives him who sent me;* for he who is least among you all is the one who is great."

130. THE STRANGE EXORCIST.

Mark 9:38–41	Luke 9:49–50
38 John said to him, "Teacher, we saw a man casting out demons in your name, and we forbade him, because he was not following us."ᶻ	49 John answered, "Master, we saw a man casting out demons in your name, and we forbade him, because he does not follow with us."
³⁹ But Jesus said, "Do not forbid him; for no one who does a mighty work in my name will be able soon after to speak evil of me.	⁵⁰ But Jesus said to him, "Do not forbid him;
⁴⁰ For he that is not against us is for us.** ⁴¹ For truly, I say to you, whoever gives you a cup of water to drink because you bear the name of Christ, will by no means lose his reward.***	for he that is not against you is for you." ** *(9:51–56, § 137, p. 101)*

* Matt. 10:40 (§ 63, p.46): "He who receives you receives me, and he who receives me receives him who sent me." Cf. also Luke 10:16 (§ 139, p.103).

** Matt. 12:30 (§ 86, p.62) = Luke 11:23 (§ 149, p.107): "He who is not with me is against me, and he who does not gather with me scatters."

*** Matt. 10:42 (§ 63, p.46): "And whoever gives to one of these little ones even a cup ot cold water because he is a disciple, truly, I say to you, he shall not lose his reward."

ᶻ text: S B C Θ syˢ syᵖ sa bo; *in your name, who does not follow (was not following: W) us, and we forbade him:* D W λ φ it vg; *in your name, who does not follow us, and we forbade him because he does not follow us:* A 𝕽.

To Mark 9:37 and Luke 9:48 cf. John 12:44-45; 13:20—⁴⁴ And Jesus cried out and said, "He who believes in me, believes not in me but in him who sent me.⁴⁵ And he who sees me sees him who sent me." 13:20 "Truly, truly, I say to you, he who receives any one whom I send receives me; and he who receives me receives him who sent me."

To Mark 9:40 and Luke 9:50 cf. *Oxyrhynchus Papyrus 1224, fol. 2 recto, col. 1:* "For he who is not against you is for you. He who today is far away will tomorrow be near you."

131. ON TEMPTATIONS.

Matt. 18:6–9	Mark 9:42–48	Luke 17:1–2 (§ 178, p. 124):
6 "But whoever causes one of these little ones who believe in me to sin,[a] it would be better for him to have a great millstone fastened round his neck and to be drowned in the depth of the sea.	42 "Whoever causes one of these little ones who believe in me to sin,[a] it would be better for him if a great millstone were hung round his neck and he were thrown into the sea.	1 And he said to his disciples, "Temptations to sin[b] are sure to come; but woe to him by whom they come! 2 It would be better for him if a millstone were hung round his neck and he were cast into the sea, than that he should cause one of these little ones to sin.[a]
7 "Woe to the world for temptations to sin![b] For it is necessary that temptations come, but woe to the man by whom the temptation comes!		
8 "And if your hand or your foot causes you to sin,[a] cut it off and throw it away; it is better for you to enter life maimed or lame than with two hands or two feet to be thrown into the eternal fire.	43 "And if your hand causes you to sin,[a] cut it off; it is better for you to enter life maimed than with two hands to go to hell,[c] to the unquenchable fire.[d] 45And if your foot causes you to sin,[a] cut it off; it is better for you to enter life lame than with two feet to be thrown into hell.[cd] 47 And	
9 And if your eye causes you to sin,[a] pluck it out and throw it away; it is better for you to enter life with one eye than with two eyes to be thrown into the hell[c] of fire." *	if your eye causes you to sin,[a] pluck it out; it is better for you to enter the kingdom of God with one eye than with two eyes to be thrown into hell,[c] * 48 where their worm does not die, and the fire is not quenched.	

* Matt. 5:29-30 (§ 23, p.22): 29 "If your right eye causes you to sin, pluck it out and throw it away; it is better that you lose one of your members than that your whole body be thrown into hell. 30 And if your right hand causes you to sin, cut it off and throw it away; it is better that you lose one of your members than that your whole body go into hell."

Mark 9:48—Isaiah 66:24

[a] Greek, *causes . . . to stumble.*   [b] Greek: *stumbling blocks.*   [c] Greek, *Gehenna.*   [d] Verses 44, 46—identical with verse 48—omitted, S B C W λ sy[s] sa bo; added, A D Θ φ 𝕽 it vg sy[p].

132. CONCERNING SALT.

Matt. 5:13 (§ 20, p. 21):	Mark 9:49–50	Luke 14:34–35 (§ 171, p. 121):
	49 "For every one will be salted with fire.[e]	
	50 Salt is good;	34 "Salt is good;
"You are the salt of the earth; but if salt has lost its taste, how shall its saltness be restored? It is no longer good for anything except to be thrown out and trodden under foot by men."	but if the salt has lost its saltness, how will you season it?	but if salt has lost its taste, how shall its saltness be restored? 35 It is fit neither for the land nor for the dunghill; men throw it away. He who has ears to hear, let him hear."
	Have salt in yourselves, and be at peace with one another."	
	(10:1–12, § 187, pp. 128–129)	

133. THE LOST SHEEP.

Matt. 18:10–14	Luke 15:3–7 (§ 172, p. 121):
10 "See that you do not despise one of these little ones; for I tell you that in heaven their angels always behold the face of my Father who is in heaven.[f]	
12 "What do you think? If a man has a hundred sheep, and one of them has gone astray, does he not leave the ninety-nine on the mountains and go in search of the one that went astray? 13 And if he finds it, truly, I say to you, he rejoices over it more than over the ninety-nine that never went astray.	3 So he told them this parable: 4 "What man of you, having a hundred sheep, if he has lost one of them, does not leave the ninety-nine in the wilderness, and go after the one which is lost, until he finds it? 5 And when he has found it, he lays it on his shoulders, rejoicing. 6 And when he comes home, he calls together his friends and his neighbors, saying to them, 'Rejoice with me, for I have found my sheep which was lost.' 7 Just so, I tell you, there will be more joy in heaven over one sinner who repents than over ninety-nine righteous persons who need no repentance."
14 So it is not the will of my[g] Father who is in heaven that one of these little ones should perish.	

Mark 9:49—Leviticus 2:13.

[e] text: S B W λ φ sy[s] sa bo; *For every one will be salted (consumed: Θ) with fire, and every sacrifice will be salted with salt:* A C Θ 𝕽 vg sy[p]; *For every sacrifice will be salted with salt:* D it.   [f] text: S B Θ λ φ sy[s] sa bo; add verse 11: *for the Son of man came to save the lost:* D W 𝕽 it vg sy[c] sy[p]. Cf. also Luke 19:10.   [g] text: B Θ φ sy[s] sa bo; *your:* S W λ 𝕽 it vg sy[c] sy[p]; *our:* D.

134. ON REPROVING ONE'S BROTHER.

Matt. 18:15–20	Luke 17:3 (§ *179, p. 124*):
15 "If your brother sins against you, go and tell him his fault, between you and him alone. If he listens to you, you have gained your brother. 16 But if he does not listen, take one or two others along with you, that every word may be confirmed by the evidence of two or three witnesses. 17 If he refuses to listen to them, tell it to the church; and if he refuses to listen even to the church, let him be to you as a Gentile and a tax collector. 18 "Truly, I say to you, whatever you bind on earth shall be bound in heaven, and whatever you loose on earth shall be loosed in heaven.* 19 "Again I say to you, if two of you agree on earth about anything they ask, it will be done for them by my Father in heaven. 20 For where two or three are gathered in my name, there am I in the midst of them."	"Take heed to yourselves; if your brother sins, rebuke him, and if he repents, forgive him;

135. ON RECONCILIATION.

Matt. 18:21–22	Luke 17:4 (§ *179, p. 124*):
21 Then Peter came up and said to him, "Lord, how often shall my brother sin against me, and I forgive him? As many as seven times?" 22 Jesus said to him, "I do not say to you seven times, but seventy times seven.[h]	"and if he sins against you seven times in the day, and turns to you seven times, and says, 'I repent,' you must forgive him."

---

* Matt. 16:19 (§ 122, p.89): "I will give you the keys of the kingdom of heaven, and whatever you bind on earth shall be bound in heaven, and whatever you loose on earth shall be loosed in heaven."

Matt. 18:16—Deuteronomy 19:15.

[h] Or, *seventy-seven times*.

To Matt. 18:18 cf. John 20:23—"If you forgive the sins of any, they are forgiven; if you retain the sins of any, they are retained."

To Matt. 18:20 cf. *Oxyrhynchus Papyrus 1, Logion 5:* Jesus said, "Where there are two, they are not without God; and where there is one alone, I say, I am with him. Raise the stone, and there you will find me; split the wood, and there I am." Cf. **Gospel of Thomas, Logion 77b**; also **Logion 30:** Jesus said, "Where there are three gods, they are gods; where there are two or one, I am with him."

To Matt. 18:21-22 (Luke 17:3-4) cf. **Gospel of the Nazaraeans** (in Jerome, *Against Pelagius, III.2*)—He says, "If your brother has sinned by a word, and repented, receive him seven times a day." Simon, his disciple, said to him, "Seven times a day?" The Lord answered, "Yes, I tell you, as much as seventy times seven times! For in the prophets also, after they were anointed by the Holy Spirit, a word of sin [sinful speech?] was found."

To Matt. 18:22 cf. **Gospel of the Nazaraeans:** The Jewish Gospel has, immediately after "seventy times seven": For in the prophets also, after they were anointed by the Holy Spirit, a word of sin [sinful speech?] was found in them.

136. THE PARABLE OF THE UNMERCIFUL SERVANT.
Matt. 18:23–35

23 "Therefore the kingdom of heaven may be compared to a king who wished to settle accounts with his servants. 24 When he began the reckoning, one was brought to him who owed him ten thousand talents;[1] 25 and as he could not pay, his lord ordered him to be sold, with his wife and children and all that he had, and payment to be made. 26 So the servant fell on his knees, imploring him, 'Lord, have patience with me, and I will pay you everything.' 27 And out of pity for him the lord of that servant released him and forgave him the debt. 28 But that same servant, as he went out, came upon one of his fellow servants who owed him a hundred denarii;[j] and seizing him by the throat he said, 'Pay what you owe.' 29 So his fellow servant fell down and besought him, 'Have patience with me, and I will pay you.' 30 He refused and went and put him in prison till he should pay the debt. 31 When his fellow servants saw what had taken place, they were greatly distressed, and they went and reported to their lord all that had taken place. 32 Then his lord summoned him and said to him, 'You wicked servant! I forgave you all that debt because you besought me; 33 and should not you have had mercy on your fellow servant, as I had mercy on you?' 34 And in anger his lord delivered him to the jailers,[k] till he should pay all his debt. 35 So also my heavenly Father will do to every one of you, if you do not forgive your brother from your heart." *

(19:1–12, § 187, pp. 128–129.)

---

* Matt. 6:15 (§ 30, p.25): "But if you do not forgive men their trespasses, neither will your Father forgive your trespasses."

---

[1] This talent was more than fifteen years' wages of a laborer.   [j] The denarius was a day's wage for a laborer.   [k] Greek: *torturers*.

II. LUKE'S SPECIAL SECTION
Luke 9:51–18:14

137. THE SAMARITAN VILLAGERS.

Luke 9:51–56

(9:49–50, § 130, p. 96)

51 When the days drew near for him to be received up, he set his face to go to Jerusalem. And he sent messengers ahead of him, 52 who went and entered a village of the Samaritans, to make ready for him; 53 but the people would not receive him, because his face was set toward Jerusalem. 54 And when his disciples James and John saw it, they said, "Lord, do you want us to bid fire come down from heaven and consume them?"1 55 But he turned and rebuked them.m 56 And they went on to another village.

138. THE NATURE OF DISCIPLESHIP.

Matt. 8:19–22 (§ 49, p. 34)	Luke 9:57–62
19 And a scribe came up and said to him, "Teacner, I will follow you wherever you go." 20 And Jesus said to him, "Foxes have holes, and birds of the air have nests; but the Son of man has nowhere to lay his head." 21 Another of the disciples said to him, "Lord, let me first go and bury my father." 22 But Jesus said to him, "Follow me, and leave the dead to bury their own dead."	57 And as they were going along the road, a man said to him, "I will follow you wherever you go." 58 And Jesus said to him, "Foxes have holes, and birds of the air have nests; but the Son of man has nowhere to lay his head." 59 To another he said, "Follow me." But he said, "Lord, let me first go and bury my father." 60 But he said to him, "Leave the dead **to** bury their own dead; but as for you, go and proclaim the kingdom of God." 61 Another said, "I will follow you, Lord; but let me first say farewell to those at my home." 62 Jesus said to him, "No one who puts his hand to the plow and looks back is fit for the kingdom of God."

Luke 9:54—II Kings 1:10, 12.

1 text: P45 P75 S B it (some MSS.) vg syc sys sa bo; add, *as Elijah did:* A C D W Θ λ φ ℜ it (some MSS.) syp.   m text: P45 P75 S A B C W sys sa bo; add, *and he said, "You do not know what manner of spirit you are of":* D; *and he said, "You do not know what manner of spirit you are of; for the Son of man came not to destroy men's lives but to save them":* Θ λ φ ℜ it vg syc syp. Cf. also Luke 19:10.

139. THE SENDING OUT OF THE SEVENTY.

Matt. 9:37–38, 10:7–16 (§ *58, pp. 39–42.*)

9:37 Then he said to his disciples, "The harvest is plentiful, but the laborers are few; [38] pray therefore the Lord of the harvest to send out laborers into his harvest." 10:16 "Lo, I send you out as sheep in the midst of wolves; so be wise as serpents and innocent as doves. [9] Take no gold, nor silver, nor copper in your belts, [10a] no bag for your journey, nor two tunics, nor sandals, nor a staff; . . . [11] And whatever town or village you enter, find out who is worthy in it, and stay with him until you depart. [12] As you enter the house, salute it. [13] And if the house is worthy, let your peace come upon it; but if it is not worthy, let your peace return to you. [10b] . . . for the laborer deserves his food. [7] And preach as you go, saying, 'The kingdom of heaven is at hand.' [8] Heal the sick, raise the dead, cleanse lepers, cast out demons. You received without paying, give without pay.

[14] And if any one will not receive you or listen to your words, shake off the dust from your feet as you leave that house or town.

[15] Truly, I say to you, it shall be more tolerable on the day of judgment for the land of Sodom and Gomorrah than for that town."

Cf. Mark 6:6b–13 = Luke 9:1–6 (§ 109, pp. 76–77)

Luke 10:1–16

1 After this the Lord appointed seventy[n] others, and sent them on ahead of him, two by two, into every town and place where he himself was about to come. [2] And he said to them, "The harvest is plentiful, but the laborers are few; pray therefore the Lord of the harvest to send out laborers into his harvest. [3] Go your way; behold, I send you out as lambs in the midst of wolves. [4] Carry no purse, no bag, no sandals; and salute no one on the road.

[5] Whatever house you enter, first say, 'Peace be to this house!'

[6] And if a son of peace is there, your peace shall rest upon him; but if not, it shall return to you. [7] And remain in the same house, eating and drinking what they provide, for the laborer deserves his wages; do not go from house to house. [8] Whenever you enter a town and they receive you, eat what is set before you; [9] heal the sick in it and say to them, 'The kingdom of God has come near to you.' [10] But whenever you enter a town and they do not receive you, go into its streets and say, [11] 'Even the dust of your town that clings to our feet, we wipe off against you; nevertheless know this, that the kingdom of God has come near.' [12] I tell you, it shall be more tolerable on that day for Sodom than for that town.

To Luke 10:7 cf. Matt. 10:10, p.41.

[n] text: S A C W Θ λ φ 𝔐 it (some MSS.) sy[p] bo; *seventy-two:* P[75] B D it (some MSS.) vg sy[c] sy[s] sa.

To Luke 10:2 cf. John 4:35—"Do you not say, 'There are yet four months, then comes the harvest'? I tell you, lift up your eyes, and see how the fields are already white for harvest."

11:21–23 (§ 66, p. 49): "Woe to you, Chorazin! woe to you, Bethsaida! for if the mighty works done in you had been done in Tyre and Sidon, they would have repented long ago in sackcloth and ashes. 22 But I tell you, it shall be more tolerable on the day of judgment for Tyre and Sidon than for you. 23 And you, Capernaum, will you be exalted to heaven? You shall be brought down to Hades."

10:40 "He who receives you receives me, and he who receives me receives him who sent me." *

13 "Woe to you, Chorazin! woe to you, Bethsaida! for if the mighty works done in you had been done in Tyre and Sidon, they would have repented long ago, sitting in sackcloth and ashes. 14 But it shall be more tolerable in the judgment for Tyre and Sidon than for you. 15 And you, Capernaum, will you be exalted to heaven? You shall be brought down to Hades. 16 He who hears you hears me, and he who rejects you rejects me, and he who rejects me rejects him who sent me." *

140. THE RETURN OF THE SEVENTY.
Luke 10:17–20

Cf.
16:
17–18
p. 191

17 The seventy° returned with joy, saying, "Lord, even the demons are subject to us in your name!" ** 18 And he said to them, "I saw Satan fall like lightning from heaven. 19 Behold, I have given you authority to tread upon serpents and scorpions, and over all the power of the enemy; and nothing shall hurt you. 20 Nevertheless do not rejoice in this, that the spirits are subject to you; but rejoice that your names are written in heaven."

141. JESUS' GRATITUDE TO THE FATHER.

Matt. 11:25–27 (§ 67, p. 49):

25 At that time Jesus declared, "I thank thee, Father, Lord of heaven and earth, that thou hast hidden these things from the wise and understanding and revealed them to babes; 26 yea, Father, for such was thy gracious will.ᵖ

Luke 10:21–22

21 In that same hour he rejoiced in the Holy Spirit and said, "I thank thee, Father, Lord of heaven and earth, that thou hast hidden these things from the wise and understanding and revealed them to babes; yea, Father, for such was thy gracious will. ᵖ

* Cf. Matt. 18:5 = Mark 9:37 = Luke 9:48 (§ 129, p.96).
** Cf. Mark 6:30 = Luke 9:10 (§ 112, p.79).

° text: P⁴⁵ S A C W Θ λ φ 𝔐 it (some MSS.) syᶜ syˢ syᵖ bo; seventy-two: P⁷⁵ B D it (some MSS.) vg sa.
ᵖ Or, so it was well-pleasing before thee.

To Luke 10:16 and Matt. 10:40 cf. John 5:23—"He who does not honor the Son does not honor the Father who sent him." And John 15:23—"He who hates me hates my Father also." Cf. also John 12:48.
To Luke 10:18 cf. John 12:31—"Now is the judgment of this world, now shall the ruler of this world be cast out."

27 All things have been delivered to me by my Father; and no one knows the Son except the Father, and no one knows the Father except the Son and any one to whom the Son chooses to reveal him."

22 All things have been delivered to me by my Father; and no one knows who the Son is except the Father, or who the Father is except the Son and any one to whom the Son chooses to reveal him."

142. THE BLESSEDNESS OF THE DISCIPLES.

Matt. 13:16–17 (§ 92, p. 66):

16 "But blessed are your eyes, for they see, and your ears, for they hear.

17 "Truly, I say to you, many prophets and righteous men longed to see what you see, and did not see it, and to hear what you hear, and did not hear it."

Luke 10:23–24

23 Then turning to the disciples he said privately, "Blessed are the eyes which see what you see!

24 "For I tell you that many prophets and kings desired to see what you see, and did not see it, and to hear what you hear, and did not hear it."

143. THE LAWYER'S QUESTION.

Matt. 22:34–40 (§ 208, p. 147)

34 But when the Pharisees heard that he had silenced the Sadducees, they came together. 35 And one of them, a lawyer, asked him a question, to test him. 36 "Teacher, which is the great commandment in the law?" 37 And he said to him,

"You shall love the Lord your God with all your heart, and with all your soul, and with all your mind. 38 This is the first and great commandment. 39 And a second is like it, You shall love your neighbor as yourself. 40 On these two commandments depend all the law and the prophets."

Mark 12:28–31 (§ 208, p. 147):

28 And one of the scribes came up and heard them disputing with one another, and seeing that he answered them well, asked him, "Which commandment is the first of all? 29 Jesus answered, "The first is, 'Hear, O Israel: The Lord our God, the Lord is one; 30 and you shall love the Lord your God with all your heart, and with all your soul, and with all your mind, and with all your strength.' 31 The second is this, 'You shall love your neighbor as yourself.' There is no other commandment greater than these."

Luke 10:25–28

25 And behold, a lawyer stood up to put him to the test, saying, "Teacher, what shall I do to inherit eternal life?" 26 He said to him, "What is written in the law? How do you read?" 27 And he answered, "You shall love the Lord your God with all your heart, and with all your soul, and with all your strength, and with all your mind; and your neighbor as yourself." 28 And he said to him, "You have answered right; do this, and you will live."

Luke 10:27—Deuteronomy 6:5, Leviticus 19:18.   10:28—Leviticus 18:5.

Luke 10:22—"no one *knew* . . ." in Marcion, Justin, Tatian, Eusebius, Clement, but not in any manuscripts.

To Luke 10:22 and Matt. 11:27 cf. John 10:15—"The Father knows me and I know the Father." Cf. also John 17:2.

144. THE PARABLE OF THE GOOD SAMARITAN.
Luke 10:29–37

29 But he, desiring to justify himself, said to Jesus, "And who is my neighbor?" 30 Jesus replied, "A man was going down from Jerusalem to Jericho, and he fell among robbers, who stripped him and beat him, and departed, leaving him half dead. 31 Now by chance a priest was going down that road; and when he saw him he passed by on the other side. 32 So likewise a Levite, when he came to the place and saw him, passed by on the other side. 33 But a Samaritan, as he journeyed, came to where he was: and when he saw him, he had compassion, 34 and went to him and bound up his wounds, pouring on oil and wine; then he set him on his own beast and brought him to an inn, and took care of him. 35 And the next day he took out two denarii q and gave them to the innkeeper, saying, 'Take care of him; and whatever more you spend, I will repay you when I come back.' 36 Which of these three, do you think, proved neighbor to the man who fell among the robbers?" 37 He said, "The one who showed mercy on him." And Jesus said to him, "Go and do likewise."

145. MARY AND MARTHA.
Luke 10:38–42

38 Now as they went on their way, he entered a village, and a woman named Martha received him into her house. 39 And she had a sister called Mary, who sat at the Lord's feet and listened to his teaching. 40 But Martha was distracted with much serving; and she went to him and said, "Lord, do you not care that my sister has left me to serve alone? Tell her then to help me." 41 But the Lord answered her, "Martha, Martha, you are anxious and troubled about many things; 42 one thing is needful.r Mary has chosen the good portion, which shall not be taken away from her."

146. THE LORD'S PRAYER.
Luke 11:1–4

Matt. 6:9–13 (§ 30, p. 25)	Luke 11:1–4
	1 He was praying in a certain place, and when he ceased, one of his disciples said to him, "Lord, teach us to pray, as John taught his disciples." 2 And he said to them, "When you pray, say:
9 "Pray then like this: Our Father who art in heaven. Hallowed be thy name.	Father,s hallowed be thy name. Thy kingdom come.
10 Thy kingdom come, Thy will be done, On earth as it is in heaven.	
11 Give us this day our daily bread,t	3 Give us each day our daily bread;t
12 And forgive us our debts, As we also have forgiven our debtors;	4 and forgive us our sins for we ourselves forgive everyone who is indebted to us;
13 And lead us not into temptation, But deliver us from evil." u v	and lead us not into temptation."

q The denarius was a day's wage for a laborer. r text: P45 P75 A C W Θ φ ℜ vg syc syp sa; *few things are needful, or only one:* P3 S B λ bo; omit, *you are anxious . . . needful:* it sys. s text: P75 S B λ vg sys Marcion, Origen; *Our Father who art in heaven:* A C D W Θ φ ℜ it syc syp sa bo. Cf. also Matthew 6:9. t Or, *our bread for the morrow.* u Or, *the evil one.* v text: S B D λ it vg bo; add, *for thine is the kingdom and the power and the glory, for ever. Amen:* W Θ φ ℜ syp; add, *for thine is the power and the glory for ever. Amen:* sa (Didache omit *Amen*); add, *for thine is the kingdom and the glory for ever. Amen:* syc.

To § 145 cf. John 11:1ff—Now a certain man was ill, Lazarus of Bethany, the village of Mary and her sister Martha.

147. THE FRIEND AT MIDNIGHT.
Luke 11:5–8

5 And he said to them, "Which of you who has a friend will go to him at midnight and say to him, 'Friend, lend me three loaves; 6 for a friend of mine has arrived on a journey, and I have nothing to set before him'; 7 and he will answer from within, 'Do not bother me; the door is now shut, and my children are with me in bed; I cannot get up and give you anything'? 8 I tell you, though he will not get up and give him anything because he is his friend, yet because of his importunity he will rise and give him whatever he needs.

148. THE ANSWER TO PRAYER.

Matt. 7:7–11 (§ 38, p. 29):	Luke 11:9–13
7 "Ask, and it will be given you; seek, and you will find; knock, and it will be opened to you. 8 For every one who asks receives, and he who seeks finds, and to him who knocks it will be opened. 9 Or what man of you, if his son asks him for bread, will give him a stone? 10 Or if he asks for a fish, will give him a serpent?	9 "And I tell you, Ask, and it will be given you; seek, and you will find; knock, and it will be opened to you. 10 For every one who asks receives, and he who seeks finds, and to him who knocks it will be opened. 11 What father among you, if his son asks for[w] a fish, will instead of a fish give him a serpent; 12 or if he asks for an egg, will give him a scorpion? 13 If you then,
11 If you then, who are evil, know how to give good gifts to your children, how much more will your Father who is in heaven give good things to those who ask him!"	who are evil, know how to give good gifts to your children, how much more will the heavenly Father give the Holy Spirit to those who ask him!"

149. THE BEELZEBUL CONTROVERSY.

Matt. 12:22–30 (§ 85, p. 61):	Mark 3:22–27 (§ 85, p. 61):	Luke 11:14–23
22 Then a blind and dumb demoniac was brought to him, and he healed him, so that the dumb man spoke and saw. 23 And all the people were amazed, and said, "Can this be the Son of David?" 24 But when the Pharisees heard it they said, 'It is only by Beelzebul, the prince of demons, that this man casts out demons." *	22 And the scribes who came down from Jerusalem said, "He is possessed by Beelzebul, and by the prince of demons he casts out the demons." *	14 Now he was casting out a demon that was dumb; when the demon had gone out, the dumb man spoke, and the people marveled.
		15 But some of them said, "He casts out demons by Beelzebul, the prince of demons"; *
		16 while others, to test him, sought from him a sign from heaven.**

* Matt. 9:32-34 (§ 57, p.39): 32 As they were going away, behold, a dumb demoniac was brought to him. 33 And when the demon had been cast out, the dumb man spoke; and the crowds marveled, saying, "Never was anything like this seen in Israel." 34 But the Pharisees said, "He casts out demons by the prince of demons."
** Cf. Matt. 12:38 (§ 87, p.63) and Matt. 16:1 = Mark 8:11 (§ 119, p. 86): see below Luke 11:29 (§ 151, p.108).

[w] text: P⁴⁵ P⁷⁵ B syˢ sa; add, *bread, will give him a stone; or if he asks for:* S A C D W Θ λ φ ℜ it vg syᶜ syᵖ bo.

25 Knowing their thoughts, he said to them,

"Every kingdom divided against itself
is laid waste, and no city or house divided against itself will stand;
26 and if Satan casts out Satan, he is divided against himself; how then will his kingdom stand? **27** And if I cast out demons by Beelzebul, by whom do your sons cast them out? Therefore they shall be your judges. **28** But if it is by the Spirit of God that I cast out demons, then the kingdom of God has come upon you.

29 "Or how can one enter a strong man's house and plunder his goods, unless he first binds the strong man? Then indeed he may plunder his house.

30 He who is not with me is against me, and he who does not gather with me scatters."

---

23 And he called them to him, and said to them in parables, "How can Satan cast out Satan? **24** If a kingdom is divided against itself, that kingdom cannot stand. **25** And if a house is divided against itself, that house will not be able to stand. **26** And if Satan has risen up against himself and is divided, he cannot stand, but is coming to an end.

27 "But no one can enter a strong man's house and plunder his goods, unless he first binds the strong man; then indeed he may plunder his house."

Cf. 9:40 = Luke 9:50 (§ 130, p. 96)

---

17 But he, knowing their thoughts, said to them,

"Every kingdom divided against itself
is laid waste, and a divided household falls."

18 And if Satan also is divided against himself, how will his kingdom stand? For you say that I cast out demons by Beelzebul. **19** And if I cast out demons by Beelzebul, by whom do your sons cast them out? Therefore they shall be your judges. **20** But if it is by the finger of God that I cast out demons, then the kingdom of God has come upon you.

21 "When a strong man, fully armed, guards his own palace, his goods are in peace; **22** but when one stronger than he assails him and overcomes him, he takes away his armor in which he trusted, and divides his spoil. **23** He who is not with me is against me, and he who does not gather with me scatters."

---

150. THE RETURN OF THE EVIL SPIRIT.

Matt. 12:43–45 (§ 88, p. 64):

43 "When the unclean spirit has gone out of a man, he passes through waterless places seeking rest, but he finds none. **44** Then he says, 'I will return to my house from which I came.' And when he comes he finds it empty, swept, and put in order. **45** Then he goes and brings with him seven other spirits more evil than himself, and they enter and dwell there; and the last state of that man becomes worse than the first. So shall it be also with this evil generation."

Luke 11:24–26

24 "When the unclean spirit has gone out of a man, he passes through waterless places seeking rest; and finding none he says, 'I will return to my house from which I came.' **25** And when he comes he finds it swept and put in order. **26** Then he goes and brings seven other spirits more evil than himself, and they enter and dwell there; and the last state of that man becomes worse than the first."

151. THE BLESSEDNESS OF JESUS' MOTHER.
Luke 11:27–28

27 As he said this, a woman in the crowd raised her voice and said to him, "Blessed is the womb that bore you, and the breasts that you sucked!" 28 But he said, "Blessed rather are those who hear the word of God and keep it!"

152. THE SIGN FOR THIS GENERATION.

Matt. 12:38–42 (§ 87, p. 63):

38 Then some of the scribes and Pharisees said to him, "Teacher, we wish to see a sign from you." 39 But he answered them, "An evil and adulterous generation seeks for a sign; but no sign shall be given to it except the sign of the prophet Jonah.* 40 For as Jonah was three days and three nights in the belly of the whale, so will the Son of man be three days and three nights in the heart of the earth.

42 The queen of the South will arise at the judgment with this generation and condemn it; for she came from the ends of the earth to hear the wisdom of Solomon, and behold, something greater than Solomon is here. 41 The men of Nineveh will arise at the judgment with this generation and condemn it; for they repented at the preaching of Jonah, and behold, something greater than Jonah is here."

Luke 11:29–32

29 When the crowds were increasing, he began to say,
Cf. 11:16
"This generation is an evil generation; it seeks a sign, but no sign shall be given to it except the sign of Jonah.* 30 For as Jonah became a sign to the men of Nineveh,
so will the Son of man be to this generation.

31 The queen of the South will arise at the judgment with the men of this generation and condemn them; for she came from the ends of the earth to hear the wisdom of Solomon, and behold, something greater than Solomon is here. 32 The men of Nineveh will arise at the judgment with this generation and condemn it; for they repented at the preaching of Jonah, and behold, something greater than Jonah is here.

153. CONCERNING LIGHT.

Matt. 5:15 (§ 20, p. 21):

15 "Nor do men light a lamp and put it under a bushel, but on a stand, and it gives light to all in the house." **

Luke 11:33–36

33 "No one after lighting a lamp puts it in a cellar or under a bushel, but on a stand, that those who enter may see the light.**

---

* Matt. 16:1, 2, 4 (§ 119, p.86): 1 And the Pharisees and Sadducees came, and to test him they asked him to show them a sign from heaven. 2 He answered them, "When it is evening, you say, 'It will be fair weather; for the sky is red.' 4 An evil and adulterous generation seeks for a sign, but no sign shall be given to it except the sign of Jonah." So he left them and departed.

** Cf. also Mark 4:21 = Luke 8:16 (§ 94, p.67).

Luke 11:31—I Kings 10:1ff.   11:32—Jonah 3:5.

Mark 8:11, 12 (§ 119, p.86): 11 The Pharisees came and began to argue with him, seeking from him a sign from heaven, to test him. 12 And he sighed deeply in his spirit, and said, "Why does this generation seek for a sign? Truly, I say to you, no sign shall be given to this generation."

6:22–23 (§ 33, p. 26): 22 "The eye is the lamp of the body. So, if your eye is sound, your whole body will be full of light; 23 but if your eye is not sound, your whole body will be full of darkness. If then the light in you is darkness, how great is the darkness!"

34 Your eye is the lamp of your body; when your eye is sound, your whole body is full of light; but when it is not sound, your body is full of darkness. 35 Therefore be careful lest the light in you be darkness. 36 If then your whole body is full of light, having no part dark, it will be wholly bright, as when a lamp with its rays gives you light."

154. DISCOURSE AGAINST THE PHARISEES.

Matt. 23 (§ 210, p. 148 ff).

25 "Woe to you, scribes and Pharisees, hypocrites! for you cleanse the outside of the cup and of the plate, but inside they are full of extortion and rapacity. 26 You blind Pharisee! first cleanse the inside of the cup and of the plate, that the outside also may be clean.

23 "Woe to you, scribes and Pharisees, hypocrites! for you tithe mint and dill and cummin, and have neglected the weightier matters of the law, justice and mercy and faith: these you ought to have done, without neglecting the others. 6 And they love the place of honor at feasts and the best seats in the synagogues, 7 and salutations in the market places,** and being called rabbi by men.

Luke 11:37–12:1

37 While he was speaking, a Pharisee asked him to dine with him; so he went in and sat at table. 38 The Pharisee was astonished to see that he did not first wash before dinner.* 39 And the Lord said to him, "Now you Pharisees cleanse the outside of the cup and of the dish, but inside you are full of extortion and wickedness. 40 You fools! Did not he who made the outside make the inside also? 41 But give for alms those things which are within; and behold, everything is clean for you.

42 "But woe to you Pharisees! for you tithe mint and rue and every herb, and neglect justice and the love of God, these you ought to have done, without neglecting the others. 43 Woe to you Pharisees! for you love the best seat in the synagogue and salutations in the market places.**

---

* Cf. Matt. 15:1ff. = Mark 7:1ff. (§ 115, p.82).
** Mark 12:38-39 (§ 210, p.148-149): 38 And in his teaching he said, "Beware of the scribes, who like to go about in long robes, and to have salutations in the market places 39 and the best seats in the synagogues and the places of honor at feasts."

Luke 11:42 (= Matt. 23:23)—Micah 6:8.

Luke 20:46 (§ 210, p.149): "Beware of the scribes, who like to go about in long robes, and love salutations in the market places and the best seats in the synagogues and the places of honor at feasts."

27 "Woe to you, scribes and Pharisees, hypocrites! for you are like white-washed tombs, which outwardly appear beautiful, but within they are full of dead men's bones and all uncleanness.

4 They bind heavy burdens, hard to bear,[z] and lay them on men's shoulders; but they themselves will not move them with their finger.

29 "Woe to you, scribes and Pharisees, hypocrites! for you build the tombs of the prophets and adorn the monuments of the righteous, 30 saying, 'If we had lived in the days of our fathers, we would not have taken part with them in shedding the blood of the prophets.' 31 Thus you witness against yourselves, that you are sons of those who murdered the prophets.

34 "Therefore I send you prophets and wise men and scribes, some of whom you will kill and crucify, and some you will scourge in your synagogues and persecute from town to town, 35 that upon you may come all the righteous blood shed on earth,

from the blood of innocent Abel to the blood of Zechariah the son of Barachiah, whom you murdered between the sanctuary and the altar. 36 Truly, I say to you, all this will come upon this generation.

13 "But woe to you, scribes and Pharisees, hypocrites! because you shut the kingdom of heaven against men; for you neither enter yourselves, nor allow those who would enter to go in."

Cf. 16:6, 12 (§ 120, p. 87)

44 "Woe to you! for you are like graves which are not seen, and men walk over them without knowing it."

45 One of the lawyers answered him, "Teacher, in saying this you reproach us also." 46 And he said, "Woe to you lawyers also! for you load men with burdens hard to bear, and you yourselves do not touch the burdens with one of your fingers. 47 Woe to you! for you build the tombs of the prophets whom your fathers killed. 48 So you are witnesses and consent to the deeds of your fathers; for they killed them, and you build their tombs.

49 "Therefore also the Wisdom of God said, 'I will send them prophets and apostles, some of whom they will kill and persecute,'

50 that the blood of all the prophets, shed from the foundation of the world, may be required of this generation, 51 from the blood of Abel to the blood of Zechariah, who perished between the altar and the sanctuary. Yes, I tell you, it shall be required of this generation.

52 "Woe to you lawyers!
     for you have taken away the key of knowledge;   you did not enter yourselves, and you hindered those who were entering."

53 As he went away from there, the scribes and the Pharisees began to press him hard, and to provoke him to speak of many things, 54 lying in wait for him, to catch at something he might say.

12:1 In the meantime, when so many thousands of the multitude had gathered together that they trod upon one another, he began to say to his disciples first, "Beware of the leaven of the Pharisees, which is hypocrisy.

Cf. 8:15 (§120, p. 87)

Luke 11:50-51 (= Matt. 23:35)—Gen. 4:8, II Chronicles 24:20-21.

[z] text: B W Θ φ 𝕽 it (some MSS.) vg sa; omit, *hard to bear:* S λ it (some MSS.) sy^c sy^s sy^p bo; *not hard to bear:* D.

To Luke 11:49 cf. Origen, *Homily on Jeremiah 14:5*—In the gospel it is written, And wisdom will send forth her children. Cf. also Tertullian, *Against Marcion IV.31*—And here it begins: And I have sent to you all my servants the prophets.

To Luke 11:52 (= Matt. 23:13) cf. **Gospel of Thomas, Logion 39.**

155. EXHORTATION TO FEARLESS CONFESSION.

Matt. 10:26–33 (§ 60, pp. 44–45)

26 "So have no fear of them; for nothing **is** covered that will not be revealed, or hidden that will not be known.* 27 What I tell you in the dark, utter in the light; and what you hear whispered, proclaim upon the housetops.

28 "And do not fear those who kill the body but cannot kill the soul;

rather fear him who can destroy both soul and body in hell.[a]

29 Are not two sparrows sold for a penny? And not one of them will fall to the ground without your Father's will. 30 But even the hairs of your head are all numbered. 31 Fear not, therefore; you are of more value than many sparrows. 32 So every one who acknowledges me before men, I also will acknowledge before my Father who is in heaven; 33 but whoever denies me before men, I also will deny before my Father who is in heaven."**

12:32 (§ 86, p. 62): "And whoever says a word against the Son of man will be forgiven; but whoever speaks against the Holy Spirit will not be forgiven, either in this age or in the age to come."***

Luke 12:2–12

2 "Nothing is covered up that will not be revealed, or hidden that will not be known.* 3 Therefore whatever you have said in the dark shall be heard in the light, and what you have whispered in private rooms shall be proclaimed upon the housetops. 4 I tell you, my friends, do not fear those who kill the body, and after that have no more that they can do. 5 But I will warn you whom to fear: fear him who, after he has killed, has power to cast into hell:[a] yes, I tell you, fear him! 6 Are not five sparrows sold for two pennies? And not one of them is forgotten before God.

7 Why even the hairs of your head are all numbered. Fear not; you are of more value than many sparrows. 8 And I tell you, every one who acknowledges me before men, the Son of man also will acknowledge before the angels of God; 9 but he who denies me before men will be denied before the angels of God.** 10 And every one who speaks a word against the Son of man will be forgiven; but he who blasphemes against the Holy Spirit will not be forgiven.***

---

* Mark 4:22 (§ 94, p.68): "For there is nothing hid, except to be made manifest; nor is anything secret, except to come to light."

** Mark 8:38 (§ 123, p.90):   "For whoever is ashamed of me and of my words in this adulterous and sinful generation, of him will the Son of man also be ashamed, when he comes in the glory of his Father with the holy angels."

Luke 8:17 (§ 94, p.68): "For nothing is hid that shall not be made manifest, nor anything secret that shall not be known and come to light."

Luke 9:26 (§ 123, p.90): "For whoever is ashamed of me and of my words, of him will the Son of man be ashamed when he comes in his glory and the glory of the Father and of the holy angels."

*** Mark 3:28, 29 (§ 86, p.62): 28 "Truly, I say to you, all sins will be forgiven the sons of men, and whatever blasphemies they utter; 29 but whoever blasphemes against the Holy Spirit never has forgiveness, but is guilty of an eternal sin."

---

[a] Greek, *Gehenna.*

To Luke 12:2 cf. *Oxyrhynchus Papyrus 654, Logion 4:*—Jesus said, "Everything that is not before you, and what is hid from you will be revealed to you. For there is nothing hid which will not be revealed; nor buried, which will not be raised." Cf **Gospel of Thomas, Logia 5 and 6.**

10:19–20 (§ *59, p. 43*): "When they deliver you up,

do not be anxious how

you are to speak or what you are to say; for what you are to say will be given to you in that hour; 20 for it is not you who speak, but the Spirit of your Father speaking through you." *

11 "And when they bring you before the synagogues and the rulers and the authorities, do not be anxious how or what you are to answer or what you are to say;

12 for the Holy Spirit will teach you in that very hour what you ought to say." *

156. THE PARABLE OF THE RICH FOOL.

Luke 12:13–21

13 One of the multitude said to him, "Teacher, bid my brother divide the inheritance with me." 14 But he said to him, "Man, who made me a judge or divider over you?" 15 And he said to them, "Take heed, and beware of all covetousness; for a man's life does not consist in the abundance of his possessions." 16 And he told them a parable, saying, "The land of a rich man brought forth plentifully; 17 and he thought to himself, 'What shall I do, for I have nowhere to store my crops?' 18 And he said, 'I will do this: I will pull down my barns, and build larger ones; and there I will store all my grain and my goods. 19 And I will say to my soul, Soul, you have ample goods laid up for many years; take your ease, eat, drink, be merry.' 20 But God said to him, 'Fool! This night your soul is required of you; and the things you have prepared, whose will they be?' 21 So is he who lays up treasure for himself, and is not rich toward God."

157. CARES ABOUT EARTHLY THINGS.

Matt. 6:25–33 (§ *35, pp. 27–28*):

25 "Therefore I tell you, do not be anxious about your life, what you shall eat or what you shall drink,bb nor about your body, what you shall put on. Is not life more than food, and the body more than clothing? 26 Look at the birds of the air: they neither sow nor reap nor gather into barns, and yet your heavenly Father feeds them. Are you not of more value than they? 27 And which of you by being anxious can add one cubit to his span of life?b

Luke 12:22–34

22 And he said to his disciples, "Therefore I tell you, do not be anxious about your life, what you shall eat, nor about your body, what you shall put on. 23 For life is more than food, and the body more than clothing. 24 Consider the ravens: they neither sow nor reap, they have neither storehouse nor barn, and yet God feeds them. Of how much more value are you than the birds? 25 And which of you by being anxious can add a cubit to his span of life?b

* Mark 13:11 (§ *215, p.154*): "And when they bring you to trial and deliver you up, do not be anxious beforehand what you are to say; but say whatever is given you in that hour, for it is not you who speak, but the Holy Spirit."

Luke 21:14–15 (§ *215, p.154*): 14 "Settle it therefore in your minds, not to meditate beforehand how to answer; 15 for I will give you a mouth and wisdom, which none of your adversaries will be able to withstand or contradict."

b Or, *to his stature.*   bb text: B W φ it (some MSS.) sa (some MSS.) bo; *what you shall eat and what you shall drink:* Θ 𝔐 syᵖ; omit, *or what you shall drink:* S λ it (some MSS.) vg syᶜ sa (some MSS.).

To Luke 12:12 cf. John 14:26—"The Counselor, the Holy Spirit, whom the Father will send in my name, he will teach you all things, and bring to your remembrance all that I have said to you."

28 And why are you anxious about clothing?

Consider the lilies of the field, how they grow; they neither toil nor spin; 29 yet I tell you, even Solomon in all his glory was not arrayed like one of these. 30 But if God so clothes the grass of the field, which today is alive and tomorrow is thrown into the oven, will he not much more clothe you, O men of little faith? 31 Therefore do not be anxious, saying, 'What shall we eat?' or 'What shall be drink?' or 'What shall we wear?' 32 For the Gentiles seek all these things; and your heavenly Father knows that you need them all. 33 But seek first his kingdom and his righteousness, and all these things shall be yours as well.

6:19–21 (§ 32, p. 26):

19 "Do not lay up for yourselves treasures on earth, where moth and rust[e] consume and where thieves break in and steal, 20 but lay up for yourselves treasures in heaven, where neither moth nor rust[e] consumes and where thieves do not break in and steal; 21 for where your treasure is, there will your heart be also."

Cf. Mark 13:32f. (p. 158)

26 If then you are not able to do as small a thing as that, why are you anxious about the rest? 27 Consider the lilies, how they grow; they neither toil nor spin,[c] yet I tell you, even Solomon in all his glory was not arrayed like one of these. 28 But if God so clothes the grass which is alive in the field today and tomorrow is thrown into the oven, how much more will he clothe you, O men of little faith! 29 And do not seek what you are to eat and what you are to drink, nor be of anxious mind. 30 For all the nations of the world seek these things; and your Father knows that you need them. 31 Instead, seek his[d] kingdom, and these things shall be yours as well. 32 Fear not, little flock, for it is your Father's good pleasure to give you the kingdom.

33 "Sell your possessions, and give alms; provide yourselves with purses that do not grow old, with a treasure in the heavens that does not fail, where no thief approaches and no moth destroys.

34 For where your treasure is, there will your heart be also."

158. WATCHFULNESS AND FAITHFULNESS.

Matt. 24:43–51 (§ 225–226, pp. 159–160)

Cf. 25:1–13 (§ 227, p. 160)

Luke 12:35–46

35 "Let your loins be girded and your lamps burning, 36 and be like men who are waiting for their master to come home from the marriage feast, so that they may open to him at once when he comes and knocks. 37 Blessed are those servants whom the master finds awake when he comes; truly, I say to you, he will gird himself and have them sit at table, and he will come and serve them. 38 If he comes in the second watch, or in the third, and finds them so, blessed are those servants!

---

[c] text: P45 P75 S A B W Θ λ φ ℜ it (some MSS.) vg sy[p] sa bo; *lilies, how they neither spin nor weave:* D sy[c] sy[s]; *how they grow; they neither toil nor spin nor weave:* it (some MSS.). [d] text: S B D sa bo; *God's:* P45 A W Θ λ φ ℜ it vg sy[c] sy[s] sy[p]; *the kingdom:* P75. [e] Or, *worm.*

To Luke 12:37 cf. John 13:4-5—Jesus . . .[4] rose from supper, laid aside his garments, and girded himself with a towel.[5] Then he poured water into a basin, and began to wash the disciples' feet, and to wipe them with the towel with which he was girded.

43 "But know this, that if the house-holder had known in what part of the night the thief was coming, he would have watched and would not have let his house be broken into. 44 Therefore you also must be ready; for the Son of man is coming at an hour you do not expect.*

45 "Who then is the faithful and wise servant, whom his master has set over his household, to give them their   food at the proper time? 46 Blessed is that servant whom his master when he comes will find so doing. 47 Truly, I say to you, he will set him over all his possessions. 48 But if that wicked servant says to himself, 'My master is delayed,'   49 and begins to beat his fellow servants,
and eats and drinks with the drunken, 50 the master of that servant will come on a day when he does not expect him and at an hour he does not know, 51 and will punishᵍ him, and put him with the hypocrites; there men will weep and gnash their teeth."

39 "But know this, that if the house-holder had known at what hour the thief was coming, heᶠ would not have left his house to be broken into.   40 You also must be ready; for the Son of man is coming at an unexpected hour." *
41 Peter said, "Lord, are you telling this parable for us or for all?" 42 And the Lord said, "Who then is the faithful and wise steward, whom his master will set over his household, to give them their portion of food at the proper time? 43 Blessed is that servant whom his master when he comes will find so doing. 44 Truly, I say to you, he will set him over all his possessions. 45 But if that servant says to himself, 'My master is delayed in coming,' and begins to beat the menservants and the maidservants, and to eat and drink and get drunk, 46 the master of that servant will come on a day when he does not expect him and at an hour he does not know, and will punish ᵍ him, and put him with the un-faithful.

159. THE SERVANT'S WAGES.
Luke 12:47–48
Cf. Luke 17:7–10 (§ 181, p. 125)

47 "And that servant who knew his master's will, but did not make ready or act according to his will, shall receive a severe beating. 48 But he who did not know, and did what deserved a beating, shall receive a light beating. Every one to whom much is given, of him will much be required; and of him to whom men commit much they will demand the more.

---

* Mark 13:35-36 (§ 222, p.158): ³⁵ "Watch therefore—for you do not know when the master of the house will come, in the evening, or at midnight, or at cockcrow, or in the morning—³⁶ lest he come suddenly and find you asleep."

ᶠ text: P⁷⁵ S D syᶜ syˢ sa; add, *would have watched and:* A B W Θ λ φ ℜ it vg syᵖ bo.   ᵍ Or, *cut him in pieces.*

160. INTERPRETING THE PRESENT TIME.

Matt. 10:34–36 (§ *61, p. 45*):

34 "Do not think that I have come to bring peace on earth; I have not come to bring peace, but a sword.

35 "For I have come to set a man against his father, and a daughter against her mother, and a daughter-in-law against her mother-in-law; 36 and a man's foes will be those of his own household."

16:2–3 (§ *119, p. 86*): 2 He answered them,[h] "When it is evening, you say, 'It will be fair weather; for the sky is red. 3 And in the morning, 'It will be stormy today, for the sky is red and threatening.'

You know how to interpret the appearance of the sky, but you cannot interpret the signs of the times."

Luke 12:49–56

49 "I came to cast fire upon the earth; and would that it were already kindled! 50 I have a baptism to be baptized with; and how I am constrained until it is accomplished! * 51 Do you think that I have come to give peace on earth? No, I tell you, but rather division; 52 for henceforth in one house there will be five divided, three against two and two against three; 53 they will be divided, father against son and son against father, mother against daughter and daughter against her mother, mother-in-law against her daughter-in-law and daughter-in-law against her mother-in-law."

54 He also said to the multitudes, "When you see a cloud rising in the west, you say at once, 'A shower is coming'; and so it happens. 55 And when you see the south wind blowing, you say, 'There will be scorching heat'; and it happens. 56 You hypocrites! You know how to interpret the appearance of earth and sky; but why do you not know how to interpret the present time?

161. AGREEMENT WITH ONE'S ACCUSER.

Matt. 5:25–26 (§ *22, p. 22*):

25 "Make friends quickly with your accuser,
while you are going with him to court, lest your accuser hand you over to the judge, and the judge to the guard, and you be put in prison;
26 truly, I say to you, you will never get out till you have paid the last penny."

Luke 12:57–59

57 "And why do you not judge for yourselves what is right? 58 As you go with your accuser before the magistrate, make an effort to settle with him on the way, lest he drag you to the judge, and the judge hand you over to the officer, and the officer put you in prison.
59 I tell you, you will never get out till you have paid the very last copper."

* Mark 10:38 (§ 192, p.133): "Are you able to drink the cup that I drink, or to be baptized with the baptism with which I am baptized?"

Luke 12:53 (= Matt. 10:35)—Micah 7:6.

[h] text: C D W Θ λ ℵ it vg sy^p bo (some MSS.); omit from here to end of v. 3: S B φ sy^c sy^s sa bo (some MSS.).

To Luke 12:50 cf. John 12:27—"Now is my soul troubled. And what shall I say? 'Father, save me from this hour'? No, for this purpose I have come to this hour."

To Luke 12:49 cf. Didymus on Psalm 89:7 and Origen, *Homily on Jeremiah, 3:3*—So the Savior speaks: "He who is near me is near the fire; and he who is far from me is far from the kingdom."

162. REPENTANCE OR DESTRUCTION.

Luke 13:1–9

1 There were some present at that very time who told him of the Galileans whose blood Pilate had mingled with their sacrifices. 2 And he answered them, "Do you think that these Galileans were worse sinners than all the other Galileans, because they suffered thus? 3 I tell you, No; but unless you repent you will all likewise perish. 4 Or those eighteen upon whom the tower in Siloam fell and killed them, do you think that they were worse offenders than all the others who dwelt in Jerusalem? 5 I tell you, No; but unless you repent you will all likewise perish."

6 And he told this parable: "A man had a fig tree planted in his vineyard; and he came seeking fruit on it and found none. 7 And he said to the vinedresser, 'Lo, these three years I have come seeking fruit on this fig tree, and I find none. Cut it down; why should it use up the ground?' 8 And he answered him, 'Let it alone, sir, this year also, till I dig about it and put on manure. 9 And if it bears fruit next year, well and good; but if not, you can cut it down.' "

163. THE HEALING OF THE WOMAN WITH A SPIRIT OF INFIRMITY.

Luke 13:10–17

Cf. Luke 14:1–6 (§ 168, p. 119)

10 Now he was teaching in one of the synagogues on the sabbath. 11 And there was a woman who had had a spirit of infirmity for eighteen years; she was bent over and could not fully straighten herself. 12 And when Jesus saw her, he called her and said to her, "Woman, you are freed from your infirmity." 13 And he laid his hands upon her, and immediately she was made straight, and she praised God. 14 But the ruler of the synagogue, indignant because Jesus had healed on the sabbath, said to the people, "There are six days on which work ought to be done; come on those days and be healed, and not on the sabbath day." 15 Then the Lord answered him, "You hypocrites! Does not each of you on the sabbath untie his ox or his ass from the manger, and lead it away to water it? 16 And ought not this woman, a daughter of Abraham whom Satan bound for eighteen years, be loosed from this bond on the sabbath day?" *
17 As he said this, all his adversaries were put to shame; and all the people rejoiced at all the glorious things that were done by him.

---

* Matt. 12:11-12 (§ 70, p.52): He said to them, "What man of you, if he has one sheep and it falls into a pit on the sabbath, will not lay hold of it and lift it out? 12 Of how much more value is a man than a sheep! So it is lawful to do good on the sabbath."

Luke 14:5 (§ 168, p. 119): And he said to them, "Which of you, having a son or an ox that has fallen into a well, will not immediately pull him out on a sabbath day?"

Luke 13:14—Exodus 20:9 and Deuteronomy 5:13.

164. THE PARABLES OF THE MUSTARD SEED AND THE LEAVEN.

Matt. 13:31–33 (§ 97, 98, p.69):	Mark 4:30–32 (§ 97, p. 69):	Luke 13:18–21
31 Another parable he put before them, saying,	30 And he said, "With what can we compare the kingdom of God, or what parable shall we use for it? 31 It is like a grain of mustard seed, which, when sown upon the ground, is the smallest of all the seeds on earth; 32 yet when it is sown it grows up and becomes the greatest of all shrubs, and puts forth large branches, so that the birds of the air can make nests in its shade."	18 He said therefore, "What is the kingdom of God like? And to what shall I compare it? 19 It is like a grain of mustard seed which a man took and sowed in his garden;
"The kingdom of heaven is like a grain of mustard seed which a man took and sowed in his field; 32 it is the smallest of all seeds,		
but when it has grown it is the greatest of shrubs and becomes a tree, so that the birds of the air come and make nests in its branches."		and it grew and became a tree, and the birds of the air made nests in its branches."
33 He told them another parable. "The kingdom of heaven is like leaven which a woman took and hid in three measures of flour, till it was all leavened."		20 And again he said, "To what shall I compare the kingdom of God? 21 It is like leaven which a woman took and hid in three measures of flour, till it was all leavened."

165. EXCLUSION FROM THE KINGDOM.

Matt. 7:13–14 (§ 40, p. 29):	Luke 13:22–30
13 "Enter by the narrow gate; for the gate is wide and the way is easy,[hh] that leads to destruction, and those who enter by it are many. 14 For the gate is narrow and the way is hard, that leads to life, and those who find it are few."	22 He went on his way through towns and villages, teaching, and journeying toward Jerusalem. 23 And some one said to him, "Lord, will those who are saved be few?" And he said to them, 24 "Strive to enter by the narrow door; for many, I tell you, will seek to enter and will not be able.
25:10b–12 (§ 227, p. 160): 10 "And the door was shut. 11 Afterward the other maidens came also, saying, 'Lord, lord, open to us.' 12 But he replied, 'Truly, I say to you, I do not know you.'" 7:22–23 (§ 42, p. 30): 22 "On that day many will say to me,	25 "When once the householder has risen up and shut the door, you will begin to stand outside and to knock at the door, saying, 'Lord, open to us.' He will answer you, 'I do not know where you come from.' 26 Then you will begin to say, 'We ate and drank in your presence, and you taught in our streets.'

Luke 13:19 (= Matt. 13:32 = Mark 4:32)—Daniel 4:21.

[hh] text: B C W Θ λ φ ℜ it (some MSS.) vg syᶜ syᵖ sa bo; *for the way is wide and easy:* S it (some MSS.) Clement, Origen.

'Lord, Lord, did we not pro-phesy in your name, and cast out demons in your name, and do many mighty works in your name?' 28 And then will I de-clare to them, 'I never knew you; depart from me, you evil-doers.' "

8:11–12 (§ 46, p. 33): 11 "I tell you, many will come from east and west and sit at table with Abraham, Isaac, and Jacob in the kingdom of heaven, 12 while the sons of the kingdom will be thrown into the outer darkness; there men will weep and gnash their teeth."

19:30 (§ 189, p. 132): "But many that are first will be last, and the last first."

20:16 (§190, p. 132): "So that the last will be first, and the first last."

10:31 (§ 189, p. 132): "But many that are first will be last, and the last first."

27 "But he will say, 'I tell you. I do not know where you come from; depart from me, all you workers of iniquity.' 28 There you will weep and gnash your teeth, when you see Abra-ham and Isaac and Jacob and all the prophets in the kingdom of God and you yourselves thrust out. 29 And men will come from east and west, and from north and south, and sit at table in the kingdom of God.

30 And behold, some are last who will be first, and some are first who will be last."

166. THE DEPARTURE FROM GALILEE.
Luke 13:31–33

31 At that very hour some Pharisees came, and said to him, "Get away from here, for Herod wants to kill you." 32 And he said to them, "Go and tell that fox. 'Behold, I cast out demons and perform cures today and tomorrow, and the third day I finish my course. 33 Nevertheless I must go on my way today and tomorrow and the day fol-lowing; for it cannot be that a prophet should perish away from Jerusalem.'

167. THE LAMENT OVER JERUSALEM.

Matt. 23:37–39 (§ 211, p. 152)

37 "O Jerusalem, Jerusalem, killing the prophets and stoning those who are sent to you! How often would I have gathered your children together as a hen gathers her brood under her wings, and you would not! 38 Behold, your house is forsaken and desolate.[i] 39 For I tell you, you will not see me again, until you say, 'Blessed is he who comes in the name of the Lord.' "

Luke 13:34–35

34, "O Jerusalem, Jerusalem, killing the pro-phets and stoning those who are sent to you! How often would I have gathered your children together as a hen gathers her brood under her wings, and you would not! 35 Behold, your house is forsaken.   And I tell you, you will not see me until you say, 'Blessed is he who comes in the name of the Lord.' "

Luke 13:27 (= Matt. 7:23)—Psalm 6:8. Luke 13:29 (= Matt. 8:11)—Psalm 107:3. Luke 13:34 (= Matt. 23:37)—Isaiah 31:5. Luke 13:35 (= Matt. 23:29)—Psalm 118:26.

[i] text: S C D W Θ λ φ 𝕽 it vg syᵖ bo (some MSS.); cf. Jeremiah 22:5; omit, *and desolate:* B syˢ sa bo (some MSS.). (Cf. Luke, *and desolate:* D Θ φ 𝕽 it vg syᶜ syᵖ.)

168. THE HEALING OF A MAN WITH DROPSY. *
Luke 14:1-6

1 One sabbath when he went to dine at the house of a ruler who belonged to the Pharisees, they were watching him. 2 And behold, there was a man before him who had dropsy. 3 And Jesus spoke to the lawyers and Pharisees, saying, "Is it lawful to heal on the sabbath, or not?" 4 But they were silent. Then he took him and healed him, and let him go. 5 And he said to them, "Which of you, having a son[ii] or an ox that has fallen into a well, will not immediately pull him out on a sabbath day?" 6 And they could not reply to this.

169. TEACHING ON HUMILITY.
Luke 14:7-14

7 Now he told a parable to those who were invited, when he marked how they chose the places of honor, saying to them, 8 "When you are invited by any one to a marriage feast, do not sit down in a place of honor, lest a more eminent man than you be invited by him; 9 and he who invited you both will come and say to you, 'Give place to this man,' and then you will begin with shame to take the lowest place. 10 But when you are invited, go and sit in the lowest place, so that when your host comes he may say to you, 'Friend, go up higher'; then you will be honored in the presence of all who sit at table with you. 11 For every one who exalts himself will be humbled, and he who humbles himself will be exalted." ** 12 He said also to the man who had invited him, "When you give a dinner or a banquet, do not invite your friends or your brothers or your kinsmen or rich neighbors, lest they also invite you in return, and you be repaid. 13 But when you give a feast, invite the poor, the maimed, the lame, the blind, 14 and you will be blessed, because they cannot repay you. You will be repaid at the resurrection of the just."

170. THE PARABLE OF THE GREAT SUPPER.

Matt. 22:1-10 (§ 205, p. 144):	Luke 14:15-24
1 And again Jesus spoke to them in parables, saying,	15 When one of those who sat at table with him heard this, he said to him, "Blessed is he who shall eat bread in the kingdom of God!" 16 But he said to him,
2 "The kingdom of heaven may be compared to a king who gave a marriage feast for his son,	"A man once gave a great banquet, and invited many;

---

* Cf. § 70, Matt. 12:9-14 = Mark 3:1-6 = Luke 6:6-11, pp. 50-51. Also § 163, p. 116, Luke 13:10-17.
** Cf. Matt. 18:4 (§ 129, p. 95); 23:12 (§ 210, p. 149); Luke 18:14 (§ 186, p. 127).

[ii] text: P45 P75 A B W ℜ (some MSS.) sa; *an ass or an ox*: S λφℜ (some MSS.) it vg bo; *a son or an ox or an ass*: sy^c; *an ass, a son or an ox*: Θ; *an ox or an ass*: sy^s; *a sheep or an ox*: D.

To Luke 14:8 cf. the addition that some MSS. (D it vg sy^c) make at Matt. 20:28—"But seek to increase from the small (insignificant), and to become less from the great. And when you enter, and are asked to dine, do not sit in the prominent places, lest someone grander than you should come in and the host should come and say to you, 'Move further down,' and you be put to shame. But if you sit down in the less conspicuous place and someone less important than you arrives the host will say, 'Come up higher'; and this will be (more—it) to your advantage."

³ and sent his servants to call those who were invited to the marriage feast; but they would not come. ⁴ Again he sent other servants, saying, 'Tell those who are invited, Behold, I have made ready my dinner, my oxen and my fat calves are killed, and everything is ready; come to the marriage feast.' ⁵ But they made light of it and went off, one to his farm, another to his business, ⁶ while the rest seized his servants, treated them shamefully, and killed them.

⁷ "The king was angry, and he sent his troops and destroyed those murderers and burned their city. ⁸ Then he said to his servants, 'The wedding is ready, but those invited were not worthy. ⁹ Go therefore to the thoroughfares, and invite to the marriage feast as many as you find.' ¹⁰ And those servants went out into the streets and gathered all whom they found, both bad and good; so the wedding hall was filled with guests."

¹⁷ and at the time for the banquet he sent his servant to say to those who had been invited, 'Come; for all is now ready.' ¹⁸ But they all alike began to make excuses. The first said to him, 'I have bought a field, and I must go out and see it; I pray you, have me excused.' ¹⁹ And another said, 'I have bought five yoke of oxen, and I go to examine them; I pray you, have me excused.' ²⁰ And another said, 'I have married a wife, and therefore I cannot come.' ²¹ So the servant came and reported this to his master. Then the householder in anger

said to his servant, 'Go out quickly to the streets and lanes of the city, and bring in the poor and maimed and blind and lame.' ²² And the servant said, 'Sir, what you commanded has been done, and still there is room.' ²³ And the master said to the servant, 'Go out to the highways and hedges, and compel people to come in, that my house may be filled. ²⁴ For I tell you,ʲ none of those men who were invited shall taste my banquet.' "

171. THE COST OF DISCIPLESHIP.

Matt. 10:37-38 (§ 62, p. 45):

Luke 14:25-35

37 "He who loves father or mother more than me is not worthy of me; and he who loves son or daughter more than me is not worthy of me; ³⁸ and he who does not take his cross and follow me is not worthy of me." *

25 Now great multitudes accompanied him; and he turned and said to them, ²⁶ "If any one comes to me and does not hate his own father and mother and wife and children and brothers and sisters, yes, and even his own life, he cannot be my disciple. 27 Whoever does not bear his own cross and come after me, cannot be my disciple.* ²⁸ For which of you, desiring to build a tower, does not first sit down and count the cost, whether he has enough to complete it? ²⁹ Otherwise, when he has laid a foundation, and is not able to finish, all who see it begin to mock him, ³⁰ saying, 'This man began to build, and was not able to finish.'

* Matt. 16:24 (§ 123, p.90): "If any man would come after me, let him deny himself and take up his cross and follow me."

Mark 8:34 (§ 123, p.90): "If any man would come after me, let him deny himself and take up his cross and follow me."

Luke 9:23 (§ 123, p.90): "If any man would come after me, let him deny himself and take up his cross daily and follow me."

ʲ The Greek word for *you* here is plural.

To Luke 14:26-27 (= Matt. 10:37-38) cf. **Gospel of Thomas, Logia 55 and 101.** For Logion 55 see note to Matt. 10:37-38, p. 45.

31 Or what king, going to encounter another king in war, will not sit down first and take counsel whether he is able with ten thousand to meet him who comes against him with twenty thousand? 32 And if not, while the other is yet a great way off, he sends an embassy and asks terms of peace. 33 So therefore, whoever of you does not renounce all that he has cannot be my disciple.

Cf. Mark 9:50 (§ 132, p. 98)

34 "Salt is good; but if salt has lost its taste, how shall its saltness be restored? 35 It is fit neither for the land nor for the dunghill; men throw it away. He who has ears to hear, let him hear."

To Luke 14:34–35 cf. Matt. 5:13 (§ 20, p. 21)

172. THE LOST SHEEP AND THE LOST COIN.

Luke 15:1–10

To Luke 15:1–2 cf. Matt. 9:10–11 = Mark 2:15–16 = Luke 5:29–30 (§ 53, p. 37)

Matt. 18:12–14 (§ 133, p. 98):

12 "What do you think? If a man has a hundred sheep, and one of them has gone astray, does he not leave the ninety-nine on the mountains and go in search of the one that went astray? 13 And if he finds it, truly, I say to you, he rejoices over it more than over the ninety-nine that never went astray.

14 So it is not the will of my[jj] Father who is in heaven that one of these little ones should perish."

1 Now the tax collectors and sinners were all drawing near to hear him. 2 And the Pharisees and the scribes murmured, saying, "This man receives sinners and eats with them."

3 So he told them this parable: 4 "What man of you, having a hundred sheep, if he has lost one of them, does not leave the ninety-nine in the wilderness, and go after the one which is lost, until he finds it? 5 And when he has found it, he lays it on his shoulders, rejoicing. 6 And when he comes home, he calls together his friends and his neighbors, saying to them, 'Rejoice with me, for I have found my sheep which was lost.' 7 Just so, I tell you, there will be more joy in heaven over one sinner who repents than over ninety-nine righteous persons who need no repentance. 8 Or what woman, having ten silver coins,[k] if she loses one coin, does not light a lamp and sweep the house and seek diligently until she finds it? 9 And when she has found it, she calls together her friends and neighbors, saying, 'Rejoice with me, for I have found the coin which I have lost.' 10 Just so, I tell you, there is joy before the angels of God over one sinner who repents."

[jj] text: B Θ φ sy[s] sa bo; *your:* S W λ ℜ it vg sy[c] sy[p]; *our:* D.   [k] The drachma, rendered here by *silver coin*, was about a day's wage for a laborer.

173. THE PRODIGAL SON.
Luke 15:11–32

11 And he said, "There was a man who had two sons; ¹² and the younger of them said to his father, 'Father, give me the share of property that falls to me." And he divided his living between them. ¹³ Not many days later, the younger son gathered all he had and took his journey into a far country, and there he squandered his property in loose living. ¹⁴ And when he had spent everything, a great famine arose in that country, and he began to be in want. ¹⁵ So he went and joined himself to one of the citizens of that country, who sent him into his fields to feed swine. ¹⁶ And he would gladly have fed on ¹the pods that the swine ate; and no one gave him anything.¹⁷ But when he came to himself he said, 'How many of my father's hired servants have bread enough and to spare, but I perish here with hunger! ¹⁸ I will arise and go to my father, and I will say to him, 'Father, I have sinned against heaven and before you; ¹⁹ I am no longer worthy to be called your son; treat me as one of your hired servants.' ²⁰ And he arose and came to his father. But while he was yet at a distance, his father saw him and had compassion, and ran and embraced him and kissed him. ²¹ And the son said to him, 'Father, I have sinned against heaven and before you; I am no longer worthy to be called your son.' ᵐ ²² But the father said to his servants, 'Bring quickly the best robe, and put it on him; and put a ring on his hand, and shoes on his feet; ²³ and bring the fatted calf and kill it, and let us eat and make merry; ²⁴ for this my son was dead, and is alive again; he was lost, and is found.' And they began to make merry.

25 "Now his elder son was in the field; and as he came and drew near to the house, he heard music and dancing. ²⁶ And he called one of the servants and asked what this meant. ²⁷ And he said to him, 'Your brother has come, and your father has killed the fatted calf, because he has received him safe and sound.' ²⁸ But he was angry and refused to go in. His father came out and entreated him, ²⁹ but he answered his father, 'Lo, these many years I have served you, and I never disobeyed your command; yet you never gave me a kid, that I might make merry with my friends. ³⁰ But when this son of yours came, who has devoured your living with harlots, you killed for him the fatted calf!' ³¹ And he said to him, 'Son, you are always with me, and all that is mine is yours. ³² It was fitting to make merry and be glad, for this your brother was dead, and is alive; he was lost, and is found.' "

174. THE UNJUST STEWARD.
Luke 16:1–13

1 He also said to the disciples, "There was a rich man who had a steward, and charges were brought to him that this man was wasting his goods. ² And he called him and said to him, 'What is this that I hear about you? Turn in the account of your stewardship, for you can no longer be steward.' ³ And the steward said to himself, 'What shall I do, since my master is taking the stewardship away from me? I am not strong enough to dig, and I am ashamed to beg. ⁴ I have decided what to do, so that people may receive me into their houses when I am put out of the stewardship. ⁵ So, summoning his master's debtors one by one, he said to the first, 'How much do you owe my master?' ⁶ He said, 'A hundred measures of oil.' And he said to him, 'Take your bill, and sit down quickly and write fifty.' ⁷ Then he said to another, 'And how much do you owe?' He said, 'A hundred measures of wheat.' He said to him, 'Take your bill, and write eighty.' ⁸ The master commended the dishonest steward for his

---

¹ text: P⁷⁵ S B D λ φ syᶜ sa; *filled his belly with:* A Θ℟ it vg s?ˢ syᵖ bo; *filled his belly and fed on:* W.
ᵐ text: P⁷⁵ A W Θ λ φ ℟ it vg syᶜ syˢ syᵖ sa bo; add, *treat me as one of your hired servants:* S B D.

shrewdness; for the sons of this world [n] are more shrewd in dealing with their own generation than the sons of light. [9] And I tell you, make friends for yourselves by means of unrighteous mammon, [nn] so when it fails they may receive you into the eternal habitations.

[10] "He who is faithful in a very little is faithful also in much; and he who is dishonest in a very little is dishonest also in much. [11] If then you have not been faithful in the unrighteous mammon, [nn] who will entrust to you the true riches? [12] And if you have not been faithful in that which is another's, who will give you that which is your own? [13] No servant can serve two masters; for either he will hate the one and love the other, or he will be devoted to the one and despise the other. You cannot serve God and mammon." [*] [nn]

175. THE HYPOCRISY OF THE PHARISEES.
Luke 16:14–15

[14] The Pharisees, who were lovers of money, heard all this, and they scoffed at him. [15] But he said to them, "You are those who justify yourselves before men, but God knows your hearts; for what is exalted among men is an abomination in the sight of God.

176. ABOUT THE LAW AND ABOUT DIVORCE.

Matt. 11:12–13 (§ 65, p. 48)	Luke 16:16–18
[12] "From the days of John the Baptist until now the kingdom of heaven has suffered violence,[o] and men of violence take it by force. [13] For all the prophets and the law prophesied until John."	[16] "The law and the prophets were until John; since then the good news of the kingdom of God is preached, and every one enters it violently.
5:18 (§ 21, p. 21): "For truly, I say to you, till heaven and earth pass away, not an iota, not a dot, will pass from the law until all is accomplished."	[17] But it is easier for heaven and earth to pass away, than for one dot of the law to become void.
5:32 (§ 24, p. 23): "But I say to you that every one who divorces his wife, except on the ground of unchastity, makes her an adulteress; and whoever marries a divorced woman commits adultery." **	[18] "Every one who divorces his wife and marries another commits adultery, and he who marries a woman divorced from her husband commits adultery.**

---

[*] Matt. 6:24 (§ 34, p.27): "No one can serve two masters; for either he will hate the one and love the other, or he will be devoted to the one and despise the other. You cannot serve God and mammon."

** Cf. Matt. 19:9 = Mark 10:11-12 (§ 187, p.129).

[n] Greek, *age*   [nn] *Mammon* is a Semitic word for money or riches.   [o] Or, *has been coming violently.*

To Luke 16:10-11 cf. II Clement 8:5—For the Lord says in the Gospel, "If you have not taken care of what is small, who will give you what is great? For I tell you, that he who is faithful in a very little, is also faithful in much."

Cf. also Irenaeus, *Against Heresies II.34.3*—Therefore the Lord said to those who were ungrateful to him, "If you have not been faithful in a little, who will give you what is great?"

177. THE RICH MAN AND LAZARUS.
Luke 16:19–31

19 "There was a rich man, who was clothed in purple and fine linen and who feasted sumptuously every day. 20 And at his gate lay a poor man named Lazarus, full of sores, 21 who desired to be fed with what fell from the rich man's table; moreover the dogs came and licked his sores. 22 The poor man died and was carried by the angels to Abraham's bosom. The rich man also died and was buried; 23 and in Hades, being in torment, he lifted up his eyes, and saw Abraham far off and Lazarus in his bosom. 24 And he called out, 'Father Abraham, have mercy upon me, and send Lazarus to dip the end of his finger in water and cool my tongue; for I am in anguish in this flame.' 25 But Abraham said, 'Son, remember that you in your lifetime received your good things, and Lazarus in like manner evil things; but now he is comforted here, and you are in anguish. 26 And besides all this, between us and you a great chasm has been fixed, in order that those who would pass from here to you may not be able, and none may cross from there to us.' 27 And he said, 'Then I beg you, father, to send him to my father's house, 28 for I have five brothers, so that he may warn them, lest they also come into this place of torment.' 29 But Abraham said, 'They have Moses and the prophets; let them hear them.' 30 And he said, 'No, father Abraham; but if some one goes to them from the dead, they will repent.' 31 He said to him, 'If they do not hear Moses and the prophets, neither will they be convinced if some one should rise from the dead.' "

178. ON CAUSING SIN.

Matt. 18:6–7 (§ *131, p. 97*):	Mark 9:42 (§ *131, p. 97*):	Luke 17:1–2
6 "But whoever causes one of these little ones who believe in me to sin, q it would be better for him to have a great millstone fastened round his neck and to be drowned in the depth of the sea. 7Woe to the world for temptations to sin! p For it is necessary that temptations come, but woe to the man by whom the temptation comes!"	"Whoever causes one of these little ones who believe in me to sin,q it would be better for him if a great millstone were hung around his neck and he were thrown into the sea."	1 And he said to his disciples, "Temptations to sin p are sure to come; but woe to him by whom they come! 2 It would be better for him if a millstone were hung around his neck and he were cast into the sea, than that he should cause one of these little ones to sin.q

179. ON FORGIVENESS.

Matt. 18:15 (§ *134, p. 99*):	Luke 17:3–4
"If your brother sins against you, go and tell him his fault, between you and him alone. If he listens to you, you have gained your brother." 18:21–22 (§ *135, p. 99*): 21 Then Peter came up and said to him, "Lord, how often shall my brother sin against me, and I forgive him? As many as seven times?" 22 Jesus said to him, "I do not say to you seven times, but seventy times seven." r	3 "Take heed to yourselves; if your brother sins, rebuke him, and if he repents, forgive him; 4 and if he sins against you seven times in the day, and turns to you seven times, and says, 'I repent,' you must forgive him."

p Greek, *stumbling blocks*   q Greek, *stumble.*   r Or, *seventy-seven times.*

180. ON FAITH.

Matt. 17:20 (§ *126, p. 94*):	Luke 17:5–6
He said to them, "Because of your little faith. For truly, I say to you, if you have faith as a grain of mustard seed, you will say to this mountain, 'Move from here to there,' and it will move; and nothing will be impossible to you." *	5 The apostles said to the Lord, "Increase our faith!" 6 And the Lord said, "If you had faith as a grain of mustard seed, you could say to this sycamine tree, 'Be rooted up, and be planted in the sea,' and it would obey you.*

181. THE SERVANT'S WAGES.
Luke 17:7–10

7 "Will any one of you, who has a servant plowing or keeping sheep, say to him when he has come in from the field, 'Come at once and sit down at table'? 8 Will he not rather say to him, 'Prepare supper for me, and gird yourself and serve me, till I eat and drink; and afterward you shall eat and drink'? 9 Does he thank the servant because he did what was commanded? 10 So you also, when you have done all that is commanded you, say, 'We are unworthy servants: we have only done what was our duty.' "

182. THE HEALING OF TEN LEPERS.
Luke 17:11–19

11 On the way to Jerusalem he was passing along between Samaria and Galilee. 12 And as he entered a village, he was met by ten lepers, who stood at a distance 13 and lifted up their voices and said, "Jesus, Master, have mercy on us." 14 When he saw them he said to them, "Go and show yourselves to the priests." And as they went they were cleansed. 15 Then one of them, when he saw that he was healed, turned back, praising God with a loud voice; 16 and he fell on his face at Jesus' feet, giving him thanks. Now he was a Samaritan. 17 Then said Jesus, "Were not ten cleansed? Where are the nine? 18 Was no one found to return and give praise to God except this foreigner?" 19 And he said to him, "Rise and go your way; your faith has made you well."

183. ON THE KINGDOM OF GOD.
Luke 17:20–21

20 Being asked by the Pharisees when the kingdom of God was coming, he answered them, "The kingdom of God is not coming with signs to be observed; 21 nor will they say, 'Lo, here it is!' or 'There!' for behold, the kingdom of God is in the midst of you." s * *

---

* Matt. 21:21 (§ 201, p.140): And Jesus answered them, "Truly, I say to you, if you have faith and never doubt, you will not only do what has been done to the fig tree, but even if you say to this mountain, 'Be taken up and cast into the sea,' it will be done."

** Matt. 24:23 (§ 217, p.156): "Then if any one says to you, 'Lo, here is the Christ!' or 'There he is!' do not believe it."

Mark 11:22-23 (§ 201, p.140): 22And Jesus answered them, "Have faith in God. 23 Truly, 1 say to you, whoever says to this mountain, 'Be taken up and cast into the sea,' and does not doubt in his heart, but believes that what he says will come to pass, it will be done for him."

Mark 13:21 (§ 217, p.156): "And then if any one says to you, 'Look, here is the Christ!' or 'Look, there he is!' do not believe it."

s Or, *within you.*

To Luke 17:21 cf. *Oxyrhynchus Papyrus 654, Logion 2:* ". . . and the kingdom of heaven is in the midst of you, and whoever knows himself shall find it. . . ." Cf. also **Gospel of Thomas, Logia 3 and 113.**

184. THE DAY OF THE SON OF MAN.

Matt. 24:26–28 (§ *218, p. 156*):

26 "So, if they say to you, 'Lo, he is in the wilderness,' do not go out; if they say, 'Lo, he is in the inner rooms,' do not believe it. 27 For as the lightning comes from the east and shines as far as the west, so will be the coming of the Son of man."

24:37–41 (§ *224, p. 159*): 37 "As were the days of Noah, so will be the coming of the Son of man. 38 For as in those days before the flood they were eating and drinking, marrying and giving in marriage, until the day when Noah entered the ark, 39 and they did not know until the flood came and swept them all away, so will be the coming of the Son of man."

10:39 (§ *62, p. 46*):
"He who finds his life will lose it, and he who loses his life for my sake, will find it."

Luke 17:22–37

22 And he said to the disciples, "The days are coming when you will desire to see one of the days of the Son of man, and you will not see it. 23 And they will say to you, 'Lo, there!' or 'Lo, here!' Do not go, do not follow them. 24 For as the lightning flashes and lights up the sky from one side to the other, so will the Son of Man be in his day[t] 25 But first he must suffer many things and be rejected by this generation. 26 And it was in the days of Noah, so will it be in the days of the Son of man. 27 They ate, they drank, they married, they were given in marriage, until the day when Noah entered the ark, and the flood came and destroyed them all. 28 Likewise as it was in the days of Lot—they ate, they drank, they bought, they sold, they planted, they built, 29 but on the day when Lot went out from Sodom fire and sulphur rained from heaven and destroyed them all— 30 so will it be on the day when the Son of man is revealed. 31 On that day, let him who is on the housetop, with his goods in the house, not come down to take them away; and likewise let him who is in the field not turn back.* 32 Remember Lot's wife. 33 Whoever seeks to gain his life will lose it, but whoever loses his life will preserve it.** 34 I tell you, in that night there will be two in one bed; one will be taken and the other left.

---

* Matt. 24:17-18 (§ 216, p.155): 17 "Let him who is on the housetop not go down to take what is in his house; 18 and let him who is in the field not turn back to take his mantle."

** Matt. 16:25 (§ 123, p.90): "For whoever would save his life will lose it, and whoever loses his life for my sake will find it."

Mark 8:35 (§ 123, p.90): "For whoever would save his life will lose it; and whoever loses his life for my sake and the gospel's will save it."

Mark 13:15-16 (§ 216, p.155): 15 "Let him who is on the housetop not go down, nor enter his house, to take anything away; 16 and let him who is in the field not turn back to take his mantle."

Luke 9:24 (§ 123, p.90): "For whoever would save his life will lose it; and whoever loses his life for my sake, he will save it."

Luke 17:26-27 (= Matt. 24:38)—Genesis 7:7.

[t] text: S A W Θ λ φ 𝕽 it (some MSS.) vg sy^c sy^s sy^p bo; omit, *in his day*: P^75 B D it (some MSS.) sa.

To Luke 17:32-33 cf. Clement of Alexandria, *Excerpts from Theodotus 2. 2:* Because of this the Savior said, "Be saved, you and your soul."

24:40 "Then two men will be in the field; one is taken and one is left. 41 Two women will be grinding at the mill; one is taken and one is left."

24:28 "Wherever the body is, there the eagles ⱽ will be gathered together."

35 There will be two women grinding together; one will be taken and the other left." ᵁ 37 And they said to him, "Where, Lord?" He said to them, "Where the body is, there the eagles ⱽ will be gathered together."

185. THE PARABLE OF THE UNJUST JUDGE.
Luke 18:1–8

1 And he told them a parable, to the effect that they ought always to pray and not lose heart. 2 He said, "In a certain city there was a judge who neither feared God nor regarded man; 3 and there was a widow in that city who kept coming to him and saying, 'Vindicate me against my adversary.' 4 For a while he refused; but afterward he said to himself, 'Though I neither fear God nor regard man, 5 yet because this widow bothers me, I will vindicate her, or she will wear me out by her continual coming.' " 6 And the Lord said, "Hear what the unrighteous judge says. 7 And will not God vindicate his elect, who cry to him day and night? Will he delay long over them? 8 I tell you, he will vindicate them speedily. Nevertheless, when the Son of man comes, will he find faith on earth?"

186. THE PARABLE OF THE PHARISEE AND THE PUBLICAN.
Luke 18:9–14

9 He also told this parable to some who trusted in themselves that they were righteous and despised others: 10 "Two men went up into the temple to pray, one a Pharisee and the other a tax collector. 11 The Pharisee stood and prayed thus with himself, 'God, I thank thee that I am not like other men, extortioners, unjust, adulterers, or even like this tax collector. 12 I fast twice a week, I give tithes of all that I get.' 13 But the tax collector, standing far off, would not even lift up his eyes to heaven, but beat his breast, saying, 'God, be merciful to me a sinner!' 14 I tell you, this man went down to his house justified rather than the other; for every one who exalts himself will be humbled, but he who humbles himself will be exalted." *
(18:15–17, § 188, pp. 129–130)

---

* Cf. Matt. 18:4 (§ 129, p.95); 23:12 (§ 210, p.149); and Luke 14:11 (§ 169, p.119).

ᵁ text: P⁷⁵ S A B W Θ λ ℵ sa bo; add verse 36: *Two men will be in the field; one will be taken and the other left:* D φ it vg syᶜ syˢ syᵖ.   ⱽ Or, *vultures.*

III. THE JUDEAN SECTION

Matthew 19–27 = Mark 10–15 = Luke 18:15–23:56

A. The Journey to Jerusalem

Matthew 19–20 = Mark 10 = Luke 18:15–19:27

187. MARRIAGE AND DIVORCE.

Matt. 19:1–12 *(18:23–35, § 136, p. 100)*

1 Now when Jesus had finished these sayings, he went away from Galilee and entered the region of Judea beyond the Jordan; 2 and large crowds followed him, and he healed them there.

3 And Pharisees came up to him and tested him by asking, "Is it lawful to divorce one's wife for any cause?"

cf. vv. 7–8

4 He answered, "Have you not read that he who made them from the beginning made them male and female, 5 and said, 'For this reason a man shall leave his father and mother and be joined to his wife, and the two shall become one flesh'? 6 So they are no longer two but one flesh. What therefore God has joined together, let not man put asunder." 7 They said to him, "Why then did Moses command one to give a certificate of divorce, and to put her away?" 8 He said to them, "For your hardness of heart Moses allowed you to divorce your wives, but from the beginning it was not so.

Mark 10:1–12 *(9:49–50, § 132, p. 98)*

1 And he left there and went to the region of Judea and beyond the Jordan, and crowds gathered to him again; and again, as his custom was, he taught them.

2 And Pharisees came up and in order to test him asked, "Is it lawful for a man to divorce his wife?" 3 He answered them, "What did Moses command you?" 4 They said, "Moses allowed a man to write a certificate of divorce, and to put her away." 5 But Jesus said to them, "For your hardness of heart he wrote you this commandment.

6 But from the beginning of creation, 'God made them male and female.' 7 'For this reason a man shall leave his father and mother and be joined to his wife,[w] 8 and the two shall become one flesh. So they are no longer two but one flesh. 9 What therefore God has joined together, let not man put asunder."

cf. vv. 3–5

Matt. 19:4 = Mark 10:6—Genesis 1:27.   Matt. 19:5 = Mark 10:7-8—Genesis 2:24.   Matt. 19:7 = Mark 10:4—Deuteronomy 24:1.

[w] text: A C D W Θ λ φ ℜ it vg sy^p sa bo; omit, *and be joined to his wife:* S B sy^s.

To Matt. 19:4 = Mark 10:6 cf. I Corinthians 7:10-11—10 To the married I give charge, not I but the Lord, that the wife should not separate from her husband 11 (but if she does, let her remain single or else be reconciled to her husband)—and that the husband should not divorce his wife.

10 And in the house the disciples asked
him again about this matter. 11 And he
9 And I said to them, "Whoever divorces his wife
say to you: whoever divorces his wife, and marries another,
except for unchastity,x and marries another, commits adultery against her; 12 and if
commits adultery." * y she divorces her husband and marries
another, she commits adultery." *

10 The disciples said to him, "If such is the
case of a man with his wife, it is not expedient
to marry." 11 But he said to them, "Not all
men can receive this saying, but only those to
whom it is given. 12 For there are eunuchs
who have been so from birth, and there are
eunuchs who have been made eunuchs by
men, and there are eunuchs who have made
themselves eunuchs for the sake of the kingdom of heaven. He who is able to receive this,
let him receive it."

188. JESUS BLESSES THE CHILDREN.

Matt. 19:13–15	**Mark 10:13–16**	**Luke 18:15–17** *(18:9–14, § 186, p. 127)*
13 Then children were brought to him that he might lay his hands on them and pray. The disciples rebuked the people; 14 but Jesus said, "Let the children come to me, and do not hinder them; for to such belongs the kingdom of heaven."	13 And they were bringing children to him, that he might touch them; and the disciples rebuked them. 14 But when Jesus saw it he was indignant, and said to them, "Let the children come to me, do not hinder them; for to such belongs the kingdom of God.	15 Now they were bringing even infants to him that he might touch them; and when the disciples saw it they rebuked them. 16 But Jesus called them to him, saying, "Let the children come to me, and do not hinder them; for to such belongs the kingdom of God.

* Matt. 5:32 (§ 24, p.23): "But I say to you that every one who divorces his wife, except on the ground of unchastity, makes her an adulteress; and whoever marries a divorced woman commits adultery."

Luke 16:18 (§ 176, p.123): "Every one who divorces his wife and marries another commits adultery, and he who marries a woman divorced from her husband commits adultery."

x text: S W Θ ℜ vg sys syp; *except on the ground of unchastity, and marries another, commits adultery (against her:* syc): D φ it sy c sa; *except on the ground of unchastity, makes her commit adultery:* P25? Bλ bo; *except for unchastity, and marries another, makes her commit adultery:* C. y text: S D it (some MSS.) syc sys sa; add, *And whoever marries a divorced woman commits adultery:* P25 B C W Θ λ φ ℜ it (some MSS.) vg syp bo (cf. Matt. 5:32).

To Matt. 19:12 cf. **Gospel of the Egyptians:** (a) The Lord said to Salome when she inquired, "How long shall death prevail?", "As long as you women bear children."—Clement of Alexandria, *Miscellanies III.6.45, 3.* . . . Salome said, "How long will men continue to die?" The Lord answered, "So long as women bear children." *Ibid. III.9.64, 1.* Cf. also on Matt. 5:17: "I came to destroy the works of the female." *Ibid. III.9.63,2.* . . . When she said, "I have done well, then, in not bearing children," the Lord answered, "Eat every plant, but do not eat the bitter ones." *Ibid III.9.66,2.* When Salome inquired when the things concerning which she asked should be known, the Lord said, "When you have trampled on the garment of shame, and when the two become one, and the male with the female neither male nor female." *Ibid. III.13.92, 2.* Cf. also II Clement 12.2, 5. Cf. also **Gospel of Thomas, Logion 22.**

18:3 (§ *129*, *p. 95*): "Truly I say to you, unless you turn and become like children, you will never enter the kingdom of heaven." 19:15 And he laid his hands on them and went away.	¹⁵ Truly, I say to you, whoever does not receive the kingdom of God like a child shall not enter it." ¹⁶ And he took them in his arms and blessed them, laying his hands upon them.	¹⁷ Truly, I say to you, whoever does not receive the kingdom of God like a child shall not enter it."

189. THE RICH YOUNG MAN.

Matt. 19:16–30	Mark 10:17–31	Luke 18:18–30
16 And behold, one came up to him, saying, "Teacher, what good deed must I do, to have eternal life?" ¹⁷ And he said to him, "Why do you ask me about what is good? One there is who is good. If you would enter life, keep the commandments." ¹⁸ He said to him, "Which?" And Jesus said, "You shall not kill, You shall not commit adultery, You shall not steal, You shall not bear false witness, ¹⁹ Honor your father and mother, and, You shall love your neighbor as yourself." ²⁰ The young man said to him, "All these I have observed; what do I still lack?" ²¹ Jesus said to him, "If you would be perfect, go, sell what you possess and give to the poor, and you will have treasure in heaven; and come, follow me." ²² When the young man heard this he went away sorrowful; for	17 And as he was setting out on his journey, a man ran up and knelt before him, and asked him, "Good Teacher, what must I do to inherit eternal life?" ¹⁸ And Jesus said to him, "Why do you call me good? No one is good but God alone. ¹⁹ You know the commandments: 'Do not kill, Do not commit adultery, Do not steal, Do not bear false witness, Do not defraud, Honor your father and mother.'" ²⁰ And he said to him, "Teacher, all these I have observed from my youth." ²¹ And Jesus looking upon him loved him, and said to him, "You lack one thing; go, sell what you have, and give to the poor, and you will have treasure in heaven; and come, follow me." ²² At that saying his countenance fell, and he went away sorrowful, for	18 And a ruler asked him, "Good Teacher, what shall I do to inherit eternal life?" ¹⁹ And Jesus said to him, "Why do you call me good? No one is good but God alone. ²⁰ You know the commandments: 'Do not commit adultery, Do not kill, Do not steal, Do not bear false witness, Honor your father and mother.'" ²¹ And he said, "All these I have observed from my youth." ²² And when Jesus heard it, he said to him, "One thing you still lack. Sell all that you have and distribute to the poor, and you will have treasure in heaven; and come, follow me." ²³ But when he heard this he became sad, for

---

Matt. 19:18-19a = Mark 10:19 = Exodus 20:12-16 and Deuteronomy 5:16-20; 24:14 (Cod. A). Matt. 19:19b—Leviticus 19:18.

To Mark 10:15 and parallels cf. John 3:3, 5.

To Matt. 19:16-24 cf. **Gospel of the Nazaraeans** (in Origen, *Commentary on Matt. 15:14* in the Latin version) The second of the rich men said to him, "Teacher, what good thing can I do and live?" He said to him "Sir, fulfil the law and the prophets." He answered, "I have." Jesus said, "Go, sell all that you have and distribute to the poor; and come, follow me." But the rich man began to scratch his head, for it did not please him. And the Lord said to him, "How can you say, I have fulfilled the law and the prophets, when it is written in the law: You shall love your neighbor as yourself; and lo, many of your brothers, sons of Abraham, are covered with filth, dying of hunger, and your house is full of many good things, none of which goes out to them?" And he turned and said to Simon, his disciple, who was sitting by him, "Simon, son of Jonah, it is easier for a camel to go through the eye of a needle than for a rich man to enter the kingdom of heaven."

To Mark 10:18 and Luke 18:19 cf. **Gospel of the Naassenes** (in Hippolytus, *Refutation of All Heresies*, V.7.26)—"Why do you call me good? One there is who is good—my Father who is in heaven—who makes his sun to rise on the just and on the unjust, and sends rain on the pure and on sinners." (Cf. also Matt. 5:45.)

he had great possessions. **23** And Jesus said to his disciples, "Truly, I say to you, it will be hard for a rich man to enter the kingdom of heaven. **24** Again I tell you, it is easier for a camel to go through the eye of a needle than for a rich man to enter the kingdom of God." **25** When the disciples heard this they were greatly astonished, saying, "Who then can be saved?" **26** But Jesus looked at them and said to them, "With men this is impossible, but with God all things are possible." **27** Then Peter said in reply, "Lo, we have left everything and followed you. What then shall we have?" **28** Jesus said to them, "Truly, I say to you, in the new world, when the Son of man shall sit on his glorious throne, you who have followed me will also sit on twelve thrones, judging the twelve tribes of Israel.	he had great possessions. **23** And Jesus looked around and said to his disciples, "How hard it will be for those who have riches to enter the kingdom of God!" **24** And the disciples were amazed at his words. But Jesus said to them again, "Children, how hard it is² to enter the kingdom of God! **25** It is easier for a camel to go through the eye of a needle than for a rich man to enter the kingdom of God." **26** And they were exceedingly astonished, and said to him,ᵃ "Then who can be saved?" **27** Jesus looked at them and said, "With men it is impossible, but not with God; for all things are possible with God." **28** Peter began to say to him, "Lo, we have left everything and followed you." **29** Jesus said, "Truly, I say to you,	he was very rich. **24** Jesus looking at him said, "How hard it is for those who have riches to enter the kingdom of God! **25** For it is easier for a camel to go through the eye of a needle than for a rich man to enter the kingdom of God." **26** Those who heard it said, "Then who can be saved?" **27** But he said, "What is impossible with men is possible with God." **28** And Peter said, "Lo, we have left our homes and followed you." **29** And he said to them, "Truly, I say to you, 22:28-30 (§ *237, p. 167):* **28** You are those who have continued with me in my trials; **29** and I assign to you, as my Father assigned to me, a kingdom, **30** that you may eat and drink at my table in my kingdom, and sit on thrones judging the twelve tribes of Israel."
29 And every one who has left houses or brothers or sisters or father or mother or children or lands, for my name's sake, will receive a hundredfold,ᵇ and inherit eternal life. **30** But many that are first will be last, and the last first." *See 20:16*	there is no one who has left house or brothers or sisters or mother or father or children or lands, for my sake and for the gospel, **30** who will not receive a hundredfold now in this time, houses and brothers and sisters and mothers and children and lands, with persecutions, and in the age to come eternal life. **31** But many that are first will be last, and the last first."	18:29b "... there is no man who has left house or wife or brothers or parents or children, for the sake of the kingdom of God, **30** who will not receive manifold more in this time, and in the age to come eternal life." 13:30 (§ *165, p. 118):* "And behold, some are last who will be first, and some are first who will be last."

ᶻ text: S B sa; add, *for those who trust in riches:* A C D Θ λ φ ℜ it vg syˢ syᵖ bo; add, *for a rich man:* W.   ᵃ text: S B C sa bo; *to one another:* A D W Θ λ φ ℜ it vg syˢ syᵖ.   ᵇ text: S C D W Θ λ φ ℜ it vg syᶜ syˢ syᵖ bo; *manifold:* B sa.

To Matt. 19:30 and parallels cf. *Oxyrhynchus Papyrus 654, Logion 3:* "... For many that are first shall be last, and the last first, and few shall find it."

To Matt. 19:30 and parallels cf. Barnabas 6:13—The Lord said, "Behold, I make the last things like the first."

190. THE PARABLE OF THE LABORERS IN THE VINEYARD.
Matt. 20:1–16

1 "For the kingdom of heaven is like a householder who went out early in the morning to hire laborers for his vineyard. 2 After agreeing with the laborers for a denarius[c] a day, he sent them into his vineyard. 3 And going out about the third hour he saw others standing idle in the market place; 4 and to them he said, 'You go into the vineyard too, and whatever is right I will give you.' So they went. 5 Going out again about the sixth hour and the ninth hour, he did the same. 6 And about the eleventh hour he went out and found others standing; and he said to them, 'Why do you stand here idle all day?' 7 They said to him, 'Because no one has hired us.' He said to them, 'You go into the vineyard too.' 8 And when evening came, the owner of the vineyard said to his steward, 'Call the laborers and pay them their wages, beginning with the last, up to the first.' 9 And when those hired about the eleventh hour came, each of them received a denarius. 10 Now when the first came, they thought they would receive more; but each of them also received a denarius. 11 And on receiving it they grumbled at the householder, 12 saying, 'These last worked only one hour, and you have made them equal to us who have borne the burden of the day and scorching heat.' 13 But he replied to one of them, 'Friend, I am doing you no wrong; did you not agree with me for a denarius? 14 Take what belongs to you, and go; I choose to give to this last as I give to you. 15 Am I not allowed to do what I choose with what belongs to me? Or do you begrudge my generosity?'[d] 16 So the last will be first, and the first last." (*See above, 19:30.*)

191. THE THIRD PREDICTION OF THE PASSION.

Matt. 20:17–19	Mark 10:32–34	Luke 18:31–34
17 And as Jesus was going up to Jerusalem,	32 And they were on the road, going up to Jerusalem, and Jesus was walking ahead of them; and they were amazed, and those who followed were afraid. And taking the twelve again, he began to tell them what was to happen to him, 33 saying, "Behold, we are going up to Jerusalem; and the Son of man will be delivered to the chief priests and the scribes, and they will condemn him to death, and deliver him to the Gentiles; 34 and they will mock him, and spit upon him, and scourge him, and kill him; and after three days he will rise."	31 And taking the twelve,
he took the twelve disciples aside, and on the way he said to them, 18 "Behold, we are going up to Jerusalem; and the Son of man will be delivered to the chief priests and scribes, and they will condemn him to death, 19 and deliver him to the Gentiles to be mocked		he said to them, "Behold, we are going up to Jerusalem, and everything that is written of the Son of man by the prophets will be accomplished. 32 For he will be delivered to the Gentiles, and will be mocked and shamefully treated and spit upon; 33 they will scourge him and kill him, and on the third day he will rise." 34 But they understood none of these things; this saying was hid from them, and they did not grasp what was said.
and scourged and crucified, and will be raised on the third day."		

---

[c] The denarius was a day's wage for a laborer.   [d] Or: *is your eye evil because I am good?*

192. JESUS AND THE SONS OF ZEBEDEE.

Matt. 20:20–28	Mark 10:35–45	Luke 22:24–27 (§ 237, p. 167)
20 Then the mother of the sons of Zebedee came up to him, with her sons, and kneeling before him she asked him for something. 21 And he said to her, "What do you want?" She said to him, "Command that these two sons of mine may sit, one at your right hand and one at your left, in your kingdom." 22 But Jesus answered, "You do not know what you are asking. Are you able to drink the cup that I am to drink?"	35 And James and John, the sons of Zebedee, came forward to him, and said to him, "Teacher, we want you to do for us whatever we ask of you." 36 And he said to them, "What do you want me to do for you?" 37 And they said to him, "Grant us to sit, one at your right hand and one at your left, in your glory." 38 But Jesus said to them, "You do not know what you are asking. Are you able to drink the cup that I drink, or to be baptized with the baptism with which I am baptized?" 39 And they said to him, "We are able." And Jesus said to them, "The cup that I drink you will drink; and with the baptism with which I am baptized, you will be baptized; 40 but to sit at my right hand or at my left is not mine to grant, but it is for those for whom it has been prepared."	
They said to him, "We are able." 23 He said to them, "You will drink my cup, but to sit at my right hand and at my left is not mine to grant, but it is for those for whom it has been prepared by my Father."		
		Luke 12:50 (§ 160, p. 115)
24 And when the ten heard it, they were indignant at the two brothers. 25 But Jesus called them to him and said, "You know that the rulers of the Gentiles lord it over them, and their great men exercise authority over them. 26 It shall not be so among you; but whoever would be great among you must be your servant, 27 and whoever would be first among you must be your slave;* 28 even as the Son of man came not to be served but to serve, and to give his life as a ransom for many."	41 And when the ten heard it, they began to be indignant at James and John. 42 And Jesus called them to him and said to them, "You know that those who are supposed to rule over the Gentiles lord it over them, and their great men exercise authority over them. 43 But it shall not be so among you; but whoever would be great among you must be your servant, 44 and whoever would be first among you must be slave of all.* 45 For the Son of man also came not to be served but to serve, and to give his life as a ransom for many."	22:24–27 (§ 237b, p. 167): 24 A dispute also arose among them, which of them was to be regarded as the greatest. 25 And he said to them, "The kings of the Gentiles exercise lordship over them; and those in authority over them are called benefactors. 26 But not so with you; rather let the greatest among you become as the youngest, and the leader as one who serves.* 27 For which is the greater, one who sits at table, or one who serves? Is it not the one who sits at table? But I am among you as one who serves."

---

* Cf. Mark 9:35 = Luke 9:48b (§ 129, p.95) and Matt. 23:11 (§ 210, p.149).

To Matt. 20:22 cf. **Gospel of the Naassenes** (in Hippolytus, *Refutation of All Heresies*, *V.8.11*)—"But" he says, "even if you drink the cup which I drink, you will not be able to enter where I go."

193. THE HEALING OF BARTIMAEUS.

Matt. 20:29–34 (cf. 9:27–31, § 56, p. 39)	Mark 10:46–52	Luke 18:35–43
29 And as they went out of Jericho, a great crowd followed him. 30 And behold, two blind men sitting by the roadside, when they heard that	46 And they came to Jericho; and as he was leaving Jericho with his disciples and a great multitude, Bartimaeus, a blind beggar, the son of Timaeus, was sitting by the roadside. 47 And when he heard that it was	35 As he drew near to Jericho, a blind man was sitting by the roadside begging; 36 and hearing a multitude going by, he inquired what this meant. 37 They told him,
Jesus was passing by, cried out,[e] "Have mercy on us, Son of David!" 31 The crowd rebuked them, telling them to be silent; but they cried out the more, "Lord, have mercy on us, Son of David!" 32 And Jesus stopped and called them, saying,	Jesus of Nazareth, he began to cry out and say, "Jesus, Son of David, have mercy on me!" 48 And many rebuked him, telling him to be silent; but he cried out all the more, "Son of David, have mercy on me!" 49 And Jesus stopped and said, "Call him." And they called the blind man, saying to him, "Take heart; rise, he is calling you." 50 And throwing off his mantle he sprang up and came to Jesus. 51 And	"Jesus of Nazareth is passing by." 38 And he cried, "Jesus, Son of David, have mercy on me!" 39 And those who were in front rebuked him, telling him to be silent; but he cried out all the more, "Son of David, have mercy on me!" 40 And Jesus stopped, and commanded him to be brought to him;
"What do you want me to do for you?" 33 They said to him, "Lord, let our eyes be opened." 34 And Jesus in pity touched their eyes, and immediately they received their sight and followed him.	Jesus said to him, "What do you want me to do for you?" And the blind man said to him, "Master,[f] let me receive my sight." 52 And Jesus said to him, "Go your way; your faith has made you well." And immediately he received his sight and followed him on the way.	and when he came near, he asked him, 41 "What do you want me to do for you?" He said, "Lord, let me receive my sight." 42 And Jesus said to him, "Receive your sight; your faith has made you well." 43 And immediately he received his sight and followed him, glorifying God; and all the people, when they saw it, gave praise to God.
(21:1–9, § 196, pp. 137–138)	(11:1–10. § 196, pp. 137–138)	

---

[e] text: D it (some MSS.) sy[c]; *Lord, have mercy on us:* P[45?] B C W λ ℜ it (some MSS.) vg sy[p] sa; *Have mercy on us, Jesus:* S Θ φ it (some MSS.); *Lord, have mercy on us, Jesus:* bo.   [f] Or, *Rabbi.*

194. ZACCHAEUS.
Luke 19:1–10

1 He entered Jericho and was passing through. 2 And there was a man named Zacchaeus; he was a chief tax collector, and rich. 3 And he sought to see who Jesus was, but could not, on account of the crowd, because he was small of stature. 4 So he ran on ahead and climbed up into a sycamore tree to see him, for he was to pass that way. 5 And when Jesus came to the place, he looked up and said to him, "Zacchaeus, make haste and come down; for I must stay at your house today." 6 So he made haste and came down, and received him joyfully. 7 And when they saw it they all murmured, "He has gone in to be the guest of a man who is a sinner." 8 And Zacchaeus stood and said to the Lord, "Behold, Lord, the half of my goods I give to the poor; and if I have defrauded any one of anything, I restore it fourfold." 9 And Jesus said to him, "Today salvation has come to this house, since he also is a son of Abraham. 10 For the Son of man came to seek and to save the lost."

195. THE PARABLE OF THE POUNDS.

Matt. 25:14-30 (§ 228, pp. 160-161):

14 "For it will be as when a man going on a journey called his servants and entrusted to them his property; 15 to one he gave five talents,[g] to another two, to another one, to each according to his ability. Then he went away. 16 He who had received the five talents went at once and traded with them; and he made five talents more. 17 So also, he who had the two talents made two talents more. 18 But he who had received the one talent went and dug in the ground and hid his master's money.

19 Now after a long time the master of those servants came and settled accounts with them.

Luke 19:11-27

11 As they heard these things, he proceeded to tell a parable, because he was near to Jerusalem, and because they supposed that the kingdom of God was to appear immediately. 12 He said therefore, "A nobleman went into a far country to receive a kingdom and then return. 13 Calling ten of his servants, he gave them ten pounds,[h] and said to them, 'Trade with these till I come.'

14 "But his citizens hated him and sent an embassy after him, saying, 'We do not want this man to reign over us.'

15 "When he returned, having received the kingdom, he commanded these servants, to whom he had given the money, to be called to him, and he might know what they had gained by trading.

Luke 19:10—Ezekiel 34:16.

[g] This talent was more than fifteen years' wages for a laborer.

[h] The mina, rendered here by *pound*, was about three months' wages for a laborer.

20 And he who had received the five talents came forward, bringing five talents more, saying, 'Master, you delivered to me five talents; here I have made five talents more.' 21 His master said to him, 'Well done, good and faithful servant; you have been faithful over a little, I will set you over much; enter into the joy of your master.' 22 And he also who had the two talents came forward, saying, 'Master, you delivered to me two talents; here I have made two talents more.' 23 His master said to him, 'Well done, good and faithful servant; you have been faithful over a little, I will set you over much; enter into the joy of your master.' 24 He also who had received the one talent came forward, saying, 'Master, I knew you to be a hard man, reaping where you did not sow, and gathering where you did not winnow; 25 so I was afraid, and I went and hid your talent in the ground. Here you have what is yours.' 26 But his master answered him, 'You wicked and slothful servant! You knew that I reap where I have not sowed, and gather where I have not winnowed? 27 Then you ought to have invested my money with the bankers, and at my coming I should have received what was my own with interest.

28 So take the talent from him, and give it to him who has the ten talents.

29 For to every one who has will more be given, and he will have abundance; but from him who has not, even what he has will be taken away.* 30 And cast the worthless servant into the outer darkness; there men will weep and gnash their teeth.' "

16 The first came before him,

saying, 'Lord, your pound has made ten pounds more.'

17 And he said to him, 'Well done, good servant! Because you have been faithful in a very little, you shall have authority over ten cities.' 18 And the second came,

saying, 'Lord, your pound has made five pounds.'

19 And he said to him,

'And you are to be over five cities.' 20 Then another came,

saying, 'Lord, here is your pound, which I have kept laid away in a napkin; 21 for I was afraid of you, because you are a severe man; you take up what you did not lay down, and reap what you did not sow.' 22 He said to him, 'I will condemn you out of your own mouth, you wicked servant! You knew that I was a severe man, taking up what I did not lay down and reaping what I did not sow? 23 Why then did you not put my money into the bank, and at my coming I should have collected it with interest?' 24 And he said to those who stood by, 'Take the pound from him, and give it to him who has the ten pounds.' 25 (And they said to him, 'Lord, he has ten pounds!') 26 'I tell you that to every one who has will more be given; but from him who has not, even what he has will be taken away.* 27 But as for these enemies of mine, who did not want me to reign over them, bring them here and slay them before me.' "

---

* Cf. Matt. 13:12 (§ 91, p.66) = Mark 4:25 = Luke 8:18 (§ 94, p.68).

B. The Days in Jerusalem

Matthew 21–25 = Mark 11–13 = Luke 19:28–21:38

196. THE ENTRY INTO JERUSALEM.

Matt. 21:1–9 (20:29–34, § 193, p. 134)	Mark 11:1–10 (10: 46–53, § 193, p. 134)	Luke 19:28–38
1 And when they drew near to Jerusalem and came to Bethphage, to the Mount of Olives, then Jesus sent two disciples, 2 saying to them "Go into the village opposite you, and immediately you will find an ass tied, and a colt with her; untie them and bring them to me. 3 If any one says anything to you, you shall say, 'The Lord has need of them,' and he will send them immediately." 4 This took place to fulfil what was spoken by the prophet, saying, 5 "Tell the daughter of Zion, Behold, your king is coming to you, humble, and mounted on an ass, and on a colt, the foal of an ass." 6 The disciples went and did	1 And when they drew near to Jerusalem, to Bethphage and Bethany, at the Mount of Olives, he sent two of his disciples, 2 and said to them, "Go into the village opposite you, and immediately as you enter it you will find a colt tied, on which no one has ever sat; untie it and bring it. 3 If any one says to you, 'Why are you doing this?' say, 'The Lord has need of it and will send it back here immediately.' "	28 And when he had said this, he went on ahead, going up to Jerusalem. 29 When he drew near to Bethphage and Bethany, at the mount that is called Olivet, he sent two of the disciples, 30 saying, "Go into the village opposite, where on entering you will find a colt tied, on which no one has ever yet sat; untie it and bring it here. 31 If any one asks you, 'Why are you untying it?' you shall say this, 'The Lord has need of it.' "
	4 And they went away, and found a colt tied at the door out in the open street; and they untied it. 5 And those who stood there said to them, "What are you doing, untying the colt?"	32 So those who were sent went away and found it as he had told them. 33 And as they were untying the colt, its owners said to them, "Why are you untying the colt?"

Matt. 21:5—Isaiah 62:11, Zechariah 9:9.

To § 196 cf. John 12:12–19.

as Jesus had directed them; ⁷ they brought the ass and the colt, and put their garments on them[i] and he sat thereon. ⁸ Most of the crowd spread their garments on the road, and others cut branches from the trees and spread them on the road.	⁶ And they told them what Jesus had said; and they let them go. ⁷ And they brought the colt to Jesus, and threw their garments on it; and he sat upon it. ⁸ And many spread their garments on the road, and others spread leafy branches which they had cut from the fields.	³⁴ And they said, "The Lord has need of it." ³⁵ And they brought it to Jesus, and throwing their garments on the colt they set Jesus upon it. ³⁶ And as he rode along, they spread their garments on the road.
		³⁷ As he was now drawing near, at the descent of the Mount of Olives, the whole multitude of the disciples began to rejoice and praise God with a loud voice for all the mighty works that they had seen, ³⁸ saying,
⁹ And the crowds that went before him and that followed him shouted, "Hosanna to the Son of David! Blessed is he who comes in the name of the Lord! Hosanna in the highest!"	⁹ And those who went before and those who followed cried out, "Hosanna! Blessed is he who comes in the name of the Lord! ¹⁰ Blessed is the kingdom of our father David that is coming! Hosanna in the highest!"	"Blessed is the King who comes in the name of the Lord! Peace in heaven and glory in the highest!"

197. PREDICTION OF THE DESTRUCTION OF JERUSALEM.
Luke 19:39–44

See below vv. 14–16	39 And some of the Pharisees in the multitude said to him, "Teacher, rebuke your disciples." ⁴⁰ He answered, "I tell you, if these were silent, the very stones would cry out." ⁴¹ And when he drew near and saw the city he wept over it, ⁴² saying, "Would that even today you knew the things that make for peace! But now they are hid from your eyes. ⁴³ For the days shall come upon you, when your enemies will cast up a bank about you and surround you, and hem you in on every side, ⁴⁴ and dash you to the ground, you and your children within you, and they will not leave one stone upon another in you; because you did not know the time of your visitation."

198. JESUS IN THE TEMPLE.

Matt. 21:10–17	Mark 11:11	Luke 19:45–46
¹⁰ And when he entered Jerusalem, all the city was stirred, saying, "Who is this?"	11 And he entered Jerusalem	

Matt. 21:9 = Mark 11:9-10 = Luke 19:38—Psalm 118:25-26. Luke 19:44—Psalm 137:9.

[i] text: S B C W λ ℜ vg sa bo; *on it:* D Θ φ it; *on the colt:* sy^p; *phrase omitted:* sy^c.

11 And the crowds said, "This is the prophet Jesus from Nazareth of Galilee."

12 And Jesus entered the temple of God [j] and drove out all who sold and bought in the temple, and he overturned the tables of the money-changers and the seats of those who sold pigeons. 13 He said to them, "It is written, 'My house shall be called a house of prayer'; but you make it a den of robbers."

14 And the blind and the lame came to him in the temple, and he healed them. 15 But when the chief priests and the scribes saw the wonderful things that he did, and the children crying out in the temple, "Hosanna to the Son of David!" they were indignant; 16 and they said to him, "Do you hear what these are saying?" And Jesus said to them, "Yes; have you never read,

'Out of the mouth of babes and sucklings thou hast brought perfect praise'?"

17 and leaving them, he went out of the city to Bethany and lodged there.

---

and went into the temple;

See below, vv. 15–19

and when he had looked round at everything, as it was already late, he went out to Bethany with the twelve.

---

45 And he entered the temple and began to drive out those who sold,

46 saying to them, "It is written, 'My house shall be a house of prayer'; but you have made it a den of robbers."

See above, vv. 39–40

---

199. THE CURSING OF THE FIG TREE.

Matt. 21:18–19

18 In the morning, as he was returning to the city, he was hungry. 19 And seeing a fig tree by the wayside he went to it

and found nothing on it but leaves only.

And he said to it, "May no fruit ever come from you again!" And the fig tree withered at once.

Mark 11:12–14

12 On the following day, when they came from Bethany, he was hungry. 13 And seeing in the distance a fig tree in leaf, he went to see if he could find anything on it. When he came to it, he found nothing but leaves, for it was not the season for figs. 14 And he said to it, "May no one ever eat fruit from you again." And his disciples heard it.

Matt. 21:13 = Mark 11:17 = Luke 19:46—Isaiah 56:7; Jeremiah 7:11. Matt. 21:16—Psalm 8:2.

[j] text: C D W λ ℜ it vg sy[c] sy[p]; omit, *of God:* S B Θ φ sa bo.

To Matt. 21:12 cf. **Gospel of the Nazaraeans,** quoted in a marginal note of a thirteenth century manuscript of the *Aurora* by Peter of Riga—In the Gospel books which the Nazarenes use it is written: From his eyes went forth rays which terrified them and put them to flight.

200. THE CLEANSING OF THE TEMPLE.

Matt. 21:12–13 (§ *198, p. 139*)	Mark 11:15–19	Luke 19:45–48
12 And Jesus entered the temple of God [k] and drove out all who sold and bought in the temple, and he overturned the tables of the money-changers and the seats of those who sold pigeons.	15 And they came to Jerusalem. And he entered the temple and began to drive out those who sold and those who bought in the temple, and he overturned the tables of the money-changers and the seats of those who sold pigeons; 16 and he would not allow any one to carry anything through the temple.	45 And he entered the temple and began to drive out those who sold,
13 He said to them, "It is written, 'My house shall be called a house of prayer'; but you make it a den of robbers."	17 And he taught, and said to them, "Is it not written, 'My house shall be called a house of prayer for all the nations'? But you have made it a den of robbers."	46 saying to them, "It is written, 'My house shall be a house of prayer'; but you have made it a den of robbers."
See 22:33	18 And the chief priests and the scribes heard it and sought a way to destroy him; for they feared him, because all the multitude was astonished at his teaching. 19 And when evening came they [l] went out of the city.	47 And he was teaching daily in the temple. The chief priests and the scribes and the principal men of the people sought to destroy him; 48 but they did not find anything they could do, for all the people hung upon his words. *Cf. 21:37 (§ 230, p. 162)*

201. THE MEANING OF THE WITHERED FIG TREE.

Matt. 21:20–22	Mark 11:20–25 (26)
20 When the disciples saw it they marveled, saying, "How did the fig tree wither at once?" 21 And Jesus answered them, "Truly, I say to you, if you have faith and never doubt, you will not only do what has been done to the fig tree, but	20 As they passed by in the morning, they saw the fig tree withered away to its roots. 21 And Peter remembered and said to him, "Master, [m] look! The fig tree which you cursed has withered." 22 And Jesus answered them, "Have faith in God. 23 Truly, I say to you,

---

Matt. 21:13 = Mark 11:17 = Luke 19:46—Isaiah 56:7, Jeremiah 7:11.

To § 200 cf. John 2:13-17.

---

[k] text: C D W λ ℜ it vg sy^c sy^p; omit, *of God:* S B Θ φ sa bo.　　[l] text: A B W it (some MSS.) sy^p; *he:* S C D Θ λ φ ℜ it (some MSS.) vg sy^s sa bo.　　[m] Or, *Rabbi.*

even if you say to this mountain, 'Be taken up and cast into the sea,' it will be done.*	whoever says to this mountain, 'Be taken up and cast into the sea,' and does not doubt in his heart, but believes that what he says will come to pass, it will be done for him. *
²² And whatever you ask in prayer, you will receive, if you have faith."	²⁴ Therefore I tell you, whatever you ask in prayer, believe that you have received [mm] it, and it will be yours. ²⁵ And whenever you stand praying, forgive, if you have anything against any one; so that your Father also who is in heaven may forgive you your trespasses." [n]
6:14 (§ 30, p. 25): "For if you forgive men their trespasses, your heavenly Father also will forgive you."	

202. THE QUESTION ABOUT AUTHORITY.

Matt. 21:23–27	Mark 11:27–33	Luke 20:1–8
23 And when he entered the temple, the chief priests and the elders of the people came up to him as he was teaching, and said, "By what authority are you doing these things, and who gave you this authority?"	27 And they came again to Jerusalem. And as he was walking in the temple, the chief priests and the scribes and the elders came to him, ²⁸ and they said to him, "By what authority are you doing these things, or who gave you this authority to do them?"	1 One day, as he was teaching the people in the temple and preaching the gospel, the chief priests and the scribes with the elders came up ² and said to him, "Tell us by what authority you do these things, or who it is that gave you this authority."
²⁴ Jesus answered them, "I also will ask you a question; and if you tell me the answer, then I also will tell you by what authority I do these things. ²⁵ The baptism of John, whence was it? From heaven or from men?" And they argued with one another, "If we say, 'From heaven,' he will say to us, 'Why then did you not believe him?'	²⁹ Jesus said to them, "I will ask you a question: answer me, and I will tell you by what authority I do these things. ³⁰ Was the baptism of John from heaven or from men? Answer me." ³¹ And they argued with one another, "If we say, 'From heaven,' he will say, 'Why then did you not believe him?'	³ He answered them, "I also will ask you a question; now tell me, ⁴ Was the baptism of John from heaven or from men?" ⁵ And they discussed it with one another, saying, "If we say, 'From heaven,' he will say, 'Why did you not believe him?'

* Matt. 17:20 (§ 126, p.94): He said to them, "Because of your little faith. For truly, I say to you, if you have faith as a grain of mustard seed, you will say to this mountain, 'Move hence to yonder place,' and it will move; and nothing will be impossible to you."	Luke 17:6 (§ 180, p.125): And the Lord said, "If you had faith as a grain of mustard seed, you could say to this sycamine tree, 'Be rooted up, and be planted in the sea,' and it would obey you."

[mm] text: S B C; *are receiving:* A φ 𝕽 sy^s sy^p; *will receive:* D Θ λ it vg.   [n] text: S B W sy^s sa bo; add verse 26: *But if you do not forgive, neither will your Father who is in heaven forgive your trespasses:* A C D Θ λ φ 𝕽 it vg sy^p Cyprian.

To Matt. 21:21-22 = Mark 11:23-24 cf. John 14:13-14—¹³ "Whatever you ask in my name, I will do it, that the Father may be glorified in the Son; ¹⁴ if you ask anything in my name, I will do it." Also John 16:23—"In that day you will ask nothing of me. Truly, truly, I say to you, if you ask anything of the Father, he will give it to you in my name."

To Matt. 21:23 and parallels cf. John 2:18—The Jews then said to him, "What sign have you to show us for doing this?"

26 But if we say, 'From men,' we are afraid of the multitude; for all hold that John was a prophet." 27 So they answered Jesus, "We do not know." And he said to them, "Neither will I tell you by what authority I do these things.	32 But shall we say, 'From men'?" — they were afraid of the people, for all held that John was a real prophet. 33 So they answered Jesus, "We do not know." And Jesus said to them, "Neither will I tell you by what authority I do these things."	6 But if we say, 'From men,' all the people will stone us; for they are convinced that John was a prophet." 7 So they answered that they did not know whence it was. 8 And Jesus said to them, "Neither will I tell you by what authority I do these things."

203. THE PARABLE OF THE TWO SONS.
Matt. 21:28–32

28 "What do you think? A man had two sons; and he went to the first and said, 'Son, go and work in the vineyard today.' 29 And he answered, 'I will not'; but afterward he repented and went. 30 And he went to the second and said the same; and he answered, 'I go, sir,' but did not go. 31 Which of the two did the will of his father?" They said, "The first." Jesus said to them, "Truly, I say to you, the tax collectors and the harlots go into the kingdom of God before you. 32 For John came to you in the way of righteousness, and you did not believe him, but the tax collectors and the harlots believed him; and even when you saw it, you did not afterward repent and believe him." * °

204. THE PARABLE OF THE WICKED TENANTS.

Matt. 21:33–46	Mark 12:1–12	Luke 20:9–19
33 "Hear another parable. There was a householder who planted a vineyard, and set a hedge around it, and dug a wine press in it, and built a tower, and let it out to tenants, and went into another country.	1 And he began to speak to them in parables. "A man planted a vineyard, and set a hedge around it, and dug a pit for the wine press, and built a tower, and let it out to tenants, and went into another country.	9 And he began to tell the people this parable: "A man planted a vineyard, and let it out to tenants, and went into another country for a long while. 10 When the time came,
34 When the season of fruit drew near, he sent his servants to the tenants, to get his fruit;	2 When the time came, he sent a servant to the tenants, to get from them some of the fruit of the vineyard.	he sent a servant to the tenants, that they should give him some of the fruit of the vineyard;
35 and the tenants took his servants and beat one, killed another, and stoned another.	3 And they took him and beat him, and sent him away empty-handed.	but the tenants beat him, and sent him away empty-handed.

---

* Luke 7:29-30 (§ 82, p.59): 29 When they heard this all the people and the tax collectors justified God, having been baptized with the baptism of John; 30 but the Pharisees and the lawyers rejected the purpose of God for themselves, not having been baptized by him.

Matt. 21:33 = Mark 12:1 = Luke 20:9—Isaiah 5:2.

° text: S B C W Θ λ φ ℜ it vg sa bo; *even when you did not see it, you afterward repented;* sy^c sy^p; *when you saw it you afterward repented:* D sy^s.

36 Again he sent other servants, more than the first; and they did the same to them.

37 Afterward he sent his son to them, saying, 'They will respect my son.' 38 But when the tenants saw the son, they said to themselves, 'This is the heir; come, let us kill him and have his inheritance.' 39 And they took him and cast him out of the vineyard, and killed him. 40 When therefore the owner of the vineyard comes, what will he do to those tenants?" 41 They said to him, "He will put those wretches to a miserable death, and let out the vineyard to other tenants who will give him the fruits in their seasons." 42 Jesus said to them, "Have you never read in the scriptures:

'The very stone which the
    builders rejected
has become the head of
    the corner;
this was the Lord's
    doing,
and it is marvelous in
    our eyes'?

43 Therefore I tell you, the kingdom of God will be taken away from you and given to a nation producing the fruits of it." ᴾ

45 When the chief priests and the Pharisees heard his parables, they perceived that he was speaking about them.

---

4 Again he sent to them another servant, and they wounded him in the head, and treated him shamefully. 5 And he sent another, and him they killed; and so with many others, some they beat and some they killed. 6 He had still one other, a beloved son; finally he sent him to them, saying, 'They will respect my son.' 7 But those tenants said to one another, 'This is the heir; come, let us kill him, and the inheritance will be ours.' 8 And they took him and killed him, and cast him out of the vineyard.

9 What will the owner of the vineyard do?

He will come and destroy the tenants, and give the vineyard to others.

10 Have you not read this scripture:

'The very stone which the
    builders rejected
has become the head of
    the corner;
11 this was the Lord's
    doing,
and it is marvelous in
    our eyes'?"

---

11 And he sent another servant; him also they beat and treated shamefully, and sent him away empty-handed. 12 And he sent yet a third; this one they wounded and cast out.

13 Then the owner of the vineyard said, 'What shall I do? I will send my beloved son; it may be they will respect him.' 14 But when the tenants saw him, they said to themselves, 'This is the heir; let us kill him, that the inheritance may be ours.'

15 And they cast him out of the vineyard and killed him.

What then will the owner of the vineyard do to them?

16 He will come and destroy those tenants, and give the vineyard to others." When they heard this, they said, "God forbid!" 17 But he looked at them and said, "What then is this that is written:

'The very stone which the
    builders rejected
has become the head of
    the corner'?

18 Every one who falls on that stone will be broken to pieces; but when it falls on any one it will crush him."

Matt. 21:42 = Mark 12:10-11 = Luke 20:17—Psalm 118:22-23.

ᴾ text: D it (some MSS.) sy ˢ; add verse 44, *And he who falls on this stone will be broken to pieces; but when it falls on any one, it will crush him:* S B C W Θ λ φ ℜ it (some MSS.) vg syᶜ syᵖ sa bo. (Cf. Luke 20:18.)

46 But when they tried to arrest him, they feared the multitudes, because they held him to be a prophet.

Cf. 22:22 (§ 206, p. 145)

12 And they tried to arrest him, but feared the multitude, for they perceived that he had told the parable against them; so they left him and went away.

19 The scribes and the chief priests tried to lay hands on him at that very hour, but they feared the people; for they perceived that he had told this parable against them.

205. THE PARABLE OF THE MARRIAGE FEAST.

Matt. 22:1–14

1 And again Jesus spoke to them in parables, saying, 2 "The kingdom of heaven may be compared to a king who gave a marriage feast for his son, 3 and sent his servants to call those who were invited to the marriage feast; but they would not come. 4 Again he sent other servants, saying, 'Tell those who are invited, Behold, I have made ready my dinner, my oxen and my fat calves are killed, and everything is ready; come to the marriage feast.' 5 But they made light of it and went off, one to his farm, another to his business, 6 while the rest seized his servants, treated them shamefully, and killed them. 7 The king was angry, and he sent his troops and destroyed those murderers and burned their city. 8 Then he said to his servants, 'The wedding is ready, but those invited were not worthy. 9 Go therefore to the thoroughfares, and invite to the marriage feast as many as you find.' 10 And those servants went out into the streets and gathered all whom they found, both bad and good; so the wedding hall was filled with guests.

11 "But when the king came in to look at the guests, he saw there a man who had no wedding garment; 12 and he said to him, 'Friend, how did you get in here without a wedding garment?' And he was speechless. 13 Then the king said to the attendants, 'Bind him hand and foot, and cast him into the outer darkness; there men will weep and gnash their teeth.' 14 For many are called, but few are chosen."

Luke 14:16–24 (§ 170, pp. 119–120)

16 But he said to him, "A man once gave a great banquet, and invited many; 17 and at the time for the banquet he sent his servant to say to those who had been invited, 'Come; for all is now ready.' 18 But they all alike began to make excuses. The first said to him, 'I have bought a field, and I must go out and see it; I pray you, have me excused.' 19 And another said, 'I have bought five yoke of oxen, and I go to examine them; I pray you, have me excused.' 20 And another said, 'I have married a wife, and therefore I cannot come.' 21 So the servant came and reported this to his master. Then the householder in anger said to his servant, 'Go out quickly to the streets and lanes of the city, and bring in the poor and maimed and blind and lame.' 22 And the servant said, 'Sir, what you commanded has been done, and still there is room.' 23 And the master said to the servant, 'Go out to the highways and hedges, and compel people to come in, that my house may be filled. 24 For I tell you,q none of those men who were invited shall taste my banquet.'"

---

q The Greek word for *you* here is plural.

To Matt. 22:14 cf. **Gospel of Thomas, Logion 23:** Jesus said, "I will choose you, one out of a thousand, and two out of ten thousand, and they will stand as a single one."

206. THE QUESTION CONCERNING TRIBUTE TO CAESAR.

Matt. 22:15–22	Mark 12:13–17	Luke 20:20–26
15 Then the Pharisees went and took counsel how to entangle him in his talk. 16 And they sent their disciples to him, along with the Herodians, saying, "Teacher, we know that you are true, and teach the way of God truthfully, and care for no man; for you do not regard the position of men. 17 Tell us, then, what you think. Is it lawful to pay taxes to Caesar, or not?"	13 And they sent to him some of the Pharisees and some of the Herodians, to entrap him in his talk. 14 And they came and said to him, "Teacher, we know that you are true, and care for no man; for you do not regard the position of men, but truly teach the way of God. Is it lawful to pay taxes to Caesar, or not? 15 Should we pay them, or should we not?" But knowing their hypocrisy, he said to them, "Why put me to the test? Bring me a coin, [r] and let me look at it." 16 And they brought one. And he said to them, "Whose likeness and inscription is this?" They said to him, "Caesar's." 17 Jesus said to them, "Render to Caesar the things that are Caesar's, and to God the things that are God's." And they	20 So they watched him, and sent spies, who pretended to be sincere, that they might take hold of what he said, so as to deliver him up to the authority and jurisdiction of the governor. 21 They asked him, "Teacher, we know that you speak and teach rightly, and show no partiality, but truly teach the way of God. 22 Is it lawful for us to give tribute to Caesar, or not?"
18 But Jesus, aware of their malice, said, "Why put me to the test, you hypocrites? 19 Show me the money for the tax." And they brought him a coin.[r] 20 And Jesus said to them, "Whose likeness and inscription is this?" 21 They said, "Caesar's." Then he said to them, "Render therefore to Caesar the things that are Caesar's and to God the things that are God's." 22 When they heard it,		23 But he perceived their craftiness, and said to them, 24 "Show me a coin.[r] Whose likeness and inscription has it?" They said, "Caesar's." 25 He said to them, "Then render to Caesar the things that are Caesar's, and to God the things that are God's." 26 And they were not able in the presence of the people to catch him by what he said; but
they marveled; and they left him and went away.	were amazed at him. *Cf. 12:12 (§ 204, p. 144)*	marveling at his answer they were silent.

---

[r] Greek, *a denarius.*

To Matt. 22:16 and parallels cf. John 3:2—This man came to Jesus by night and said to him, "Rabbi, we know that you are a teacher come from God; for no one can do these signs that you do, unless God is with him."

To Matt. 22:15ff. cf. *Egerton Papyrus 2*—And they, coming to him to test him, said, "Teacher Jesus, we know that you are from God, for what you do testifies above all the prophets. Tell us, therefore, is it lawful to give to kings what pertains to their rule? Shall we pay them or not?" And Jesus, knowing their thoughts, being moved with indignation, said to them, "Why do you call me teacher with your mouth and do not hear what I say? Well did Isaiah prophesy of you, when he said: 'This people honors me with their lips, but their heart is far from me; in vain do they worship me, teaching as doctrines the precepts of men.'" . . . (Cf. Matt. 15:7-8 = Mark 7:6-7, § 115, p.82.)

To Matt. 22:17ff. and parallels cf. **Gospel of Thomas, Logion 100:** They showed Jesus a gold (coin) and said to him, "Caesar's men demand taxes from us." He said to them, "Give to Caesar what belongs to Caesar, give to God what belongs to God, and give to me what is mine."

207. THE QUESTION CONCERNING THE RESURRECTION.

Matt. 22:23–33	Mark 12:18–27	Luke 20:27–40
23 The same day Sadducees came to him, who say that there is no resurrection; and they asked him a question, 24 saying, "Teacher, Moses said, 'If a man dies, having no children, his brother must marry the widow, and raise up children for his brother.' 25 Now there were seven brothers among us; the first married, and died, and having no children left his wife to his brother. 26 So too the second and third, down to the seventh. 27 After them all, the woman died. 28 In the resurrection, therefore, to which of the seven will she be wife? For they all had her." 29 But Jesus answered them, "You are wrong, because you know neither the scriptures nor the power of God.	18 And Sadducees came to him, who say that there is no resurrection; and they asked him a question, 19 "Teacher, Moses wrote for us that if a man's brother dies and leaves a wife, but leaves no child, the man [s] must take the wife, and raise up children for his brother. 20 There were seven brothers; the first took a wife, and when he died left no children; 21 and the second took her, and died, leaving no children; and the third likewise; 22 and the seven left no children. Last of all the woman also died. 23 In the resurrection [t] whose wife will she be? For the seven had her as wife." 24 Jesus said to them, "Is not this why you are wrong, that you know neither the scriptures nor the power of God?	27 There came to him some Sadducees, those who say that there is no resurrection, 28 and they asked him a question, saying, "Teacher, Moses wrote for us that if a man's brother dies, having a wife but no children, the man [s] must take the wife and raise up children for his brother. 29 Now there were seven brothers; the first took a wife, and died without children; 30 and the second 31 and the third took her, and likewise all seven left no children and died. 32 Afterward the woman also died. 33 In the resurrection, therefore, whose wife will the woman be? For the seven had her as wife." 34 And Jesus said to them, "The sons of this age marry and are given in marriage; 35 but those who are accounted worthy to attain to that age and to the resurrection from the dead neither marry
30 For in the resurrection they neither marry nor are given in marriage, but are like angels [u] in heaven.	25 For when they rise from the dead, they neither marry nor are given in marriage, but are like angels in heaven.	nor are given in marriage, 36 for they cannot die any more, because they are equal to angels and are sons of God, being sons of the resurrection. 37 But that
31 And as for the resurrection of the dead, have you not read what was said to you by God, 32 'I am the God of Abraham, and the God of Isaac, and the God of Jacob'? He is not God of the dead, but of the living." 33 And when the crowd heard it, they were astonished at his teaching.	26 And as for the dead being raised, have you not read in the book of Moses, in the passage about the bush, how God said to him, 'I am the God of Abraham, and the God of Isaac, and the God of Jacob'? 27 He is not God of the dead, but of the living; you are quite wrong."	the dead are raised, even Moses showed, in the passage about the bush, where he calls the Lord the God of Abraham, and the God of Isaac, and the God of Jacob. 38 Now he is not God of the dead, but of the living; for all live to him." 39 And some of the scribes answered, "Teacher, you have spoken well." 40 For they no longer dared to ask him any question.
See v. 46	*See 11:18b* *See 12:32a* *See 12:34b*	

Matt. 22:24 = Mark 12:19 = Luke 20:28—Deuteronomy 25:5-6, Genesis 38:8.   Matt. 22:32 = Mark 12:26 = Luke 20:37—Exodus 3:6.

[s] Greek, *his brother.*   [t] text: S B C D W sy[p] sa bo; add, *when they shall arise:* A Θ λ φ ℜ it vg sy[s].
[u] text: B D Θ λ it (some MSS.) sy[c] sy[s] sa Origen; add, *of God:* S W φ ℜ it (some MSS.) vg sy[p] bo.

208. THE GREAT COMMANDMENT.

Matt. 22:34–40	Mark 12:28–34	Luke 10:25–28 (§ 143, p. 104)
34 But when the Pharisees heard that he had silenced the Sadducees, they came together. 35 And one of them, a lawyer, asked him a question, to test him. 36 "Teacher, which is the great commandment in the law?" 37 And he said to him,	28 And one of the scribes came up and heard them disputing with one another, and seeing that he answered them well, asked him, "Which commandment is the first of all?" 29 Jesus answered, "The first is, 'Hear, O Israel: The Lord our God, the Lord is one; 30 and you shall love the Lord your God with all your heart, and with all your soul, and with all your mind, and with all your strength.'	25 And behold, a lawyer stood up to put him to the test, saying, "Teacher, what shall I do to inherit eternal life?" 26 He said to him, "What is written in the law? How do you read?" 27 And he answered, "You shall love the Lord your God with all your heart, and with all your soul, and with all your strength, and with all your mind;
"You shall love the Lord your God with all your heart, and with all your soul, and with all your mind.		
38 This is the great and first commandment. 39 And a second is like it, You shall love your neighbor as yourself. 40 On these two commandments depend all the law and the prophets."	31 The second is this, 'You shall love your neighbor as yourself.' There is no other commandment greater than these."	and your neighbor as yourself." 28 And he said to him, "You have answered right; do this, and you will live."
	32 And the scribe said to him, "You are right, Teacher; you have truly said that he is one, and there is no other but he; 33 and to love him with all the heart, and with all the understanding, and with all the strength, and to love one's neighbor as oneself, is much more than all whole burnt offerings and sacrifices." 34 And when Jesus saw that he answered wisely, he said to him, "You are not far from the kingdom of God." And after that no one dared to ask him any question.	*See 20:39*
See v. 46		*See 20:40*

Matt. 22:37 = Mark 12:30 = Luke 10:27—Deuteronomy 6:5.   Mark 12:29—Deuteronomy 6:4.
Matt. 22:39 = Mark 12:31 = Luke 10:27b—Leviticus 19:18.   Mark 12:33—cf. I Samuel 15:22.

209. ABOUT DAVID'S SON.

Matt. 22:41–46	**Mark 12:35–37a**	**Luke 20:41–44**
41 Now when the Pharisees were gathered together, Jesus asked them a question, 42 saying, "What do you think of the Christ? Whose son is he?" They said to him, "The son of David." 43 He said to them, "How is it then that David, inspired by the Spirit,ᵛ calls him Lord, saying,	35 And as Jesus taught in the temple, he said, "How can the scribes say that the Christ is the son of David? 36 David himself, inspired by the Holy Spirit,ᵛᵛ declared,	41 But he said to them, "How can **they say** that the Christ is David's son? 42 For David himself says in the Book of Psalms,
44 'The Lord said to my Lord, Sit at my right hand, till I put thy enemies under thy feet'?	'The Lord said to my Lord, Sit at my right hand, till I put thy enemies under thy feet.'	'The Lord said to my Lord, Sit at my right hand, 43 till I make thy enemies a stool for thy feet.'
45 If David thus calls him Lord, how is he his son?" 46 And no one was able to answer him a word, nor from that day did any one dare to ask him any more questions.	37 David himself calls him Lord; so how is he his son?" *See above, v. 34*	44 David thus calls him Lord; so how is he his son?" *See above 20:40*

210. WOES AGAINST THE PHARISEES.

Matt. 23:1–36	**Mark 12:37b–40**	**Luke 20:45–47**
1 Then said Jesus to the crowds and to his disciples, 2 "The scribes and the Pharisees sit on Moses' seat; 3 so practice and observe whatever they tell you, but not what they do; for they preach, but do not practice. 4 They bind heavy burdens, hard to bear,ʷ and lay them on men's shoulders; but they themselves will not move them with their finger. 5 They do all their deeds to be seen by men; for they make their phylacteries **broad** and their fringes long,	37b And the great throng heard him gladly. 38 And in his teaching he said,	20:45 And in the hearing of all the people he said to his disciples, . . . 11:46 (*§ 154, p. 110*): And he said, "Woe to you lawyers also! for you load men with burdens hard to bear, and you yourselves do not touch the burdens with one of your fingers."

Matt. 22:44 = Mark 12:36 = Luke 20:42-43—Psalm 110:1.   Matt. 23:5 cf. Numbers 15:38-39.

ᵛ Or, *David in the Spirit.*   ᵛᵛ Or, *himself, in the Holy Spirit.*   ʷ text: B W Θ λ 𝔐 it (some MSS.) vg sa; omit, *hard to bear:* S λ it (some MSS.) syᶜ syˢ syᵖ bo; *not hard to bear:* D.

20:46

"Beware of the scribes, who like to go about in long robes, and to have salutations in the market places **39** and the best seats in the synagogues and the places of honor at feasts,* | "Beware of the scribes, who like to go about in long robes, and love salutations in the market places and the best seats in the synagogues and the places of honor at feasts, . . ." *

6 and they love the place of honor at feasts and the best seats in the synagogues, **7** and salutations in the market places,* and being called rabbi by men. **8** But you are not to be called rabbi, for you have one teacher, and you are all brethren. **9** And call no man your father on earth, for you have one Father, who is in heaven. **10** Neither be called masters, for you have one master, the Christ. **11** He who is greatest among you shall be your servant;** **12** whoever exalts himself will be humbled, and whoever humbles himself will be exalted.

Cf. Mark 9:35 (§ 129, p. 95)

Cf. Luke 9:48b (§ 129, p. 96)

Cf. Matt. 18:4 (§ 129, p. 95), and Luke 14:11 (§ 169, p. 119), and Luke 18:14 (§ 186, p. 127).

13 "But woe to you, scribes and Pharisees, hypocrites! because you shut the kingdom of heaven against men; for you neither enter yourselves, nor allow those who would enter to go in.ˣ

11:52 *(§ 154, p. 110)*: "Woe to you lawyers! for you have taken away the key of knowledge; you did not enter yourselves, and you hindered those who were entering."

40 who devour widows' houses and for a pretense make long prayers. They will receive the greater condemnation." | 20:47 ". . . who devour widows' houses and for a pretense make long prayers. They will receive the greater condemnation."

(Mark 12:41–44 = Luke 21:1–4, § 212, p. 152)

15 "Woe to you, scribes and Pharisees, hypocrites! for you traverse sea and land to make a single proselyte, and when he becomes a proselyte, you make him twice as much a child of hellʸ as yourselves.

---

* Luke 11:43 (§ 154, p.109): "Woe to you Pharisees! for you love the best seat in the synagogues and salutations in the market places."
** Cf. also Matt. 20:26-27 = Mark 10:43-44 (§ 192, p.133) = Luke 22:26 (§ 237b, p.167).

ˣ text: S B D Θ λ it (some MSS.) vg (some MSS.) syˢ sa bo Origen; add verse 14 (sometimes put after verse 12)—*Woe to you, scribes and Pharisees, hypocrites! for you devour widows' houses and for a pretense you make long prayers; therefore you will receive the greater condemnation*—(= Mark 12:40 and Luke 20:47): W φ ℵ it (some MSS.) vg (some MSS.) syᶜ syᵖ.   ʸ Greek, *Gehenna*.

To Matt. 23:13 (= Luke 11:52) cf. **Gospel of Thomas, Logion 39.**

16 "Woe to you, blind guides, who say, 'If any one swears by the temple, it is nothing; but if any one swears by the gold of the temple, he is bound by his oath.' 17 You blind fools! For which is greater, the gold or the temple that has made the gold sacred? 18 And you say, 'If any one swears by the altar, it is nothing; but if any one swears by the gift that is on the altar, he is bound by his oath.' 19 You blind men! For which is greater, the gift or the altar that makes the gift sacred? 20 So he who swears by the altar, swears by it and by everything on it; 21 and he who swears by the temple, swears by it and by him who dwells in it; 22 and he who swears by heaven, swears by the throne of God and by him who sits upon it.

23 "Woe to you, scribes and Pharisees, hypocrites! for you tithe mint and dill and cummin, and have neglected the weightier matters of the law, justice and mercy and faith; these you ought to have done, without neglecting the others. 24 You blind guides, straining out a gnat and swallowing a camel!

25 "Woe to you, scribes and Pharisees, hypocrites! for you cleanse the outside of the cup and of the plate, but inside they are full of extortion and rapacity. 26 You blind Pharisee! first cleanse the inside of the cup and of the plate, that the outside also may be clean.

11:39–42, 44, 47–51
(§ *154, p. 109f*):
42 "But woe to you Pharisees!   for you tithe mint and rue and every herb, and neglect

             justice
and the love of God; these you ought to have done, without neglecting the others.

39 "Now you Pharisees cleanse the outside of the cup and of the dish, but inside you are full of extortion and wickedness. 40 You fools! Did not he who made the outside make the inside also? 41 But give for alms those things which are within; and behold, everything is clean for you.

27 "Woe to you, scribes and Pharisees, hypocrites! for you are like whitewashed tombs, which outwardly appear beautiful, but within they are full of dead men's bones and all uncleanness. 28 So you also outwardly appear righteous to men, but within you are full of hypocrisy and iniquity.

29 "Woe to you, scribes and Pharisees, hypocrites! for you build the tombs of the prophets and adorn the monuments of the righteous, 30 saying, 'If we had lived in the days of our fathers, we would not have taken part with them in shedding the blood of the prophets.' 31 Thus you witness against yourselves, that you are sons of those who murdered the prophets.

32 "Fill up, then, the measure of your fathers. 33 You serpents, you brood of vipers, how are you to escape being sentenced to hell?[z] 34 Therefore I send you prophets and wise men and scribes, some of whom you will kill and crucify, and some you will scourge in your synagogues and persecute from town to town, 35 that upon you may come all the righteous blood shed on earth, from the blood of innocent Abel to the blood of Zechariah the son of Barachiah, whom you murdered between the sanctuary and the altar. 36 Truly, I say to you, all this will come upon this generation.

44 "Woe to you!

for

you are like graves which are not seen, and men walk over them without knowing it.

47 "Woe to you!

for

you build the tombs of the prophets whom your fathers killed. 48 So you are witnesses and consent to the deeds of your fathers; for they killed them, and you build their tombs.

To Matt. 23:33 cf. Matt. 3:7b

= *Luke 3:7b (§ 2, p. 9)*
49 Therefore also the Wisdom of God said, 'I will send them prophets and apostles, some of whom they will kill

and persecute,'
50 that the blood of all the prophets, shed from the foundation of the world, may be required of this generation, 51 from the blood of Abel to the blood of Zechariah, who perished between the altar and the sanctuary. Yes, I tell you, it will be required of this generation.

Matt. 23:35 = Luke 11:50-51—cf. Genesis 4:8, II Chronicles 24:20-21, Zechariah 1:1.

---

[z] Greek, *Gehenna.*

To Matt. 23:27 cf. **Gospel of the Naassenes** (in Hippolytus, *Refutation of All Heresies, V.8.23*)—"You are whitewashed tombs filled within with dead men's bones," that is, there is not within you the living man.

To Matt. 23:35 cf. **Gospel of the Nazaraeans** (in Jerome, *Commentary on Matthew 23:35*)—In the gospel which the Nazarenes use, for "son of Barachiah" we find written, "son of Jehoiada." Cf. also—And Zechariah the son of Jehoiada said, "For he was of two names"—Peter of Laodicea *Commentary on Matthew 23:35* ed. Heinrici V. 267.

211. THE LAMENT OVER JERUSALEM.

Matt. 23:37–39	Luke 13:34–35 (§ *167, p. 118*)
37 "O Jerusalem, Jerusalem, killing the prophets and stoning those who are sent to you! How often would I have gathered your children together as a hen gathers her brood under her wings, and you would not! [38] Behold, your house is forsaken and desolate.[a] [39] For I tell you, you will not see me again, until you say, 'Blessed is he who comes in the name of the Lord.' "	34 "O Jerusalem, Jerusalem, killing the prophets and stoning those who are sent to you! How often would I have gathered your children together as a hen gathers her brood under her wings, and you would not! [35] Behold, your house is forsaken! And I tell you, you will not see me until you say, 'Blessed is he who comes in the name of the Lord.' "

212. THE WIDOW'S GIFT.

Mark. 12:41–44 (*12:38–40, § 210, pp. 148–149*)	Luke 21:1–4 (*20:45–47, § 210, pp. 148–149*)
41 And he sat down opposite the treasury, and watched the multitude putting money into the treasury. Many rich people put in large sums. [42] And a poor widow came, and put in two copper coins, which make a penny. [43] And he called his disciples to him, and said to them, "Truly, I say to you, this poor widow has put in more than all those who are contributing to the treasury. [44] For they all contributed out of their abundance; but she out of her poverty has put in everything she had, her whole living."	1 He looked up and saw the rich putting their gifts into the treasury; [2] and he saw a poor widow put in two copper coins. [3] And he said, "Truly I tell you, this poor widow has put in more than all of them; [4] for they all contributed out of their abundance, but she out of her poverty put in all the living that she had."

213. PREDICTION OF THE DESTRUCTION OF THE TEMPLE.

Matt. 24:1–3	Mark 13:1–4	Luke 21:5–7
1 Jesus left the temple and was going away, when his disciples came to point out to him the buildings of the temple. [2] But he answered them, "You see all these, do you not? Truly, I say to you, there will not be left here one stone upon another, that will not be thrown down."	1 And as he came out of the temple, one of his disciples said to him, "Look, Teacher, what wonderful stones and what wonderful buildings!" [2] And Jesus said to him, "Do you see these great buildings? There will not be left here one stone upon another, that will not be thrown down."[c]	5 And as some spoke of the temple, how it was adorned with noble stones and offerings, he said, [6] "As for these things which you see, the days will come when there shall not be left here[b] one stone upon another that will not be thrown down."

Matt. 23:37 = Luke 13:34—Isaiah 31:5.
Matt. 23:39 = Luke 13:35—Psalm 118:26.

[a] text: S C D W Θ λ φ 𝕽 it vg sy^p bo (some MSS.); cf. Jeremiah 22:5, omit, *and desolate:* B sy^s sa bo (some MSS.) (Cf. Luke, *and desolate:* D Θ φ 𝕽 it vg sy^c sy^p.)   [b] text: S B λ φ sy^c sy^s sa bo; omit, *here:* A W Θ 𝕽 vg sy^p; *one stone upon another in the wall here:* D it.   [c] text: S A B λ φ 𝕽 vg sa bo; add, *and after three days another will be raised up without hands:* D W it Cyprian Cf. Mark 14:58 and John 2:19.

152

3 As he sat on the Mount of Olives, the disciples came to him privately saying,

"Tell us, when will this be, and what will be the sign of your coming and of the close of the age?"

3 And as he sat on the Mount of Olives opposite the temple, Peter and James and John and Andrew asked him privately, 4 "Tell us, when will this be, and what will be the sign when these things are all to be accomplished?"

7 And they asked him, "Teacher, when will this be, and what will be the sign when this is about to take place?"

The Synoptic Apocalypse

Matthew 24:4–36 = Mark 13:5–37 = Luke 21:8–36

214. Ia. THE SIGNS OF THE PAROUSIA

Matt. 24:4–8	Mark 13:5–8	Luke 21:8–11
4 And Jesus answered them, "Take heed that no one leads you astray. ⁵ For many will come in my name, saying, 'I am the Christ,' and they will lead many astray. *	5 And Jesus began to say to them, "Take heed that no one leads you astray. ⁶ Many will come in my name, saying, 'I am he!' and they will lead many astray. *	8 And he said, "Take heed that you are not led astray; for many will come in my name, saying, 'I am he!' and, 'The time is at hand!' Do not go after them. *
⁶ And you will hear of wars and rumors of wars; see that you are not alarmed; for this must take place, but the end is not yet.	⁷ And when you hear of wars and rumors of wars, do not be alarmed; this must take place, but the end is not yet.	⁹ And when you hear of wars and tumults, do not be terrified; for this must take place, but the end will not be at once." ¹⁰ Then he said to them, "Nation will rise
⁷ For nation will rise against nation, and kingdom against kingdom, and there will be famines and earthquakes in various places:	⁸ For nation will rise against nation, and kingdom against kingdom; there will be earthquakes in various places, there will be famines;	against nation, and kingdom against kingdom; ¹¹ there will be great earthquakes, and in various places famines and pestilences; and there will be terrors and great signs from heaven.
⁸ all this is but the beginning of the birth-pangs.	this is but the beginning of the birth-pangs.	

215. Ib. THE BEGINNINGS OF THE TROUBLES.

Matt. 24:9–14	Mark 13:9–13	Luke 21:12–19
9ª "Then they will deliver you up to tribulation, . . ."	9 "But take heed to yourselves; for they will deliver you up to councils; and you will be beaten in synagogues; and you will stand before governors and kings for my sake, to bear testimony before them. ¹⁰ And the gospel must first be preached to all nations.	12 "But before all this they will lay their hands on you and persecute you, delivering you up to the synagogues and prisons, and you will be brought before kings and governors for my name's sake.
10:17–21 (§ 59, p. 43): ¹⁷ "Beware of men; for they will deliver you up to councils, and flog you in their synagogues, ¹⁸ and you will be dragged before governors and kings for my sake, to bear testimony before them and the Gentiles.	(= Matt. 24:14)	¹³ This will be a time for you to bear testimony.
¹⁹ When they deliver you up, do not be anxious how you are to speak or what you are to say; for what you are to say will be given to you in that hour; ²⁰ for it is not you who speak, but the Spirit of your Father speaking through you. **	¹¹ And when they bring you to trial and deliver you up, do not be anxious beforehand what you are to say; but say whatever is given you in that hour, for it is not you who speak but the Holy Spirit. **	¹⁴ Settle it therefore in your minds, not to meditate beforehand how to answer; ¹⁵ for I will give you a mouth and wisdom, which none of your adversaries will be able to withstand or contradict. **

---

* Cf. Matt. 24:23-26 = Mark 13:21-22 (§ 217, p.156) = Luke 17:23 (§ 184, p.126).

** Luke 12:11-12 (§ 155, p.112): ¹¹ "And when they bring you before the synagogues and the rulers and the authorities, do not be anxious how or what you are to answer or what you are to say; ¹² for the Holy Spirit will teach you in that very hour what you ought to say."

Matt. 24:6 = Mark 13:7 = Luke 21:9—Daniel 2:28.　　Matt. 24:7 = Mark 13:8 = Luke 21:10 cf. Isaiah 19:2, II Chronicles 15:6.

Matt. 10:19-20 = Mark 13:11 = Luke 21:14 cf. John 14:26—"But the Counselor, the Holy Spirit, whom the Father will send in my name, he will teach you all things, and bring to your remembrance all that I have said to you."

21 Brother will deliver up brother to death, and the father his child, and children will rise against parents and have them put to death;

9b . . . and put you to death; and you will be hated by all nations for my name's sake. * 10 And then many will fall away,d and betray one another, and hate one another. 11 And many false prophets will arise and lead many astray. 12 And because wickedness is multiplied, most men's love will grow cold. 13 But he who endures to the end will be saved. *** 14 And this gospel of the kingdom will be preached throughout the whole world, as a testimony to all nations; and then the end will come.

12 And brother will deliver up brother to death, and the father his child, and children will rise against parents and have them put to death;

13 and you will be hated by all for my name's sake. *

But he who endures to the end will be saved. ***

Cf. above v. 10

16 You will be delivered up even by parents and brothers and kinsmen and friends, and some of you they will put to death;

17 you will be hated by all for my name's sake. * 18 But not a hair of your head will perish. **

19 By your endurance you will gain your lives. ***

216. IIa. THE DESOLATING SACRILEGE.

Matt. 24:15–22

15 "So when you see the desolating sacrilege spoken of by the prophet Daniel, standing in the holy place (let the reader understand), 16 then let those who are in Judea flee to the mountains; 17 let him who is on the housetop not go down to take what is in his house; 18 and let him who is in the field not turn back to take his mantle. ****

Mark 13:14–20

14 "But when you see the desolating sacrilege

set up where it ought not to be (let the reader understand), then let those who are in Judea flee to the mountains; 15 let him who is on the housetop not go down, nor enter his house, to take anything away; 16 and let him who is in the field not turn back to take his mantle. ****

Luke 21:20–24

20 "But when you see Jerusalem surrounded by armies, then know that its desolation has come near.

21 Then let those who are in Judea flee to the mountains, and let those who are inside the city depart, and let not those who are out in the country enter it; **** 22 for these are days of vengeance, to fulfil all that is written.

---

* Matt. 10:22a (§ 59, p.43): "And you will be hated by all for my name's sake."
** Matt. 10:30 (§ 60, p.44): "But even the hairs of your head are all numbered." | Luke 12:7 (§ 155, p. 111): "Why, even the hairs of your head are all numbered."
*** Matt. 10:22b (§ 59, p.43): "But he who endures to the end will be saved."
**** Luke 17:31 (§ 184, p.126): "On that day, let him who is on the housetop, with his goods in the house, not come down to take them away; and likewise let him who is in the field not turn back."

Mark 13:12 = Matt. 10:21—cf. Micah 7:6.   Matt. 24:15 = Mark 13:14—Daniel 9:27; 11:31; 12:11; 1 Macc. 1:54.   Matt. 24:16 = Mark 13:14b—cf. Ezekiel 7:16.   Luke 21:22—Deuteronomy 32:35.

---

d Or, stumble.

To Matt. 24:9b = Mark 13:13 = Luke 21:17 cf. John 15:21 "But all this they will do to you on my account, because they do not know him who sent me." Also John 16:2 "They will put you out of the synagogues; indeed, the hour is coming when whoever kills you will think he is offering service to God."

19 And alas for those who are with child and for those who give suck in those days! 20 Pray that your flight may not be in winter or on a sabbath. 21 For then there will be great tribulation, such as has not been from the beginning of the world until now, no, and never will be. 22 And if those days had not been shortened, no human being would be saved; but for the sake of the elect those days will be shortened.	17 And alas for those who are with child and for those who give suck in those days! 18 Pray that it may not happen in winter. 19 For in those days there will be such tribulation as has not been from the beginning of the creation which God created until now, and never will be. 20 And if the Lord had not shortened the days, no human being would be saved; but for the sake of the elect, whom he chose, he shortened the days.	23 Alas for those who are with child and for those who give suck in those days! For great distress shall be upon the earth and wrath upon this people; 24 they will fall by the edge of the sword, and be led captive among all nations; and Jerusalem will be trodden down by the Gentiles, until the times of the Gentiles are fulfilled.

217. IIb. THE CULMINATION OF THE TROUBLES.

Matt. 24:23–25	Mark 13:21–23	
23 "Then if any one says to you, 'Lo, here is the Christ!' or 'There he is!' do not believe it. 24 For false Christs and false prophets will arise and show great signs and wonders, so as to lead astray, if possible, even the elect. 25 Lo, I have told you beforehand.	21 "And then if any one says to you, 'Look, here is the Christ!' or 'Look, there he is!' do not believe it. 22 False Christs and false prophets will arise and show signs and wonders, to lead astray, if possible, the elect. 23 But take heed; I have told you all things beforehand.	*17:21, 23* (§ *183 f., p. 125 f.*)

218. IIc. THE DAY OF THE SON OF MAN.

Matt. 24:26–28	Luke 17:23–24, 37 (§ *184, pp. 126–127*)
26 "So, if they say to you, 'Lo, he is in the wilderness,' do not go out; if they say, 'Lo, he is in the inner rooms,' do not believe it. 27 For as the lightning comes from the east and shines as far as the west, so will be the coming of the Son of man. 28 Wherever the body is, there the eagles [f] will be gathered together.	23 "And they will say to you, 'Lo, there!' or 'Lo, here!' Do not go; do not follow them. 24 For as the lightning flashes and lights up the sky from one side to the other, so will the Son of man be in his day. [e] 37 Where the body is, there the eagles [f] will be gathered together.

Matt. 24:21 = Mark 13:19—Daniel 12:1. Luke 21:24—Zechariah 12:3. Matt. 24:24 = Mark 13:22—Deuteronomy 13:2.

[e] text: S A W Θ λ φ ℜ it (some MSS.) vg sy[c] sy[s] sy[p] bo; omit, *in his day:* P[75] B D it (some MSS.) sa.   [f] Or, *vultures.*

219. IIIa. THE PAROUSIA OF THE SON OF MAN.

Matt. 24:29–31	Mark 13:24–27	Luke 21:25–28
29 "Immediately after the tribulation of those days the sun will be darkened, and the moon will not give its light, and the stars will fall from heaven,	24 "But in those days, after that tribulation, the sun will be darkened, and the moon will not give its light, 25 and the stars will be falling from heaven,	25 "And there will be signs in sun and moon and stars, and upon the earth distress of nations in perplexity at the roaring of the sea and the waves, 26 men fainting with fear and with foreboding of what is coming on the world;
and the powers of the heavens will be shaken; 30 then will appear the sign of the Son of man in heaven, and then all the tribes of the earth will mourn, and they will see the Son of man coming on the clouds of heaven with power and great glory; 31 and he will send out his angels with a loud trumpet call, and they will gather his elect from the four winds, from one end of heaven to the other.	and the powers in the heavens will be shaken. 26 And then they will see the Son of man coming in clouds with great power and glory. 27 And then he will send out the angels, and gather his elect from the four winds, from the ends of the earth to the ends of heaven.	for the powers of the heavens will be shaken. 27 And then they will see the Son of man coming in a cloud with power and great glory. 28 Now when these things begin to take place, look up and raise your heads, because your redemption is drawing near."

220. IIIb. THE PARABLE OF THE FIG TREE.

Matt. 24:32–33	Mark 13:28–29	Luke 21:29–31
32 "From the fig tree learn its lesson: as soon as its branch becomes tender and puts forth its leaves, you know that summer is near. 33 So also, when you see all these things you know that he is near, at the very gates.	28 "From the fig tree learn its lesson: as soon as its branch becomes tender and puts forth its leaves, you know that summer is near. 29 So also, when you see these things taking place, you know that he is near, at the very gates.	29 And he told them a parable: "Look at the fig tree, and all the trees; 30 as soon as they come out in leaf, you see for yourselves and know that the summer is already near. 31 So also, when you see these things taking place, you know that the kingdom of God is near.

Matt. 24:30—cf. Revelation 1:7.

Matt. 24:29 = Mark 13:24-25 = Luke 21:26—Isaiah 13:10; 34:4.   Matt. 24:30—cf. Zechariah 12:12-14.   Matt. 24:30 = Mark 13:26 = Luke 21:27—Daniel 7:13-14.   Matt. 24:31 = Mark 13:27—Deuteronomy 30:4, Isaiah 27:13, Zechariah 2:6.   Luke 21:25—Psalm 65:7.

To Matt. 24:30-31 and parallels cf. I Thessalonians 4:15-16—15 For this we declare to you by the word of the Lord, that we who are alive, who are left until the coming of the Lord, shall not precede those who have fallen asleep. 16 For the Lord himself will descend from heaven with a cry of command, with the archangel's call, and with the sound of the trumpet of God.

221. IIIc. THE TIME OF THE PAROUSIA.

Matt. 24:34–36	Mark 13:30–32	Luke 21:32–33
34 "Truly I say to you, this generation will not pass away till all these things take place. * 35 Heaven and earth will pass away, but my words will not pass away. ** 36 But of that day and hour no one knows, not even the angels of heaven, nor the Son,ᵍ but the Father only.	30 "Truly, I say to you, this generation will not pass away before all these things take place. * 31 Heaven and earth will pass away, but my words will not pass away. ** 32 But of that day or that hour no one knows, not even the angels in heaven, nor the Son, but only the Father.	32 "Truly, I say to you, this generation will not pass away till all has taken place. * 33 Heaven and earth will pass away, but my words will not pass away. **

222. MARK'S ENDING TO THE DISCOURSE.

Matt. 25:14–15b (§ 228, p. 160)	Mark 13:33–37	Luke 19:12–13 (§ 195, p. 135)
14 "For it will be as when a man going on a journey called his servants and entrusted to them his property; 15b . . . to each according to his ability. Then he went away."	33 "Take heed, watch;ʰ for you do not know when the time will come. 34 It is like a man going on a journey, when he leaves home and puts his servants in charge, each with his work, and commands the doorkeeper to be on the watch. 35 Watch therefore — for you do not know when the master of the house will come, in the evening, or at midnight, or at cockcrow, or in the morning — 36 lest he come suddenly and find you asleep. 37 And what I say to you I say to all: Watch."	12 He said therefore, "A nobleman went into a far country to receive kingly powerⁱ and then return. 13 Calling ten of his servants, he gave them ten pounds."
24:42 (§ 225, p. 159): "Watch therefore, for you do not know on what day your Lord is coming."		
25:13 (§ 227, p. 160): "Watch therefore, for you know neither the day nor the hour."		12:38 (§ 158, p. 113): "If he comes in the second watch, or in the third, and finds them so, blessed are those servants!"
	(14:1–2, § 231, p. 163)	

223. LUKE'S ENDING TO THE DISCOURSE.
Luke 21:34–36

34 "But take heed to yourselves lest your hearts be weighed down with dissipation and drunkenness and cares of this life, and that day come upon you suddenly like a snare; 35 for it will come upon all who dwell upon the face of the whole earth. 36 But watch at all times, praying that you may have strength to escape all these things that will take place, and to stand before the Son of man."

---

* Cf. Matt. 16:28 = Mark 9:1 = Luke 9:27 (§ 123, p.90).
** Cf. Matt. 5:17 (§ 21, p.21) = Luke 16:17 (§ 176, p.123).

Luke 21:35—Isaiah 24:17.

ᵍ text: S B D Θ φ it Irenaeus; omit, *nor the son:* W λ 𝔐 vg syˢ syᵖ sa bo Didymus.   ʰ text: B D it (some MSS.); add, *and pray:* S A C W Θ λ φ 𝔐 it (some MSS.) vg syˢ syᵖ sa bo.   ⁱ Greek, *a kingdom.*

224. THE NEED FOR WATCHFULNESS.

Matt. 24:37–41

37 "As were the days of Noah, so will be the coming of the Son of man. 38 For as in those days before the flood they were eating and drinking, marrying and giving in marriage, until the day when Noah entered the ark, 39 and they did not know until the flood came and swept them all away, so will be the coming of the Son of man.

40 Then two men will be in the field; one is taken and one is left. 41 Two women will be grinding at the mill; one is taken and one is left.

Luke 17:26–27, 30, 34–35 (§ 184, pp. 126–127)

26 "As it was in the days of Noah, so will it be in the days of the Son of man.

27 They ate, they drank, they married, they were given in marriage, until the day when Noah entered the ark,

and the flood came and destroyed them all. 30 so will it be on the day when the Son of man is revealed.

34 I tell you, in that night there will be two in one bed; one will be taken and the other left. 35 There will be two women grinding together; one will be taken and the other left."

225. THE WATCHFUL HOUSEHOLDER.

Matt. 24:42–44

42 "Watch therefore, for you do not know on what day your Lord is coming.* 43 But know this, that if the householder had known in what part of the night the thief was coming, he would have watched and would not have let his house be broken into. 44 Therefore you also must be ready; for the Son of man is coming at an hour you do not expect.

Luke 12:39–40 (§ 158, p. 114)

39 "But know this, that if the householder had known at what hour the thief was coming, he [j] would not have left his house to be broken into.
40 You also must be ready; for the Son of man is coming at an unexpected hour."

226. THE FAITHFUL AND WISE SERVANT.

Matt. 24:45–51

45 "Who then is the faithful and wise servant, whom his master has set over his household, to give them their food at the proper time? 46 Blessed is that servant whom his master when he comes will find so doing. 47 Truly, I say to you, he will set him over all his possessions. 48 But if that wicked servant says to himself, 'My master is

Luke 12:42–46 (§ 158, p. 114)

42 "Who then is the faithful and wise steward, whom his master will set over his household, to give them their portion of food at the proper time? 43 Blessed is that servant whom his master when he comes will find so doing. 44 Truly, I say to you, he will set him over all his possessions. 45 But if that servant says to himself, "My master is

---

* Cf. Mark 13:33, 35 (§ 222, p.158).

Matt. 24:38 = Luke 17:26-27—Genesis 7:7.

---

[j] text: P[75] S D sy[c] sy[s] sa; add, *would have watched and:* A B W Θ λ φ ℜ it vg sy [p] bo.

To Matt. 24:42-43 cf. I Thessalonians 5:2—For you yourselves know well that the day of the Lord will come like a thief in the night. Cf. also Revelation 16:15—"Lo, I am coming like a thief!" Epiphanius, *Ancoratus 21:2*—For he (the Son) said, "That day will come like a thief in the night." Cf. also Didymus, *On the Trinity, III.22.*

delayed,'   [49] and begins to beat his fellow servants, and eats and drinks with the drunken, [50] the master of that servant will come on a day when he does not expect him and at an hour he does not know, [51] and will punish[k] him, and put him with the hypocrites; there men will weep and gnash their teeth.

delayed in coming,' and begins to beat the menservants and the maid-servants, and to eat and drink and get drunk, [46] the master of that servant will come on a day when he does not expect him and at an hour he does not know, and will punish[k] him, and put him with the unfaithful."

227. THE PARABLE OF THE TEN MAIDENS.*
Matt. 25:1–13

1 "Then the kingdom of heaven shall be compared to ten maidens who took their lamps and went to meet the bridegroom.[l] [2] Five of them were foolish, and five were wise. [3] For when the foolish took their lamps, they took no oil with them; [4] but the wise took flasks of oil with their lamps. [5] As the bridegroom was delayed, they all slumbered and slept. [6] But at midnight there was a cry, 'Behold, the bridegroom! Come out to meet him.' [7] Then all those maidens rose and trimmed their lamps. [8] And the foolish said to the wise, 'Give us some of your oil, for our lamps are going out.' [9] But the wise replied, 'Perhaps there will not be enough for us and for you; go rather to the dealers and buy for yourselves.' [10] And while they went to buy, the bridegroom came, and those who were ready went in with him to the marriage feast; and the door was shut. [11] Afterward the other maidens came also, saying, 'Lord, lord, open to us.' [12] But he replied, 'Truly, I say to you, I do not know you.' ** [13] Watch therefore, for you know neither the day nor the hour.

13: 35–37 (§ 222, p. 158)

228. THE PARABLE OF THE TALENTS.

Matt. 25:14–30

14 "For it will be as when a man going on a journey called his servants and entrusted to them his property; [15] to one he gave five talents,[m] to another two, to another one, to each according to his ability. Then he went away. [16] He who had received the five talents went at once and traded with them; and he made five talents more. [17] So also, he who had the two talents made two talents more.

Cf. Mark 13:34 (§ 222, p. 158)

Luke 19:12–27 (§ 195, pp. 135–136)

12 He said therefore, "A nobleman went into a far country to receive a kingdom and then return. [13] Calling ten of his servants, he gave them ten pounds,[n] and said to them, 'Trade with these till I come.' [14] But his citizens hated him and sent an embassy after him, saying, 'We do not want this man to reign over us.'

---

* Luke 12:35–36 (§ 158, p.113): [35] "Let your loins be girded and your lamps burning, [36] and be like men who are waiting for their master to come home from the marriage feast, so that they may open to him at once when he comes and knocks."

** Luke 13:25 (§ 165, p.117): "When once the householder has risen up and shut the door, you will begin to stand outside and to knock at the door, saying, 'Lord, open to us.' He will answer you, 'I do not know where you come from.' "

---

[k] Or, *cut him in pieces.*   [l] text: S B C W φ 𝔐 sa bo; add, *and the bride:* D Θ λ it vg sy^s sy^p.   [m] This talent was more than fifteen years' wages for a laborer.   [n] The mina, rendered here by *pound,* was about three months' wages for a laborer.

To Matt. 25:14-30 cf. Clement of Alexandria, *Miscellanies I.28.177* and frequently elsewhere—"Be skilful bankers, rejecting some things but retaining what is good."

18 But he who had received the one talent went and dug in the ground and hid his master's money. 19 Now after a long time the master of those servants came and settled accounts with them. 20 And he who had received the five talents came forward, bringing five talents more, saying, 'Master, you delivered to me five talents; here I have made five talents more.' 21 His master said to him, 'Well done, good and faithful servant; you have been faithful over a little, I will set you over much; enter into the joy of your master.' 22 And he also who had the two talents came forward, saying, Master, you delivered to me two talents; here I have made two talents more.' 23 His master said to him, 'Well done, good and faithful servant; you have been faithful over a little, I will set you over much; enter into the joy of your master.' 24 He also who had received the one talent came forward, saying, 'Master, I knew you to be a hard man, reaping where you did not sow, and gathering where you did not winnow; 25 so I was afraid, and I went and hid your talent in the ground. Here you have what is yours.' 26 But his master answered him, 'You wicked and slothful servant! You knew that I reap where I have not sowed, and gather where I have not winnowed? 27 Then you ought to have invested my money with the bankers, and at my coming I should have received what was my own with interest. 28 So take the talent from him, and give it to him who has the ten talents.

29 For to every one who has will more be given, and he will have abundance; but from him who has not, even what he has will be taken away.* 30 And cast the worthless servant into the outer darkness; there men will weep and gnash their teeth.'

15 "When he returned, having received the kingdom, he commanded these servants, to whom he had given the money, to be called to him, that he might know what they had gained by trading. 16 The first came before him, saying, 'Lord, your pound has made ten pounds more.'

17 And he said to him, 'Well done, good servant! Because you have been faithful in a very little, you shall have authority over ten cities. 18 And the second came, saying, 'Lord, your pound has made five pounds.'

19 And he said to him, 'And you are to be over five cities.'

20 Then another came, saying, 'Lord, here is your pound, which I kept laid away in a napkin; 21 for I was afraid of you, because you are a severe man; you take up what you did not lay down, and reap what you did not sow.'

22 He said to him, 'I will condemn you out of your own mouth, you wicked servant! You knew that I was a severe man, taking up what I did not lay down and reaping what I did not sow? 23 Why then did you not put my money into the bank, and at my coming I should have collected it with interest?' 24 And he said to those who stood by, 'Take the pound from him, and give it to him who has the ten pounds.' 25 (And they said to him, 'Lord, he has ten pounds!') 26 'I tell you, that to every one who has will more be given.

but from him who has not, even what he has will be taken away.* 27 But as for these enemies of mine, who did not want me to reign over them, bring them here and slay them before me.'

---

* Cf. Matt. 13:12 (§ 91, p.66) = Mark 4:25 = Luke 8:18 (§ 94, p.68).

To Matt. 25:22ff. cf. **Gospel of the Nazaraeans** (in Eusebius, *Theophany on Matt. 25:14f.*)—But the Gospel [written] in Hebrew letters which has reached our hands turns the threat not against the man who had hid [the talent], but against him who had lived dissolutely—for it told of three servants: one who wasted his master's possessions with harlots and flute-girls, one who multiplied his gains, and one who hid the talent; and accordingly, one was accepted, one was only rebuked, and one was shut up in prison.

229. THE LAST JUDGMENT.
Matt. 25:31–46

31 "When the Son of man comes in his glory, and all the angels with him, then he will sit on his glorious throne. 32 Before him will be gathered all the nations, and he will separate them one from another as a shepherd separates the sheep from the goats, 33 and he will place the sheep at his right hand, but the goats at the left. 34 Then the King will say to those at his right hand, 'Come, O blessed of my Father, inherit the kingdom prepared for you from the foundation of the world; 35 for I was hungry and you gave me food, I was thirsty and you gave me drink, I was a stranger and you welcomed me, 36 I was naked and you clothed me, I was sick and you visited me, I was in prison and you came to me.' 37 Then the righteous will answer him 'Lord, when did we see thee hungry and feed thee, or thirsty and give thee drink? 38 And when did we see thee a stranger and welcome thee, or naked and clothe thee? 39 And when did we see thee sick or in prison and visit thee?' 40 And the King will answer them, 'Truly, I say to you, as you did it to one of the least of these my brethren, you did it to me.' 41 Then he will say to those at his left hand, 'Depart from me, you cursed, into the eternal fire prepared for the devil and his angels; 42 for I was hungry and you gave me no food, I was thirsty and you gave me no drink, 43 I was a stranger and you did not welcome me, naked and you did not clothe me, sick and in prison and you did not visit me.' 44 Then they also will answer, 'Lord, when did we see thee hungry or thirsty or a stranger or naked or sick or in prison, and did not minister to thee?' 45 Then he will answer them, 'Truly, I say to you, as you did it not to one of the least of these, you did it not to me.' 46 And they will go away into eternal punishment, but the righteous into eternal life."

230. A SUMMARY OF THE DAYS SPENT IN JERUSALEM.
Luke 21:37–38 *(34–36, § 223, p. 158)*.

21:17   *11:19*   37 And every day he was teaching in the temple, but at night he went out and
(§ 198,   *(§ 200,*   lodged on the mount called Olivet. 38 And early in the morning all the people came
p. 139)   *p. 140)*   to him in the temple to hear him.

To Matt. 25:46 cf. John 5:28-29—28 ". . . the hour is coming when all who are in the tombs will hear his voice 29 and come forth, those who have done good, to the resurrection of life, and those who have done evil, to the resurrection of judgment."

To Matt. 25:31 cf. Origen, *Commentary on Matthew 13:2*—And Jesus said, "Because of the sick they were sick, and because of the hungry they were hungry, and because of the thirsty they were thirsty."

To Matt. 25:40 cf. Clement of Alexandria, *Miscellanies* I.19.94, 5—"For," he said, "you have seen your brother, you have seen your God." Cf. also Ibid. II.15.70, 5 and Tertullian *On Prayer 26*: He said, "You have seen your brother; you have seen your Lord."

C. The Passion Narrative

Matthew 26–27 = Mark 14–15 = Luke 22–23

231. THE CONSPIRACY AGAINST JESUS.

Matt. 26:1–5	Mark 14:1–2 *(13:33–37, § 222, p. 158)*	Luke 22:1–2
1 When Jesus had finished all these sayings, he said to his disciples, 2 "You know that after two days the Passover is coming, and the Son of man will be delivered up to be crucified."		
	1 It was now two days before the Passover and the feast of Unleavened Bread.	1 Now the feast of Unleavened Bread drew near, which is called the Passover.
3 Then the chief priests and the elders of the people gathered in the palace of the high priest, who was called Caiaphas, 4 and took counsel together in order to arrest Jesus by stealth and kill him. 5 But they said, "Not during the feast, lest there be a tumult among the people."	And the chief priests and the scribes were seeking how to arrest him by stealth, and kill him; 2 for they said, "Not during the feast, lest there be a tumult of the people."	2 And the chief priests and the scribes were seeking how to put him to death; for they feared the people.

232. THE ANOINTING AT BETHANY.

Matt. 26:6–13	Mark 14:3–9	
6 Now when Jesus was at Bethany in the house of Simon the leper,	3 And while he was at Bethany in the house of Simon the leper, as he sat at table, a woman came with an alabaster flask of ointment of pure nard, very costly, and she broke the flask and poured it over his head. 4 But there were some who said to themselves indignantly, "Why was the ointment thus wasted? 5 For this ointment might have been sold for more than three hundred denarii,° and given to the poor." And they reproached her. 6 But Jesus said, "Let her alone; why do you trouble her? She has done a beautiful thing to me. 7 For you always have the poor with you, and whenever you will, you can do good to them; but you will not always have me. 8 She has done what she could; she has anointed my body beforehand for burying. 9 And truly, I say to you, wherever the gospel is preached in the whole world, what she has done will be told in memory of her."	*Cf. 7: 36–50 (§ 83, p. 60)*
7 a woman came up to him with an alabaster flask of very expensive ointment, and she poured it on his head, as he sat at table. 8 But when the disciples saw it, they were indignant, saying, "Why this waste? 9 For this ointment might have been sold for a large sum, and given to the poor. 10 But Jesus, aware of this, said to them, "Why do you trouble the woman? For she has done a beautiful thing to me. 11 For you always have the poor with you, but you will not always have me. 12 In pouring this ointment on my body she has done it to prepare me for burial. 13 Truly, I say to you, wherever this gospel is preached in the whole world, what she has done will be told in memory of her."		

° The denarius was a day's wage for a laborer.

To § 231 cf. John 11:47–53.
To § 232 cf. John 12:1–8.

233. THE BETRAYAL BY JUDAS.

Matt. 26:14–16	Mark 14:10–11	Luke 22:3–6
14 Then one of the twelve, who was called Judas Iscariot,	10 Then Judas Iscariot, who was one of the twelve,	3 Then Satan entered into Judas called Iscariot, who was of the number of the twelve; [4] he went away and conferred with the chief priests and officers how he might betray him to them. [5] And they were glad, and engaged to give him money. [6] So he agreed, and sought an opportunity to betray him to them in the absence of the multitude.
went	went	
to the chief priests [15] and said, "What will you give me if I deliver him to you?" And they paid him thirty pieces of silver. [16] And from that moment he sought an opportunity to betray him.	to the chief priests in order to betray him to them. [11] And when they heard it they were glad, and promised to give him money. And he sought an opportunity to betray him.	

234. PREPARATION FOR THE PASSOVER.

Matt. 26:17–19	Mark 14:12–16	Luke 22:7–13
17 Now on the first day of Unleavened Bread	12 And on the first day of Unleavened Bread, when they sacrificed the passover lamb,	7 Then came the day of Unleavened Bread, on which the passover lamb had to be sacrificed. [8] So Jesus[p] sent Peter and John, saying, "Go and prepare the passover for us, that we may eat it." [9] They said to him, "Where will you have us prepare it?"
the disciples came to Jesus, saying, "Where will you have us prepare for you to eat the passover?" [18] He said,	his disciples said to him, "Where will you have us go and prepare for you to eat the passover?" [13] And he sent two of his disciples, and said to them,	
"Go into the city to a certain one,	"Go into the city, and a man carrying a jar of water will meet you; follow him,	[10]He said to them, "Behold, when you have entered the city, a man carrying a jar of water will meet you; follow him into the house which he enters,
and say to him, 'The Teacher says, My time is at hand; I will keep the passover at your house with my disciples.' "	[14] and wherever he enters, say to the householder, 'The Teacher says Where is my guest room, where I am to eat the passover with my disciples?' [15] And he will show you a large upper room furnished and ready; there prepare for us." [16] And the	[11] and tell the householder, 'The Teacher says to you, Where is the guest room, where I am to eat the passover with my disciples?' [12] And he will show you a large upper room furnished; there make ready."
[19] And the disciples did as Jesus had directed them, and they prepared the passover.	disciples set out and went to the city, and found it as he had told them; and they prepared the passover.	[13] And they went, and found it as he had told them; and they prepared the passover.

Matt. 26:15—Zechariah 11:12.

[p] Greek, *he.*

To Matt. 26:17 (Luke 22:9,15) cf. **Gospel of the Ebionites** (in Epiphanius, *Against Heresies, XXX.22.4*)—But leaving the proper sequence of the words and perverting the meaning . . ., they make the disciples say: "Where will you have us prepare for you to eat the passover?" And he (Jesus) asks, "Have I earnestly desired to eat this passover meat (flesh?) with you?"

The Last Supper

Matthew 26:20–29 = Mark 14:17–25 = Luke 22:14–38

235. THE TRAITOR.

Matt. 26:20–25	Mark 14:17–21	Luke 22:14, 21–23
20 When it was evening, he sat at table with the twelve disciples;q 21 and as they were eating, he said, "Truly, I say to you, one of you will betray me." 22 And they were very sorrowful, and began to say to him one after another, "Is it I, Lord?" 23 He answered, "He who has dipped his hand in the dish with me, will betray me. 24 The Son of man goes as it is written of him, but woe to that man by whom the Son of man is betrayed! It would have been better for that man if he had not been born." 25 Judas, who betrayed him, said, "Is it I, Master?"r He said to him, "You have said so."	17 And when it was evening he came with the twelve. 18 And as they were at table eating, Jesus said, "Truly, I say to you, one of you will betray me, one who is eating with me." 19 They began to be sorrowful, and to say to him one after another, "Is it I?" 20 He said to them, "It is one of the twelve, one who is dipping bread into the dish with me. 21 For the Son of man goes as it is written of him, but woe to that man by whom the Son of man is betrayed! It would have been better for that man if he had not been born."	14 And when the hour came, he sat at table, and the apostles with him. 22:21–23 (§ 237a, p. 166): 21 But behold the hand of him who betrays me is with me on the table. 22 For the Son of man goes as it has been determined; but woe to that man by whom he is betrayed!" 23 And they began to question one another, which of them it was that would do this.

236. THE INSTITUTION OF THE LORD'S SUPPER.

Matt. 26:26–29	Mark 14:22–25	Luke 22:15–20
		15 And he said to them, "I have earnestly desired to eat this passover with you before I suffer; 16 for I tell you I shall not eat its until it is fulfilled in the kingdom of God.

Mark 14:18—Psalm 41:9.

q text: S A W Θ it vg syᵖ sa bo; omit, *disciples:* P³⁷ᵗ P⁴⁵ᵗ B D λ φ 𝕽 syˢ.   r Or, *Rabbi.*   s text: P⁷⁵ᵗ S A B Θ λ sa bo; *never eat it again:* C D W φ 𝕽 it vg syᶜ syˢ syᵖ.

To § 236 cf. John 13:21–30.

| | | ¹⁷ And he took a cup, and when he had given thanks he said, "Take this, and divide it among yourselves; ¹⁸ for I tell you that from now on I shall not drink of the fruit of the vine until the kingdom of God comes." |

See below, v. 29 | *See below, v. 25* | ¹⁷ And he took a cup, and when he had given thanks he said, "Take this, and divide it among yourselves; ¹⁸ for I tell you that from now on I shall not drink of the fruit of the vine until the kingdom of God comes."

26 Now as they were eating, Jesus took bread, and blessed, and broke it, and gave it to the disciples and said, "Take, eat; this is my body." ²⁷ And he took a cup, and when he had given thanks he gave it to them, saying, "Drink of it, all of you; ²⁸ for this is my blood of the^u covenant, which is poured out for many for the forgiveness of sins.* ²⁹ I tell you I shall not drink again of this fruit of the vine until that day when I drink it new with you in my Father's kingdom."

22 And as they were eating, he took bread, and blessed, and broke it, and gave it to them   and said, "Take; this is my body." ²³ And he took a cup, and when he had given thanks he gave it to them, and they all drank of it. ²⁴ And he said to them, "This is my blood of the^v covenant, which is poured out for many.* ²⁵ Truly, I say to you, I shall not drink again of the fruit of the vine until that day when I drink it new in the kingdom of God."

¹⁹ And he took bread, and when he had given thanks he broke it and gave it to them, saying,

"This is my body which is given for you. Do this in remembrance of me." ²⁰ And likewise the cup after supper, saying, "This cup which is poured out for you is the new covenant in my blood."^t *

See vv. 16, 18

237. LAST WORDS.
Luke 22:21-38
a) The Betrayal Foretold.
Luke 22:21-23

See vv. 21-25 (§ 235, p. 165) | *See vv. 18-21* | 21 "But behold the hand of him who betrays me is with me on the table. ²² For the Son of man goes as it has been determined; but woe to that man by whom he is betrayed!" ²³ And they began to question one another, which of them it was that would do this.

---

* I Corinthians 11:23-25: ²³ For I received of the Lord what I also delivered to you, that the Lord Jesus on the night when he was betrayed took bread, ²⁴ and when he had given thanks, he broke it, and said, "This is my body which is broken for you. Do this in remembrance of me." ²⁵ In the same way also the cup, after supper, saying, "This cup is the new covenant in my blood. Do this, as often as you drink it, in remembrance of me."

Matt. 26:28 = Mark 14:24 = [Luke 22:20]—cf. Exodus 24:8, Jeremiah 31:31, Zechariah 9:11.

---

^t text: P⁷⁵ S A B C W Θ λ φ ℜ it (some MSS.) vg sa bo; omit, *which is given for you* through verse 20: D it (some MSS.); verses 19, 17, 18: sy^c; verses 19, 20: sy^p; verses 19, 20a *(after supper)*, 17, 20b *(This blood of mine is the new covenant):* sy^s.   ^u text: P³⁷ P ^{45?} S B Θ; add, *new:* A C D W λ φ ℜ it vg sy^s sy^p sa bo.   ^v text S B C D W Θ bo; add, *new:* A λ φ ℜ it vg sy^s sy^p sa.

To Matt. 26:27-28 cf. Justin, *Apology I.66.3*—For the apostles, in the writings composed by them which are called gospels, have thus delivered what was demanded of them: that Jesus took bread, gave thanks and said, "Do this in remembrance of me; this is my body." And likewise he took the cup, and when he had given thanks he said, "This is my blood."

b) Greatness in the Kingdom of God.

Matt. 20:25–28 (*§ 192, p. 133*)	Mark 10:42–45 (*§ 192, p. 133*)	Luke 22:24–30
25 But Jesus called them to him and said, "You know that the rulers of the Gentiles lord it over them, and their great men exercise authority over them. **26** It shall not be so among you; but whoever would be great among you must be your servant, **27** and whoever would be first among you must be your slave; **28** even as the Son of man came not to be served but to serve, and to give his life as a ransom for many."	**42** And Jesus called them to him and said to them, "You know that those who are supposed to rule over the Gentiles lord it over them, and their great men exercise authority over them. **43** But it shall not be so among you; but whoever would be great among you must be your servant, **44** and whoever would be first among you must be slave of all. **45** For the Son of man also came not to be served but to serve, and to give his life as a ransom for many."	**24** A dispute also arose among them, which of them was to be regarded as the greatest. **25** And he said to them, "The kings of the Gentiles exercise lordship over them; and those in authority over them are called benefactors. **26** But not so with you; rather let the greatest among you become as the youngest, and the leader as one who serves." *Cf. 9:48b- = Mark 9:35 (§ 129, p. 95)* **27** "For which is the greater, one who sits at table, or one who serves? Is it not the one who sits at table? But I am among you as one who serves.
19:28 (*§ 189, p. 131*): Jesus said to them, "Truly I say to you, in the new world, when the Son of man shall sit on his glorious throne, you who have followed me will also sit on twelve thrones judging the twelve tribes of Israel."		**28** "'You are those who have continued with me in my trials; **29** and I assign to you, as my Father assigned to me, a kingdom, **30** that you may eat and drink at my table in my kingdom, and sit on thrones judging the twelve tribes of Israel.

c) Peter's Denial Prophesied.
Luke 22:31–34

See vv. 30–35	See vv. 26–31 (§ 238, pp. 168–169)	
		31 "Simon, Simon, behold, Satan demanded to have you,[w] that he might sift you[w] like wheat, **32** but I have prayed for you that your faith may not fail; and when you have turned again, strengthen your brethren." **33** And he said to him, "Lord, I am ready to go with you to prison and to death." **34** He said, "I tell you, Peter, the cock will not crow this day, until you three times deny that you know me."

[w] The Greek word for *you* here is plural; in verse 32 it is singular.

To Luke 22:27 and parallels cf. John 13:4-5, 12-14—(Jesus) **4** rose from supper, laid aside his garments, and girded himself with a towel. **5** Then he poured water into a basin, and began to wash the disciples' feet, and to wipe them with the towel with which he was girded. . . .**12** When he had washed their feet, and taken his garments, and resumed his place, he said to them, "Do you know what I have done to you? **13** You call me Teacher and Lord; and you are right, for so I am.**14** If I then, your Lord and Teacher, have washed your feet, you also ought to wash one another's feet."

To § 237c cf. John 13:36-38—**36** Simon Peter said to him, "Lord, where are you going?" Jesus answered, "Where I am going you cannot follow me now; but you shall follow afterward." **37** Peter said to him, "Lord, why cannot I follow you now? I will lay down my life for you." **38** Jesus answered, "Will you lay down your life for me? Truly, truly, I say to you, the cock will not crow, till you have denied me three times."

d) The Two Swords.
Luke 22:35–38

35 And he said to them, "When I sent you out with no purse or bag or sandals, did you lack anything?" They said, "Nothing." 36 He said to them, "But now, let him who has a purse take it, and likewise a bag. And let him who has no sword sell his mantle and buy one. 37 For I tell you that this scripture must be fulfilled in me, 'And he was reckoned with transgressors'; for what is written about me has its fulfillment." 38 And they said, "Look, Lord, here are two swords." And he said to them, "It is enough."

238. THE WAY TO GETHSEMANE; PETER'S DENIAL PROPHESIED.

Matt. 26:30–35	Mark 14:26–31	Luke 22:39
30 And when they had sung a hymn, they went out to the Mount of Olives. 31 Then Jesus said to them, "You will all fall away because of me this night; for it is written, 'I will strike the shepherd, and the sheep of the flock will be scattered.' 32 But after I am raised up, I will go before you to Galilee."	26 And when they had sung a hymn, they went out to the Mount of Olives. 27 And Jesus said to them, "You will all fall away; for it is written, 'I will strike the shepherd, and the sheep will be scattered.' 28 But after I am raised up, I will go before you to Galilee." x	39 And he came out, and went as was his custom, to the Mount of Olives; and the disciples followed him.
		22:31–34 (§ 237c, p. 167): 31 "Simon, Simon, behold, Satan demanded to have you, that he might sift you like wheat, 32 but I have prayed for you that your faith may not fail; and when you have turned again, strengthen your brethren."

Matt. 26:31 = Mark 14:27—Zechariah 13:7.   Luke 22:37—Isaiah 53:12.

x Verse 28 omitted in the Fayum Fragment.

To Matt. 26:30 and parallels cf. John 18:1—When Jesus had spoken these words, he went forth with his disciples across the Kidron valley, where there was a garden, which he and his disciples entered.

To Matt. 26:31 and parallels cf. John 16:32—"The hour is coming, indeed it has come, when you will be scattered, every man to his home, and will leave me alone; yet I am not alone, for the Father is with me."

To Mark 14:27–30 cf. Fayum Fragment— . . . . . while he was going out he said, "This night you will all fall away, as it is written, 'I will strike the shepherd, and the sheep will be scattered.' " When Peter said, "Even though all, not I," Jesus said, "Before the cock crows twice, you will this day deny me three times."

33 Peter declared to him, "Though they all fall away because of you, I will never fall away." 34 Jesus said to him, "Truly, I say to you, this very night, before the cock crows, you will deny me three times." 35 Peter said to him, "Even if I must die with you, I will not deny you." And so said all the disciples.	29 Peter said to him, "Even though they all fall away, I will not." 30 And Jesus said to him, "Truly, I say to you, this very night, before the cock crows twice,y you will deny me three times." 31 But he said vehemently, "If I must die with you, I will not deny you." And they all said the same.	33 And he said to him "Lord, I am ready to go with you to prison and to death." 34 He said, "I tell you, Peter, the cock will not crow this day, until you three times deny that you know me."

239. JESUS IN GETHSEMANE.

Matt. 26:36-46	Mark 14:32-42	Luke 22:40-46
36 Then Jesus went with them to a place called Gethsemane, and he said to his disciples, "Sit here, while I go yonder and pray." 37 And taking with him Peter and the two sons of Zebedee, he began to be sorrowful and troubled. 38 Then he said to them, "My soul is very sorrowful, even to death; remain here, and watchz with me." 39 And going a little farther, he fell on his face and prayed,	32 And they went to a place which was called Gethsemane; and he said to his disciples, "Sit here, while I pray." 33 And he took with him Peter and James and John, and began to be greatly distressed and troubled. 34 And he said to them, "My soul is very sorrowful, even to death; remain here, and watch."z 35 And going a little farther, he fell on the ground and prayed that, if it were possible, the hour might pass from him.	40 And when he came to the place he said to them, "Pray that you may not enter into temptation." 41 And he withdrew from them about a stone's throw, and knelt down and prayed,

Matt. 26:38 = Mark 14:34—Psalm 42:5-6, 11; 43:5.

y text: A B Θ λ φ ℜ vg sys syp sa bo; omit, *twice:* S C D W it. z Or, *keep awake.*

To Matt. 26:33 and parallels cf. John 13:36-38—36 Simon Peter said to him, "Lord, where are you going?" Jesus answered, "Where I am going you cannot follow me now; but you shall follow me afterward." 37 Peter said to him, "Lord, why cannot I follow you now? I will lay down my life for you." 38 Jesus answered, "Will you lay down your life for me? Truly, truly, I say to you, the cock will not crow, till you have denied me three times."

To Matt. 26:36 and parallels cf. John 18:1.

To Matt. 26:38 = Mark 14:34 cf. John 12:27—"Now is my soul troubled. And what shall I say? 'Father, save me from this hour'? No, for this purpose I have come to this hour."

"My Father, if it be possible, let this cup pass from me; nevertheless, not as I will, but as thou wilt." 40 And he came to the disciples and found them sleeping; and he said to Peter, "So you could not watch b with me one hour? 41 Watch b and pray that you may not enter into temptation; the spirit indeed is willing, but the flesh is weak." 42 Again, for the second time, he went away and prayed, "My Father, if this cannot pass unless I drink it, thy will be done." 43 And again he came and found them sleeping, for their eyes were heavy.

44 So, leaving them again, he went away and prayed for the third time, saying the same words. 45 Then he came to the disciples and said to them, "Are you still sleeping and taking your rest? Behold, the hour is at hand, and the Son of man is betrayed into the hands of sinners. 46 Rise, let us be going; see, my betrayer is at hand."

36 And he said, "Abba, Father, all things are possible to thee; remove this cup from me; yet not what I will, but what thou wilt." 37 And he came and found them sleeping, and he said to Peter, "Simon, are you asleep? Could you not watch b one hour? 38 Watch b and pray that you may not enter into temptation; the spirit indeed is willing, but the flesh is weak." 39 And again he went away and prayed, saying the same words.

40 And again he came and found them sleeping, for their eyes were very heavy; and they did not know what to answer him.

41 And he came the third time, and said to them, "Are you still sleeping and taking your rest? It is enough; the hour has come; the Son of man is betrayed into the hands of sinners. 42 Rise, let us be going; see, my betrayer is at hand."

42 "Father, if thou art willing, remove this cup from me; nevertheless not my will, but thine, be done." a 45 And when he rose from prayer, he came to the disciples and found them sleeping for sorrow, 46 and he said to them, "Why do you sleep?

Rise and pray that you may not enter into temptation."

---

a text: P75 A B W sy s sa bo Marcion, Clement, Origen; add verses 43-44, 43 *And there appeared to him an angel from heaven, strengthening him.* 44 *And being in an agony he prayed more earnestly; and his sweat became like great drops of blood falling down upon the ground:* S D Θ λ ℜ it vg sy c sy p Justin, Irenaeus, Hippolytus. b Or, *keep awake.*

To Matt. 26:39b and parallels cf. John 18:11—Jesus said to Peter, " . . . shall I not drink the cup which the Father has given me?"
To Matt. 26:46 = Mark 14:42 cf. John 14:31—"Rise, let us go hence."

240. JESUS TAKEN CAPTIVE.

Matt. 26:47-56	Mark 14:43-52	Luke 22:47-53
47 While he was still speaking, Judas came, one of the twelve, and with him a great crowd with swords and clubs, from the chief priests and the elders of the people. 48 Now the betrayer had given them a sign, saying, "The one I shall kiss is the man; seize him."	43 And immediately, while he was still speaking, Judas came, one of the twelve, and with him a crowd with swords and clubs, from the chief priests and the scribes and the elders. 44 Now the betrayer had given them a sign, saying, "The one I shall kiss is the man; seize him and lead him away under guard." 45 And when he came, he went up to him at once, and said,	47 While he was still speaking, there came a crowd, and the man called Judas, one of the twelve, was leading them. *Cf. v. 52*
49 And he came up to Jesus at once and said, "Hail, Master!" c And he kissed him. 50 Jesus said to him, "Friend, why are you here?" d Then they came up and laid hands on Jesus and seized him.	"Master!" c And he kissed him. 46 And they laid hands on him and seized him.	He drew near to Jesus to kiss him; 48 but Jesus said to him, "Judas, would you betray the Son of man with a kiss?" 49 And when those who were about him saw what would follow, they said, "Lord, shall we strike with the sword?"
51 And behold, one of those who were with Jesus stretched out his hand and drew his sword, and struck the slave of the high priest, and cut off his ear. 52 Then Jesus said to him, "Put your sword back into its place; for all who take the sword will perish by the sword. 53 Do you think that I cannot appeal to my Father, and he will at once send me more than twelve legions of angels? 54 But how then should the scriptures be fulfilled, that it must be so?" 55 At that hour Jesus said to the crowds,	47 But one of those who stood by drew his sword, and struck the slave of the high priest and cut off his ear.	50 And one of them struck the slave of the high priest and cut off his right ear. 51 But Jesus said, "No more of this!" And he touched his ear and healed him.
	48 And Jesus said to them, *Cf. v. 43*	52 Then Jesus said to the chief priests and officers of the temple and elders, who had come out against him,
"Have you come out as against a robber, with swords and clubs to capture me?	"Have you come out as against a robber, with swords and clubs to capture me?	"Have you come out as against a robber, with swords and clubs?

c Or, *Rabbi.* d Or, *do that for which you have come.*

To § 240 cf. John 18:2-11.

Day after day I sat
  in the temple teaching,
and you did not seize me.

56 But all this has taken place, that the scriptures of the prophets might be fulfilled." Then all the disciples forsook him and fled.

49 Day after day I was with you in the temple teaching, and you did not seize me.

But let the scriptures
    be fulfilled." 50 And they all   forsook him and fled.

51 And a young man followed him, with nothing but a linen cloth about his body; and they seized him, 52 but he left the linen cloth and ran away naked.

53 When I was with you day after day in the temple, you did not lay hands on me. But this is your hour, and the power of darkness."

241. JESUS BEFORE THE SANHEDRIN. PETER'S DENIAL.

| Matt. 26:57–75 | Mark 14:53–72 | Luke 22:54–71 |

57 Then those who had seized Jesus led him to Caiaphas the high priest, where the scribes and the elders had gathered. 58 But Peter followed him at a distance, as far as the courtyard of the high priest, and going inside he sat with the guards to see the end.

53 And they led Jesus to the high priest; and all the chief priests and the elders and the scribes were assembled. 54 And Peter had followed him at a distance, right into the courtyard of the high priest; and he was sitting with the guards, and warming himself at the fire.

54 Then they seized him and led him away, bringing him e into the high priest's house.

Peter followed at a distance; 55 and when they had kindled a fire in the middle of the courtyard and sat down together, Peter sat among them.

---

e text: S A B W φ 𝔏 sa bo; omit, *bringing him:* D Θ λ it vg sy^e sy^s.

To Matt. 26:55b, and parallels cf. John 18:20—Jesus answered him, "I have spoken openly to the world; I have always taught in synagogues and in the temple, where all Jews come together; I have said nothing secretly."

To Matt. 26:57 and parallels, cf. John 18:12-14—12 So the band of soldiers and their captain and the officers of the Jews seized Jesus and bound him. 13 First they led him to Annas; for he was the father-in-law of Caiaphas, who was high priest that year. 14 It was Caiaphas who had given counsel to the Jews that it was expedient that one man should die for the people.

To Matt. 26:58 and parallels, cf. John 18:15-16—15 Simon Peter followed Jesus, and so did another disciple. As this disciple was known to the high priest, he entered the court of the high priest along with Jesus, 16 while Peter stood outside at the door. So the other disciple, who was known to the high priest, went out and spoke to the maid who kept the door, and brought Peter in.

		56 Then a maid, seeing him as he sat in the light and gazing at him, said, "This man also was with him." 57 But he denied it, saying, "Woman, I do not know him." 58 And a little later some one else saw him and said, "You also are one of them." But Peter said, "Man, I am not." 59 And after an interval of about an hour still another insisted, saying, "Certainly this man also was with him; for he is a Galilean." 60 But Peter said, "Man, I do not know what you are saying." And immediately, while he was still speaking, the cock crowed. 61 And the Lord turned and looked at Peter. And Peter remembered the word of the Lord, how he had said to him, "Before the cock crows today, you will deny me three times." 62 And he went out. and wept bitterly.
See vv. 69–75 (§ 241, pp. 174–175).	*See vv. 66–72 (§ 241, pp. 174–175).*	
See v. 67	*See v. 65*	63 Now the men who were holding Jesus mocked him and beat him; 64 they also blindfolded him and asked him, "Prophesy! Who is it that struck you?" 65 And they spoke many other words against him, reviling him.
See 27:1	*See 15:1*	66 When day came, the assembly of the elders of the people gathered together, both chief priests and scribes; and they led him away to their council,
59 Now the chief priests and the whole council sought false testimony against Jesus that they might put him to death, 60 but they found none, though many false witnesses came forward.	55 Now the chief priests and the whole council sought testimony against Jesus to put him to death; but they found none. 56 For many bore false witness against him, and their witness did not agree.	

To Matt. 26:59 = Mark 14:55, cf. John 18:19-24.

At last two came forward ⁶¹ and said, "This fellow said, 'I am able to destroy the temple of God, and to build it in three days.' "

⁶² And the high priest stood up and said "Have you no answer to make? What is it that these men testify against you?" ⁶³ But Jesus was silent.

And the high priest said to him, "I adjure you by the living God, tell us if you are the Christ, the Son of God."

⁶⁴ Jesus said to him, "You have said so. But I tell you, hereafter you will see the Son of man seated at the right hand of Power, and coming on the clouds of heaven."

⁶⁵ Then the high priest tore his robes, and said, "He has uttered blasphemy. Why do we still need witnesses? You have now heard his blasphemy. ⁶⁶ What is your judgment?" They answered, "He deserves death." ⁶⁷ Then they spat in his face, and struck him; and some slapped him, ⁶⁸ saying, "Prophesy to us, you Christ! Who is it that struck you?"

---

⁵⁷ And some stood up and bore false witness against him, saying, ⁵⁸ "We heard him say, 'I will destroy this temple that is made with hands, and in three days I will build another, not made with hands.' " ⁵⁹ Yet not even so did their testimony agree. ⁶⁰ And the high priest stood up in the midst, and asked Jesus, "Have you no answer to make? What is it that these men testify against you?" ⁶¹ But he was silent and made no answer. Again the high priest asked him,

"Are you the Christ, the Son of the Blessed?"

⁶² And Jesus said, "I am;

and you will see the Son of man seated at the right hand of Power, and coming with the clouds of heaven."

⁶³ And the high priest tore his garments, and said,

"Why do we still need witnesses? ⁶⁴ You have heard his blasphemy. What is your decision?" And they all condemned him as deserving death. ⁶⁵ And some began to spit on him, and to cover his face, and to strike him, saying to him, "Prophesy!"

And the guards received him with blows.

---

and they said,

⁶⁷ "If you are the Christ, tell us." But he said to them, "If I tell you, you will not believe; ⁶⁸ and if I ask you, you will not answer.

⁶⁹ But from now on the Son of man shall be seated at the right hand of the Power of God."

⁷⁰ And they all said, "Are you the Son of God, then?" And he said to them, "You say that I am." ⁷¹ And they said,

"What further testimony do we need? We have heard it ourselves from his own lips."

⁶³ (See above, p. 173): Now the men who were holding Jesus mocked him and beat him; ⁶⁴ they also blindfolded him and asked him, "Prophesy! Who is it that struck you?" ⁶⁵ And they spoke many other words against him, reviling him.

Matt. 26:64 (24:30) = Mark 14:62 (13:26) = Luke 22:69 (21:27)—Psalm 110:1, Daniel 7:13. Matt. 26:65f. = Mark 14:64, cf. Leviticus 24:16.

To Matt. 26:61 and Mark 14:58 cf. John 2:19—Jesus answered them, "Destroy this temple, and in three days I will raise it up."

69 Now Peter was sitting outside in the courtyard. And a maid　　came up to him,

and said, "You also were with Jesus the Galilean." 70 But he denied it before them all, saying, "I do not know what you mean." 71 And when he went out to the porch, another maid saw him, and she said　　to the bystanders, "This man was with　Jesus　of　Nazareth." 72 And again he denied it with an oath, "I do not know the man." 73 After a little while the bystanders came up and said to Peter, "Certainly　you　are also one of them, for your accent betrays you." 74 Then he began to invoke a curse on himself and to swear, "I do not know the man."
　　　　　　And immediately the cock crowed.

75 And Peter remembered the saying of Jesus,

"Before the cock crows, you will deny me three times." And he went out and wept bitterly.

66 And as Peter was below in the courtyard, one of the maids of the high priest came; 67 and seeing Peter warming himself, she looked at him, and said, "You also were with the Nazarene, Jesus." 68 But he denied it, saying, "I neither know nor understand what you mean." And he went out into the gateway.[f] 69 And the maid saw him, and began again to say to the bystanders, "This man is one of them." 70 But again he denied it.

And after a little while again the bystanders　　said to Peter, "Certainly　you　are　one of them; for you are a Galilean. 71 But he began to invoke a curse on himself and to swear, "I do not know this man of whom you speak." 72 And immediately　the　cock　crowed a second time.[g]

　　　　　　And Peter remembered how Jesus had said to him, "Before the cock crows twice, you will deny me three times." And he broke down and wept.

56 (See above, p. 173): Then a maid, seeing him as he sat in the light and gazing at him,

said, "This man also was with him." 57 But he denied it, saying, "Woman, I do not know him."

58 And a little later some one else saw him and said, "You also are one of them." But Peter said, "Man, I am not."

59 And after an interval of about an hour still another insisted, saying, "Certainly this man also was with him; for he is a Galilean." 60 But Peter said,

"Man, I do not know what you are saying." And immediately, while he was still speaking, the cock crowed. 61 And the Lord turned and looked at Peter. And Peter remembered the word of the Lord, how he had said to him, "Before the cock crows today, you will deny me three times." 62 And he went out and wept bitterly.

---

[f] text: S B W syˢ sa bo; add, and the cock crowed: A C D Θ λ φ � it vg syᵖ　　　[g] text: A B D W Θ λ φ � it vg syˢ syᵖ sa bo (see 14:68); omit, a second time: S C (see Matt. 26:74; Luke 22:60; John 18:27).

To Matt. 26:69ff and parallels, cf. John 18:17, 25-27: 17 The maid who kept the door said to Peter, "Are not you also one of this man's disciples?" He said, "I am not." . . . . 25 Now Simon Peter was standing and warming himself. They said to him, "Are not you also one of his disciples?" He denied it and said, "I am not." 26 One of the servants of the high priest, a kinsman of the man whose ear Peter had cut off, asked, "Did I not see you in the garden with him?" 27 Peter again denied it; and at once the cock crowed.

To Matt. 26:74 cf. **Gospel of the Nazaraeans:** The Jewish Gospel has: And he denied, and he swore [i.e., took an oath], and he cursed.

242. JESUS DELIVERED TO PILATE.

Matt. 27:1–2	Mark 15:1	Luke 23:1
1 When morning came, all the chief priests and the elders of the people took counsel against Jesus to put him to death; 2 and they bound him and led him away and delivered him to Pilate, the governor.	1 And as soon as it was morning the chief priests, with the elders and scribes, and the whole council held a consultation; and they bound Jesus and led him away and delivered him to Pilate.	22:66 (See above, p. 173): When day came, the assembly of the elders of the people gathered together, both chief priests and scribes; and they led him away to their council. 23:1 Then the whole company of them arose, and brought him before Pilate.

243. THE DEATH OF JUDAS.
Matt. 27:3–10

3 When Judas, his betrayer, saw that he was condemned, he repented and brought back the thirty pieces of silver to the chief priests and the elders, 4 saying, "I have sinned in betraying innocent blood." They said, "What is that to us? See to it yourself." 5 And throwing down the pieces of silver in the temple, he departed; and he went and hanged himself. 6 But the chief priests, taking the pieces of silver, said, "It is not lawful to put them into the treasury, since they are blood money." 7 So they took counsel, and bought with them the potter's field, to bury strangers in. 8 Therefore that field has been called the Field of Blood to this day. 9 Then was fulfilled what had been spoken by the prophet Jeremiah, saying, "And they took the thirty pieces of silver, the price of him on whom a price had been set by some of the sons of Israel, 10 and they gave them for the potter's field, as the Lord directed me."

244. THE TRIAL BEFORE PILATE.

Matt. 27:11–14	Mark 15:2–5	Luke 23:2–5
11 Now Jesus stood before the governor;		2 And they began to accuse him, saying, "We found this man perverting our nation, and forbidding us to give tribute to Caesar, and saying that he himself is Christ a king."

Matt. 27:9-10—Zechariah 11:12-13; Jeremiah 32:6-15; 18:2-3.

To § 242, cf. John 18:28-32. To § 243 cf. Acts 1:18-19.

and the governor asked him, "Are you the King of the Jews?" Jesus said, "You have said so." 12 But when he was accused by the chief priests and elders, he made no answer. 13 Then Pilate said to him, "Do you not hear how many things they testify against you?" 14 But he gave them no answer, not even to a single charge; so that the governor wondered greatly.

2 And Pilate asked him, "Are you the King of the Jews?" And he answered him, "You have said so." 3 And the chief priests accused him of many things.

4 And Pilate again asked him, "Have you no answer to make? See how many charges they bring against you." 5 But Jesus made no further answer,

so that Pilate wondered.

3 And Pilate asked him, "Are you the King of the Jews?" And he answered him. "You have said so."

4 And Pilate said to the chief priests and the multitudes, "I find no crime in this man." 5 But they were urgent, saying, "He stirs up the people, teaching throughout all Judea, from Galilee even to this place."

245. JESUS BEFORE HEROD.
Luke 23:6–16

v. 12 | v. 3

6 When Pilate heard this, he asked whether the man was a Galilean. 7 And when he learned that he belonged to Herod's jurisdiction, he sent him over to Herod, who was himself in Jerusalem at that time. 8 When Herod saw Jesus, he was very glad, for he had long desired to see him, because he had heard about him, and he was hoping to see some sign done by him. 9 So he questioned him at some length; but he made no answer. 10 The chief priests and the scribes stood by, vehemently accusing him. 11 And Herod with his soldiers treated him with contempt and mocked him; then, arraying him in gorgeous apparel, he sent him back to Pilate. 12 And Herod and Pilate became friends with each other that very day, for before this they had been at enmity with each other.

To Matt. 27:11ff and parallels, cf. John 18:33-37. To Matt. 27:14 and Mark 15:5 cf. John 19:9-10— 9 He entered the praetorium again and said to Jesus, "Where are you from?" But Jesus gave no answer. 10 Pilate therefore said to him, "You will not speak to me? Do you not know that I have power to release you, and power to crucify you?" To Luke 23:4-5 cf. John 19:6—When the chief priests and the officers saw him, they cried out, "Crucify him, crucify him!" Pilate said to them, "Take him yourselves and crucify him, for I find no crime in him."

13 Pilate then called together the chief priests and the rulers and the people, 14 and said to them, "You brought me this man as one who was perverting the people; and after examining him before you, behold, I did not find this man guilty of any of your charges against him; 15 neither did Herod, for he sent him back to us. Behold, nothing deserving death has been done by him; 16 I will therefore chastise him and release him."

246. THE SENTENCE OF DEATH.

Matt. 27:15–26	Mark 15:6–15	Luke 23:17–25
15 Now at the feast the governor was accustomed to release for the crowd any one prisoner whom they wanted. 16 And they had then a notorious prisoner called Barabbas.[i]	6 Now at the feast he used to release for them one prisoner for whom they asked. 7 And among the rebels in prison, who had committed murder in the insurrection, there was a man called Barabbas. 8 And the crowd came up and began to ask Pilate to do as he was wont to do for them. 9 And he answered them, "Do you want me to release for you the King of the Jews?" 10 For he perceived that it was out of envy that the chief priests had delivered him up.	(17)[h] Cf. v. 19
17 So when they had gathered, Pilate said to them, "Whom do you want me to release for you, Barabbas[i] or Jesus who is called Christ?" 18 For he knew that it was out of envy that they had delivered him up. 19 Besides, while he was sitting on the judgment seat, his wife sent word to him, "Have nothing to do with that righteous man, for I have suffered much over him today in a dream." 20 Now the chief priests and the elders persuaded the people to ask for Barabbas and destroy Jesus.	11 But the chief priests stirred up the crowd to have him release for them Barabbas instead.	18 But they all cried out together, "Away with this man, and release to us Barabbas"— 19 a man who had been thrown into prison for an insurrection started in the city, and for murder. 20 Pilate addressed them once more, desiring to release Jesus;
21 The governor again said to them, "Which of the two do you want me to release for you?" And they said, "Barabbas." 22 Pilate said to	12 And Pilate again said to them,	

[h] text: P75 A B sa bo; add verse 17, *Now he was obliged to release one man to them at the festival:* S W Θ λ φ ℜ it vg syp; verse 17 follows verse 19: D syc sys.   [i] text: S A B D W φ ℜ it vg syp sa bo; *Jesus Barabbas:* Θ λ sys Origen.

To § 246 cf. John 18:38–40; 19:4–16.

To Matt. 27:16 cf. **Gospel of the Nazaraeans** (in Jerome, *Commentary on Matthew 27:16*)—In the Gospel according to the Hebrews Barabbas is interpreted as "son of their master (teacher?)." He had been condemned because of insurrection and murder.

them, "Then what shall I do with Jesus who is called Christ?" They all said, "Let him be crucified." **23** And he said, 'Why, what evil has he done?"	"Then what shall I do with the man whom you call the King of the Jews?" **13** And they cried out again, "Crucify him." **14** And Pilate said to them, "Why, what evil has he done?"	**21** but they shouted out, "Crucify, crucify him!" **22** A third time he said to them, "Why, what evil has he done? I have found in him no crime deserving death; I will therefore chastise him and release him." **23** But they were urgent, demanding with loud cries that he should be crucified. And their voices prevailed.
But they shouted all the more, "Let him be crucified."	But they shouted all the more, "Crucify him."	
24 So when Pilate saw that he was gaining nothing, but rather that a riot was beginning, he took water and washed his hands before the crowd, saying, "I am innocent of this man's blood,ʲ see to it yourselves." **25** And all the people answered, "His blood be on us and on our children!"		
26 Then he released for them Barabbas,	**15** So Pilate, wishing to satisfy the crowd, released for them Barabbas;	**24** So Pilate gave sentence that their demand should be granted. **25** He released the man who had been thrown into prison for insurrection and murder, whom they asked for;
and having scourged Jesus, delivered him to be crucified.	and having scourged Jesus, he delivered him to be crucified.	but Jesus he delivered up to their will.

To Matt. 27:24 cf. Deuteronomy 21:6-8.

ʲ text: B D Θ it (some MSS.) syˢ sa; *this righteous (innocent) man's blood*: S A W λ φ 𝔑 it (some MSS.) vg syᵖ bo.

To Matt. 27:23 and parallels, cf. John 19:6, 7, 15—⁶ When the chief priests and the officers saw him, they cried out, "Crucify him, crucify him!" Pilate said to them, "Take him yourselves and crucify him, for I find no crime in him." ⁷ The Jews answered him, "We have a law, and by that law he ought to die, because he has made himself the Son of God.". . . . ¹⁵ They cried out, "Away with him, away with him, crucify him!" Pilate said to them, "Shall I crucify your King?" The chief priests answered, "We have no king but Caesar."

To Matt. 27:26 and parallels, cf. John 19:16—Then he handed him over to them to be crucified.

To Matt. 27:26b-31 = Mark 15:15b-20 cf. **Gospel of Peter 2.5b—3.9**—And he delivered him to the people before the first day of Unleavened Bread, their feast day. **3.** ⁶ And having taken the Lord, they pushed him as they ran and said, "Let us drag around the Son of God now that we have power over him." ⁷ And they put a purple robe on him, and made him sit on the seat of judgment, saying, "Judge justly, king of Israel." ⁸ And one of them brought a crown of thorns and put it on the Lord's head; ⁹ and others stood and spat in his eyes and still others slapped his cheeks; others pricked him with a reed, and some of them scourged him, saying, "With this honor let us honor the Son of God."

247. THE MOCKING BY THE SOLDIERS.

Matt. 27:27–31	Mark 15:16–20
27 Then the soldiers of the governor took Jesus into the praetorium, and they gathered the whole battalion before him. 28 And they stripped him and put a scarlet robe upon him, 29 and plaiting a crown of thorns they put it on his head, and put a reed in his right hand. And kneeling before him they mocked him, saying, "Hail, King of the Jews!" 30 And they spat upon him, and took the reed and struck him on the head. 31 And when they had mocked him, they stripped him of the robe, and put his own clothes on him, and led him away to crucify him.	16 And the soldiers led him away inside the palace (that is, the praetorium); and they called together the whole battalion. 17 And they clothed him in a purple cloak, and plaiting a crown of thorns they put it on him. 18 And they began to salute him, "Hail, King of the Jews!" 19 And they struck his head with a reed, and spat upon him, and they knelt down in homage to him. 20 And when they had mocked him, they stripped him of the purple cloak, and put his own clothes on him. And they led him out to crucify him. *See v. 26*

248. THE ROAD TO GOLGOTHA.

Matt. 27:32	Mark 15:21	Luke 23:26–32
32 As they went out, they came upon a man of Cyrene, Simon by name; this man they compelled to carry his cross.	21 And they compelled a passer-by, Simon of Cyrene, who was coming in from the country, the father of Alexander and Rufus, to carry his cross.	26 And as they led him away, they seized one Simon of Cyrene, who was coming in from the country, and laid on him the cross, to carry it behind Jesus. 27 And there followed him a great multitude of the people, and of women who bewailed and lamented him. 28 But Jesus turning to them said, "Daughters of Jerusalem, do not weep for me, but weep for yourselves and for your children. 29 For behold, the days are coming when they will say, 'Blessed are the barren, and the wombs that never bore, and the breasts that never gave suck!' 30 Then they will begin to say to the mountains, 'Fall on us'; and to the hills, 'Cover us.' 31 For if they do this when the wood is green, what will happen when it is dry?" 32 Two others also, who were criminals, were led away to be put to death with him.
See v. 38	*See v. 27*	

Luke 23:30—Hosea 10:8.

To § 247 cf. John 19:1–3.

249. THE CRUCIFIXION.

Matt. 27:33–44	Mark 15:22–32	Luke 23:33–43
33 And when they came to a place called Golgotha, (which means the place of a skull), 34 they offered him wine to drink, mingled with gall; but when he tasted it, he would not drink it. 35 And when they had crucified him,	22 And they brought him to the place called Golgotha (which means the place of a skull). 23 And they offered him wine mingled with myrrh; but he did not take it. 24 And they crucified him,	33 And when they came to the place which is called The Skull, there they crucified him, and the criminals, one on the right and one on the left. 34 And Jesus said, "Father, forgive them; for they know not what they do." k And they
See v. 38	*See v. 27*	cast lots to divide his garments. 35 And the people stood by, watching;
they divided his garments among them by casting lots; 36 then they sat down and kept watch over him there. 37 And over his head they put the charge against him, which read, "This is Jesus the King of the Jews." 38 Then two robbers were crucified with him, one on the right and one on the left. 39 And those who passed by derided him, wagging their heads 40 and saying, "You who would destroy the temple and build it in three days, save yourself! If you are the Son of God, come down m from the cross."	and divided his garments among them, casting lots for them, to decide what each should take. 25 And it was the third hour, when they crucified him. 26 And the inscription of the charge against him read, "The King of the Jews." 27 And with him they crucified two robbers, one on his right and one on his left.l 29 And those who passed by derided him, wagging their heads, and saying, "Aha! You who would destroy the temple and build it in three days, 30 save yourself, and come down from the cross!"	*See v. 38*

See vv. 32, 33

See v. 37 |

Matt. 27:34 (= Mark 15:23) = Luke 23:36—cf. Psalm 69:21.   Matt. 27:35 = Mark 15:24 = Luke 23:34b—Psalm 22:18.   Matt. 27:39 = Mark 15:29 = Luke 23:35—Psalm 22:7.

k text: S A C λ φ ℜ it vg syᶜ syᵖ Marcion, Irenaeus, Origen; omit, *And Jesus said, "Father, forgive them; for they know not what they do"*: P⁷⁵ B D W Θ syˢ sa bo.   l text: S A B C D syˢ sa bo; add verse 28, *And the scripture was fulfilled which says, "He was reckoned with transgressors"*: Θ λ φ ℜ it vg syᵖ. (Cf. Luke 22:37; Isaiah 53:12.)   m text: B W Θ λ φ ℜ it (some MSS.) vg sa bo; *save yourself, if you are the Son of God, and come down*: S A D it (some MSS.) syˢ syᵖ.

To Matt. 27:33 and parallels cf. John 19:17—So they took Jesus, and he went out, bearing his own cross, to the place called the place of a skull, which is called in Hebrew Golgotha.

To Matt. 27:35 and parallels cf. John 19:23–24.

To Matt. 27:37 and parallels cf. John 19:19—Pilate also wrote a title and put it on the cross; it read, "Jesus of Nazareth, the King of the Jews."

To Matt. 27:38 and parallels cf. John 19:18—There they crucified him, and with him two others, one on either side, and Jesus between them.

To Luke 23:34 cf. **Gospel of the Nazaraeans** (in Haimo of Auxerre, *Commentary on Isaiah 53:12*)—As it is said in the Gospel of the Nazarenes: At this word of the Lord, many thousands of Jews standing around the cross, believed.

41 So also the chief priests, with the scribes and elders, mocked him, saying, 42 "He saved others; he cannot save himself.
He is the King of Israel; let him come down now from the cross, and we will believe in him. 43 He trusts in God; let God deliver him now, if he desires him; for he said, 'I am the Son of God.' "

31 So also the chief priests mocked him to one another with the scribes, saying, "He saved others; he cannot save himself. 32 Let the Christ, the King of Israel, come down now from the cross, that we may see and believe."

but the rulers scoffed at him saying, "He saved others; let him save himself, if he is the Christ of God, his Chosen One!"

See v. 48

See v. 40

See v. 37

See v. 36

See v. 30

See v. 26

36 The soldiers also mocked him, coming up and offering him vinegar, 37 and saying, "If you are the King of the Jews, save yourself!" 38 There was also an inscription over him,[n] "This is the King of the Jews."

44 And the robbers who were crucified with him also reviled him in the same way.

Those who were crucified with him also reviled him.

39 One of the criminals who were hanged railed at him, saying, "Are you not the Christ? Save yourself and us!" 40 But the other rebuked him, saying, "Do you not fear God, since you are under the same sentence of condemnation? 41 And we indeed justly; for we are receiving the due reward of our deeds; but this man has done nothing wrong." 42 And he said, "Jesus, remember me when you come into [o] your kingdom." 43 And he said to him, "Truly, I say to you, today you will be with me in Paradise."

Matt. 27:43—Psalm 22:8.

[n] text: P[75] B C sy[c] sy[s] sa bo; add, *in letters of Greek and Latin and Hebrew:* S A D W Θ λ φ 𝔐 it vg sy[p]. (Cf. John 19:20.)   [o] text: P[75] B it (some MSS.) vg; *in your kingdom:* SAC it (some MSS.) sy[c] sy[s] sy[p] sa bo.

To Matt. 27:33-44 cf. **Gospel of Peter 4.10-14**—10 And they brought two criminals and crucified the Lord between them; and he was silent, as one having no pain. 11 And when they had set up the cross, they wrote on it, "This is the King of Israel." 12 And they laid his garments before him, and divided them, and cast lots for them. 13 But one of those criminals reviled them, saying, "We have suffered in this way for the evils we have done; but in what way has this man injured you, who has become the Savior of men?" 14 And they were angry with him and commanded that his legs should not be broken in order that he might die in agony.

250. THE DEATH ON THE CROSS.

Matt. 27:45-56	Mark 15:33-41	Luke 23:44-49
45 Now from the sixth hour there was darkness over all the land P until the ninth hour.	33 And when the sixth hour had come, there was darkness over the whole land P until the ninth hour.	44 It was now about the sixth hour, and there was darkness over the whole land P until the ninth hour, 45 while the sun's light failed; q and the curtain of the temple was torn in two.
See v. 51a	*See v. 38*	
46 And about the ninth hour Jesus cried with a loud voice, "Eli, Eli, lama sabachthani?" that is, "My God, my God, why hast thou forsaken me?" 47 And some of the bystanders hearing it said, "This man is calling Elijah." 48 And one of them at once ran and took a sponge, filled it with vinegar, and put it on a reed, and gave it to him to drink. 49 But the others said, "Wait, let us see whether Elijah will come to save him." r 50 And Jesus cried again with a loud voice and yielded up his spirit.	34 And at the ninth hour Jesus cried with a loud voice, "Eloi, Eloi, lama sabachthani?" which means, "My God, my God, why hast thou forsaken me?" 35 And some of the bystanders hearing it said, "Behold, he is calling Elijah." 36 And one ran and, filling a sponge full of vinegar, put it on a reed and gave it to him to drink, saying, "Wait, let us see whether Elijah will come to take him down." 37 And Jesus uttered a loud cry, and breathed his last.	*See v. 36* 46 Then Jesus, crying with a loud voice, said, "Father, into thy hands I commit my spirit!" And having said this he breathed his last.

Matt. 27:46 = Mark 15:34—Psalm 22:1.   Matt. 27:48 = Mark 15:36—Psalm 69:21.   Luke 23:46—Psalm 31:5.

P Or, *earth.*   q text: B sa bo; *after the sun's light failed:* P[75] S C?; *and the sun was darkened:* A D W Θ λ φ ℜ it vg sy[c] sy[s] sy[p].   r text: A D W Θ λ φ ℜ it vg sy[s] sy[p] sa bo; add, *and another took a spear and pierced his side, and there came out water and blood:* S B C. Cf. John 19:34.

To Matt. 27:48 and parallels cf. John 19:29—A bowl full of vinegar stood there; so they put a sponge full of the wine on hyssop and held it to his mouth.

To Luke 23:46 cf. John 19:30—When Jesus had received the vinegar, he said, "It is finished"; and he bowed his head and gave up his spirit. Cf. also John 19:31-37.

To Matt. 27:45-51 cf. **Gospel of Peter 5.15-20**—[15] Now it was noonday, and darkness prevailed over all Judea, and they were afraid and distressed for fear the sun had set while he was still alive. For it is written for them that the sun should not set upon one put to death. [16] And one of them said, "Give him gall with vinegar to drink." And they mixed them and gave it to him. [17] And they fulfilled all things and brought their sins to an end upon their own heads. [18] And many went about with lamps, supposing it was night, and fell. [19] And the Lord cried out, "My power, my power, thou hast forsaken me." And, saying this, he was taken up. [20] And in the same hour the curtain of the temple of Jerusalem was torn in two.

51 And behold, the curtain of the temple was torn in two, from top to bottom; and the earth shook, and the rocks were split; 52 the tombs also were opened, and many bodies of the saints who had fallen asleep were raised. 53 and coming out of the tombs after his resurrection they went into the holy city and appeared to many. 54 When the centurion and those who were with him, keeping watch over Jesus, saw the earthquake and what took place, they were filled with awe, and said, "Truly this was the Son [t] of God!"	38 And the curtain of the temple was torn in two, from top to bottom.	*See v. 45*
	39 And when the centurion, who stood facing him, saw that he thus [s] breathed his last,	47 Now when the centurion saw what had taken place, he praised God,
	he said "Truly this man was the Son [t] of God!"	and said, "Certainly this man was innocent!" 48 And all the multitudes who assembled to see the sight, when they saw what had taken place, returned home beating their breasts. 49 And all his acquaintances and the women who had followed him from Galilee stood at a distance and saw these things.
55 There were also many women there, looking on from afar, who had followed Jesus from Galilee, ministering to him; 56 among whom were Mary Magdalene, and Mary the mother of James and Joseph, and the mother of the sons of Zebedee.	40 There were also women looking on from afar, among whom were Mary Magdalene and Mary the mother of James the younger and of Joses, and Salome, 41 who, when he was in Galilee, followed him, and ministered to him; and also many other women who came up with him to Jerusalem.	*To Matt. 27:55 f = Mark 15:40 f cf. Luke 8:3 (§ 84, p. 60); also Luke 23:55.*

Luke 23:49—Psalm 38:11

[s] text: S B sa; *saw that he having thus cried out breathed his last:* A C λ φ 𝕽 it vg sy[p]; *saw him having thus cried out and breathed his last:* D; *saw that he having cried out breathed his last:* W Θ sy[s]; *saw that he breathed his last:* bo.
[t] Or, *a son.*

To Matt. 25:55 and parallels cf. John 19:25—Standing by the cross of Jesus were his mother, and his mother's sister, Mary the wife of Clopas, and Mary Magdalene.

To Matt. 27:51 cf. **Gospel of the Nazaraeans** (in Jerome, *Letter 120 to Hedibia* and *Commentary on Matthew 27:51*): In the Gospel that is written in Hebrew letters we read, not that the curtain of the temple was torn, but that the astonishingly large lintel of the temple collapsed.
To Luke 23:48 cf. **Gospel of Peter 7.25**—Then the Jews and the elders and the priests, when they perceived what great evil they had done to themselves, began to lament and to say, "Woe for our sins; the judgment and the end of Jerusalem has drawn near."
To Matt. 27:55ff. and parallels, cf. Tatian, *Diatessaron* in Dura Parchment 24—. . . of Zebedee and Salome, and the women who followed him from Galilee seeing him who had been crucified. It was the day of Preparation; the sabbath was beginning. And when it was evening on the day of Preparation, that is, the day before the sabbath, there came a man from Erinmathaias, a city of Judea, whose name was Joseph. He was good and righteous, being a disciple of Jesus, but had been condemned secretly on account of the fear of the Jews, and looked for the kingdom of God. He had not consented to the purpose. . . .

251. THE BURIAL OF JESUS.

Matt. 27:57–61	Mark 15:42–47	Luke 23:50–56
57 When it was evening, there came a rich man from Arimathea, named Joseph, who also was a disciple of Jesus.	42 And when evening had come, since it was the day of Preparation, that is, the day before the sabbath, 43 Joseph of Arimathea, a respected member of the council, who was also himself looking for the kingdom of God, took courage and	50 Now there was a man named Joseph from the Jewish town of Arimathea. He was a member of the council, a good and righteous man, 51 who had not consented to their purpose and deed, and he was looking for the king-dom of God. 52 This man
58 He went to Pilate and asked for the body of Jesus.	went to Pilate, and asked for the body of Jesus. 44 And Pilate wondered if he were already dead; and summoning the centurion, he asked him whether he was already dead.[u] 45 And when he learned from the centurion that he was dead, he granted the body to Joseph.	went to Pilate and asked for the body of Jesus.
Then Pilate ordered it to be given to him. 59 And Joseph took the body, and wrapped it in a clean linen shroud, 60 and laid it in his own new tomb, which he had hewn in the rock; and he rolled a great stone to the door of the tomb, and departed. 61 Mary Magdalene and the other Mary were there, sitting opposite the sepulchre.	46 And he bought a linen shroud, and taking him down, wrapped him in the linen shroud, and laid him in a tomb which had been hewn out of the rock; and he rolled a stone against the door of the tomb. 47 Mary Magdalene and Mary the mother of Joses saw where he was laid. *Cf. 16:1*	53 Then he took it down and wrapped it in a linen shroud, and laid him in a rock-hewn tomb, where no one had ever yet been laid. 54 It was the day of Preparation, and the sabbath was beginning.[v] 55 The women who had come with him from Galilee followed, and saw the tomb, and how his body was laid; 56 then they re-turned, and prepared spices and ointments. On the sabbath they rested according to the commandment.

Matt. 27:57-60 = Mark 15:43-46 = Luke 23:50-54—cf. Deuteronomy 21:22-23, Exodus 34:25. Luke 23:56—cf. Exodus 12:16; 20:9-10; Deuteronomy 5:13-14.

---

[u] text: B D W Θ it vg bo; *whether he had been some time dead:* S A C λ φ ℵ sy[p] sa; *whether he was dead:* sy[s].   [v] Greek, *was dawning.*

To § 251 cf. John 19:38-42.

To Matt. 27:57ff. and parallels, cf. **Gospel of Peter 6.21-24**—21 And then they drew out the nails from the hands of the Lord and laid him upon the earth. And the whole earth was shaken and there came a great fear. 22 Then the sun shone and it was found to be the ninth hour. 23 And the Jews rejoiced and gave his body to Joseph, to bury it, because he had seen all the good things which he did. 24 And he he took the Lord, and washed him, and wrapped him in a linen shroud, and brought him to his own tomb, called the garden of Joseph.

252. THE GUARD AT THE TOMB.
Matt. 27:62–66

62 Next day, that is, after the day of Preparation, the chief priests and the Pharisees gathered before Pilate 63 and said, "Sir, we remember how that imposter said, while he was still alive, 'After three days I will rise again.' 64 Therefore order the sepulchre to be made secure until the third day, lest his disciples go and steal him away, and tell the people, 'He has risen from the dead,' and the last fraud will be worse than the first." 65 Pilate said to them, "You have a guard ʷ of soldiers; go, make it as secure as you can." ˣ 66 So they went and made the sepulchre secure by sealing the stone and setting a guard.

253. THE EMPTY TOMB.

Matt. 28:1–10	**Mark 16:1–8**	**Luke 24:1–11 (12)**
1 Now after the sabbath, toward the dawn of the first day of the week, Mary Magdalene and the other Mary went to see the sepulchre.	1 And when the sabbath was past, Mary Magdalene, and Mary the mother of James, and Salome, bought spices, so that they might go and anoint him. 2 And very early on the first day of the week they went to the tomb when the sun had risen.	*See 23:56b* 1 But on the first day of the week, at early dawn, they went to the tomb, taking the spices which they had prepared.
2 And behold, there was a great earthquake; for an angel of the Lord descended from heaven and came and rolled back the stone, and sat upon it. 3 His appearance was like lightning, and his raiment white as snow. 4 And for fear of him the guards trembled and became like dead men.		

ʷ Or, *take a guard.*   ˣ Greek, *know.*

To § 253 cf. John 20:1-10.

To Matt. 27:62-66 cf. **Gospel of Peter 8.28-33**—28 When the scribes and Pharisees and elders had gathered with each other, ... 29 they came to Pilate, entreating him, 30 "Give us soldiers that we may watch his tomb for three days, lest his disciples come and steal him away, and the people suppose that he is risen from the dead, and do evil things to us." 31 And Pilate gave them Petronius, the centurion, with soldiers, to watch the tomb. And the elders and scribes came with them to the tomb. 32 And when they, with the centurion and the soldiers, had rolled a great stone, all who were there together set it against the door of the tomb, 33 and having spread seven wax seals on it and pitched a tent, they kept watch.
To Matt. 27:65 cf. **Gospel of the Nazaraeans,** as recorded in a marginal note of some mss: The Jewish Gospel has: And he delivered armed men to them, that they might sit opposite the cave and guard it day and night.

3 And they were saying to one another, "Who will roll away the stone for us from the door of the tomb?" 4 And looking up, they saw that the stone was rolled back—it was very large. 5 And entering the tomb,

2 And they found the stone rolled away from the tomb, 3 but when they went in they did not find the body.ʸ 4 While they were perplexed about this, behold, two men stood by them in dazzling apparel; 5 and as they were frightened and bowed their faces to the ground, the men said to them, "Why do you seek the living among the dead?ᶻ

5 But the angel said to the women, "Do not be afraid; for I know that you seek Jesus who was crucified. 6 He is not here; for he has risen, as he said. Come, see the place where he ª lay. 7 Then go quickly and tell his disciples that he has risen from the dead, and behold, he is going before you to Galilee; there you will see him. Lo, I have told you."

they saw a young man sitting on the right side, dressed in a white robe; and they were amazed. 6 And he said to them, "Do not be amazed; you seek Jesus of Nazareth, who was crucified. He has risen, he is not here; see the place where they laid him. 7 But go, tell his disciples and Peter that he is going before you to Galilee; there you will see him, as he told you."

6 Remember how he told you while he was still in Galilee, 7 that the Son of man must be delivered into the hands of sinful men, and be crucified, and on the third day rise." 8 And they remembered his words, 9 and returning from the tomb they told all this to the eleven and to all the rest.

8 So they departed quickly from the tomb with fear and great joy, and ran to tell his disciples.

8 And they went out and fled from the tomb; for trembling and astonishment had come upon them; and they said nothing to any one, for they were afraid.

ʸ text: D it (some MSS.) Eusebius; add, *of Jesus:* syᶜ syˢ syᵖ; add, *of the Lord Jesus:* P⁷⁵ S A B C W Θ λ φ 𝔐it (some MSS.) vg sa bo. ᶻ text: D it (some MSS.); add, *He is not here but has risen:* P⁷⁵ S A B C W Θ λ φ 𝔐it (some MSS.) vg syᶜ syˢ syᵖ sa bo. ª text: S B Θ syˢ sa bo; *the Lord:* A C D W λ φ 𝔐it vg syᵖ.

To Matt. 28:1, 5-8 = Mark 16:1-8 = Luke 24:1-11 cf. **Gospel of Peter 12.50-13.57**—[50] Now early on the Lord's day Mary Magdalene, a disciple of the Lord—who was afraid because of the Jews, for they were inflamed with anger and had not done at the tomb of the Lord the things which women usually do to their loved ones when they die—[51] took friends with her, and came to the tomb where he was laid. [52] And they feared lest the Jews see them, and said, "Even if we were not able to weep and lament him on the day on which he was crucified, yet let us now do so at his tomb. [53] But who will roll away the stone for us that is set against the door of the tomb, that we may enter and sit beside him and perform our obligations?" [54] For the stone was large. "We fear lest some one see us. But if we cannot, then let us lay beside the door the things which we have brought in remembrance of him, and we will weep and lament until we get home." **13** [55] And they went and found the tomb open; and they went near and looked in there, and saw there a young man sitting in the middle of the tomb, handsome, and dressed in a brilliant robe. And he said to them, [56] "Why have you come? Whom do you seek? Not him who was crucified, for he has risen and gone. But if you do not believe it, look in and see the place where he lay, that he is not here. For he has risen and gone to the place from which he was sent." [57] Then the women were afraid and fled.

10 Now it was Mary Magdalene and Joanna and Mary the mother of James and the other women with them who told this to the apostles; 11 but these words, seemed to them an idle tale, and they did not believe them.[b]

9 And behold, Jesus met them and said, "Hail!" And they came up and took hold of his feet and worshiped him. 10 Then Jesus said to them, "Do not be afraid; go and tell my brethren to go to Galilee, and there they will see me."

APPEARANCES OF THE RISEN LORD

A. The Matthean Narrative

Matt. 28:11–20

1. The Bribing of the Soldiers.

Matt. 28:11–15

11 While they were going, behold, some of the guard went into the city and told the chief priests all that had taken place. 12 And when they had assembled with the elders and taken counsel, they gave a sum of money to the soldiers 13 and said, "Tell people, 'His disciples came by night and stole him away while we were asleep.' 14 And if this comes to the governor's ears, we will satisfy him and keep you out of trouble." 15 So they took the money and did as they were directed; and this story has been spread among the Jews to this day.

[b] text: D it (some MSS.) add verse 12, *But Peter rose and ran to the tomb; stooping and looking in, he saw the linen cloths by themselves; and he went home wondering at what had happened:* P75 S A B W Θ λ φ ℵ it (some MSS.) vg syc sys syp sa bo. (Cf. John 20:3-10.)

To Matt. 28:11-15 cf. **Gospel of Peter 11.45-49**—45 Those who were with the centurion, seeing these things, hastened to go at night to Pilate, and left the tomb which they were watching. They told all that they had seen, greatly disturbed, saying, "Truly he was a son of God." 46 Pilate answered, "I am clear from the blood of the son of God, but this thing seemed good to you." 47 And they all came and asked him and begged him to order the centurion and the soldiers to tell no one what they had seen. 48 "For," they said, "it is better for us to incur the greatest sin before God, than to fall into the hands of the people of the Jews and be stoned." 49 Pilate then ordered the centurion and the soldiers to say nothing.

2. The Command to Baptize.
Matt. 28:16–20

16 Now the eleven disciples went to Galilee, to the mountain to which Jesus had directed them. 17 And when they saw him they worshiped him; but some doubted. 18 And Jesus came and said to them, "All authority in heaven and on earth has been given to me. 19 Go therefore and make disciples of all nations, baptizing them in the name of the Father and of the Son and of the Holy Spirit, 20 teaching them to observe all that I have commanded you; and lo, I am with you always, to the close of the age."

B. The Lucan Narrative

Luke 24:13–53

1. The Road to Emmaus.
Luke 24:13–35

13 That very day two of them were going to a village named Emmaus, about seven miles [c] from Jerusalem, 14 and talking with each other about all these things that had happened. 15 While they were talking and discussing together, Jesus himself drew near and went with them. 16 But their eyes were kept from recognizing him. 17 And he said to them, "What is this conversation which you are holding with each other as you walk?" And they stood still, looking sad. 18 Then one of them, named Cleopas, answered him, "Are you the only visitor to Jerusalem who does not know the things that have happened there in these days?" 19 And he said to them, "What things?" And they said to him, "Concerning Jesus of Nazareth, who was a prophet mighty in deed and word before God and all the people, 20 and how our chief priests and rulers delivered him up to be condemned to death, and crucified him. 21 But we had hoped that he was the one to redeem Israel. Yes, and besides all this, it is now the third day since this happened. 22 Moreover, some women of our company amazed us. They were at the tomb early in the morning 23 and did not find his body; and they came back saying that they had even seen a vision of angels, who said that he was alive. 24 Some of those who were with us went to the tomb, and found it just as the women had said; but him they did not see." 25 And he said to them, "O foolish men, and slow of heart to believe all that the prophets have spoken! 26 Was it not necessary that the Christ should suffer these things and enter into his glory?" 27 And beginning with Moses and all the prophets, he interpreted to them in all the scriptures the things concerning himself.

28 So they drew near to the village to which they were going. He appeared to be going further, 29 but they constrained him, saying, "Stay with us, for it is toward evening and the day is now far spent." So he went in to stay with them. 30 When he was at table with them, he took the bread and blessed, and broke it, and gave it to them. 31 And their eyes were opened and they recognized him; and he vanished out of their sight. 32 They said to each other, "Did not our hearts burn within us [cc] while he talked to us on the road, while he opened to us the scriptures?" 33 And they rose that same hour and returned to Jerusalem; and they found the eleven gathered together and those who were with them, 34 who said, "The Lord has risen indeed, and has appeared to Simon!" 35 Then they told what had happened on the road, and how he was known to them in the breaking of the bread.

[c] Greek (most MSS) *sixty stadia; a hundred and sixty stadia:* S Θ.   [cc] text: S A λ φ 𝔐 vg sy^p sa bo; omit, *within us:* P^75 B D sy^c sy^s.

To Matt. 28:20 cf. John 14:23—"If a man loves me, he will keep my word, and my Father will love him, and we will come to him and make our home with him."

2. The Appearance of the Risen Christ in Jerusalem.
Luke 24:36-49

36 As they were saying this, Jesus himself stood among them.[d] [37] But they were startled and frightened, and supposed that they saw a spirit. [38] And he said to them, "Why are you troubled, and why do questionings rise in your hearts? [39] See my hands and my feet, that it is I myself; handle me, and see; for a spirit has not flesh and bones as you see that I have. [e] [41] And while they still disbelieved for joy, and wondered, he said to them, "Have you anything here to eat?" [42] They gave him a piece of broiled fish, [43] and he took it and ate before them.

44 Then he said to them, "These are my words which I spoke to you, while I was still with you, that everything written about me in the law of Moses and the prophets and the psalms must be fulfilled." [45] Then he opened their minds to understand the scriptures [46] and said to them, "Thus it is written, that the Christ should suffer and on the third day rise from the dead, [47] and that repentance and forgiveness of sins should be preached in his name to all nations,[f] beginning from Jerusalem. [48] You are witnesses of these things. [49] And behold, I send the promise of my Father upon you; but stay in the city, until you are clothed with power from on high."

3. The Ascension.
Luke 24:50-53

50 Then he led them out as far as Bethany, and lifting up his hands he blessed them. [51] While he blessed them, he parted from them, and was carried up into heaven.[g] [52] And they[h] returned to Jerusalem with great joy, [53] and were continually in the temple blessing God.

Luke 24:46—cf. Hosea 6:2.

---

[d] text: D it (some MSS.); add, *and he said to them, "Peace be with you"*: P[75] S A B Θ λ φ ℜ sy[c] sy[s] sa bo (cf. John 20:19, 26); add, *and he said to them, "Peace be with you; it is I, do not be afraid"*: it (some MSS.) vg sy[p] (cf. John 6:20); add, *and he said to them, "It is I, do not be afraid; peace be with you"*: W.   [e] text: D it (some MSS.) sy[c] sy[s]; add verse 40, *And when he had said this, he showed them his hands and his feet*: P[75] S A B W Θ λ φ ℜ it (some MSS.) vg sy[p] sa bo (cf. John 20:20).   [f] Or, *nations. Beginning from Jerusalem you are witnesses . . .*   [g] text: P[75] A B C W Θ λ φ ℜ it (some MSS.) vg sy[p] sa bo; omit, *and was carried up into heaven*: S D it (some MSS.) sy[s].   [h] text: D it sy[s]; add, *worshiped him and*: P[75] S A B C W Θ λ φ ℜ vg sy[p] sa bo.

To § 2 cf. John 20:19-23.

Cf. Gospel according to the Hebrews (in Jerome, *On Illustrious Men, 2*—Also the gospel called according to the Hebrews, recently translated by me into Greek and Latin, which Origen often uses, says, after the resurrection of the Savior: "Now the Lord, when he had given the linen cloth to the servant of the priest, went to James and appeared to him (for James had sworn that he would not eat bread from that hour in which he had drunk the Lord's cup until he should see him risen from among them that sleep)." And a little further on the Lord says, "Bring a table and bread." And immediately it is added, "He took bread and blessed and broke and gave it to James the Just and said to him, 'My brother, eat your bread, for the Son of man is risen from among them that sleep.' "

To Luke 24:39 cf. Ignatius, *Epistle to the Smyrneans 3:2*—And when he came to those with Peter, he said to them, "Take hold of me, handle me, and see that I am not a bodiless ghost."

C. The Longer Ending of Mark

Mark 16:9–20

9 Now when he rose early on the first day of the week, he appeared first to Mary Magdalene, from whom he had cast out seven demons. 10 She went and told those who had been with him, as they mourned and wept. 11 But when they heard that he was alive and had been seen by her, they would not believe it.

12 After this he appeared in another form to two of them, as they were walking into the country. 13 And they went back and told the rest, but they did not believe them.*

14 Afterward he appeared to the eleven themselves as they sat at table; and he upbraided them for their unbelief and hardness of heart, because they had not believed those who saw him after he had risen. 15 And he said to them, "Go into all the world and preach the gospel to the whole creation. 16 He who believes and is baptized will be saved; but he who does not believe will be condemned.** 17 And these signs will accompany those who believe: in my name they will cast out demons; they will speak in new tongues; 18 they will pick up serpents, and if they drink any deadly thing, it will not hurt them; they will lay their hands on the sick, and they will recover."

19 So then the Lord Jesus, after he had spoken to them, was taken up into heaven, and sat down at the right hand of God.*** 20 And they went forth and preached everywhere, while the Lord worked with them and confirmed the message by the signs that attended it. Amen.

* Mark 16:12f—Luke 24:13-35.   ** 14-16—Matt. 28:16-20.   *** 19—Luke 24:50-51.

The Longer Ending is not found in: S B sy* Clement, Origen; it is found in: A C D (to v.16) W Θ λ φ ℜ it vg sy^e sy^p sa bo.

The Shorter Ending reads as follows: But they reported briefly to Peter and those with him all that they had been told. And after this, Jesus himself sent out by means of them, from east to west, the sacred and imperishable proclamation of eternal salvation.

This ending is found in only a few manuscripts.

After v.14 W has a gloss, the so-called Freer Ending, the beginning of which is quoted in Latin by Jerome. An English translation of the Greek text follows:

And they replied saying, "This age of lawlessness and unbelief is under Satan, who by means of unclean spirits does not allow men to comprehend the true power of God; therefore reveal now thy righteousness." Thus they spoke to Christ; and Christ answered them: "The limit of the years of the authority of Satan is fulfilled; but other afflictions draw near, even for those sinners on whose behalf I was delivered up to death, in order that they might return to the truth and sin no more; that they might inherit the spiritual and incorruptible glory of righteousness which is in heaven."

To Mark 16:9-11 cf. John 20:11-18   To Mark 16-14 cf. John 20:19-23.

VR-467